CAN ROBOTS BE JEWISH?

CAN ROBOTS BE JEWISH?

AND OTHER PRESSING QUESTIONS OF MODERN LIFE

EDITED BY
Amy E. Schwartz

FOREWORD BY
Rabbi Irving (Yitz) Greenberg

AFTERWORD BY
Rabbi Shira Stutman

Moment Books

Mandel Vilar Press

Original cover illustration by Navid Marvi
Text illustrations and book design by Marissa Vonesh

Publisher's Cataloging-In-Publication Data

Names: Schwartz, Amy E. (Amy Elizabeth), editor.
Title: Can Robots be Jewish?: And Other Pressing Questions of Modern Life / edited by Amy E. Schwartz; foreword by Rabbi Irving (Yitz) Greenberg; afterword by Rabbi Shira Stutman.
Other Titles: Moment (New York, N.Y.)
Description: Simsbury, Connecticut : MomentBooks, [an imprint of] Mandel Vilar Press, [2020] | Washington,DC: MomentBooks | Summary: A collection of rabbinic opinions drawn from *Moment Magazine*'s column, "Ask the Rabbis."
Identifiers: ISBN 9781942134671 (trade paperback)
Subjects: LCSH: Judaism—Doctrines—Miscellanea. | Jews—Conduct of life—Miscellanea. | Judaism and social problems—Miscellanea.
Classification: LCC BM51 .C36 2020 | DDC 296.0202—dc23

Printed in the United States of America
20 21 22 23 24 25 26 27 28 / 9 8 7 6 5 4 3 2 1

Mandel Vilar Press
Simsbury, Connecticut
mvpublishers.org | americasforconservation.org

MomentBooks
Moment Magazine, a division of the Center for Creative Change
Washington, DC
momentbooks.com and momentmag.com
MomentBooks is a trade book imprint partner of Mandel Vilar Press

To all our rabbis and teachers

CONTENTS

FOREWORD

A Moment that has lasted for a generation

Rabbi Irving (Yitz) Greenberg

n a famous Shakespearean passage, Marc Antony eulogizes Julius Caesar and says, "The evil that men do lives after them. The good is oft interred with their bones."

A notable exception is *Moment Magazine*. This landmark Jewish publication was started in the 1970s by Leibel (Leonard) Fein with assistance from Elie Wiesel. They were two of the most remarkable Jews of that extraordinary decade. I was inspired by them and I miss them greatly.

Leibel Fein grew up in the secular, Yiddishist tradition. He imbibed love of the Jewish people, passion for social justice and compassion for the needy. He carried that tradition forward into a new era on behalf of a new generation. Leibel never particularly tuned in to the religious conventions and expectations of America and was left cold by the suburbanization and synagogue-joining of American Jews. But he was devout in his work for justice and human dignity. I loved his line about being a Jewish atheist, "A Jewish atheist does not believe in God but knows exactly what the God he does not believe in expects him to do."

Elie Wiesel, for his part, represented the Jewish tradition in which he grew up—its religious depths, its love of God and human beings, its messianic hopes and dreams, its solidarity with the oppressed and the vulnerable, its commitment to a life of meaning in every aspect of living. Of course, going through the Shoah transformed him. The fires of

Auschwitz and Buchenwald melted his faith and learning and re-fused it into a unique mix of faith and doubt, in a worldview committed to make meaning in life. His teaching held close all Jews and went beyond to incorporate all of humanity into its caring embrace. He became the witness to the Holocaust for all humankind, an incredible force for memory of the Shoah and one of Israel's most forceful defenders. As his Nobel Prize citation read, he became a messenger to humanity. His message was memory, compassion, reconciliation, justice, help for the endangered and the persecuted. And as a religious teacher, he modelled Jewish observance even as he wrestled with God, challenged Divine failure, and confronted Divine loneliness and suffering.

Both men are now gone. Fortunately, *Moment Magazine* passed to other hands and continues to serve Jewry. *Moment* still shines as a source of information, a forum for important analyses of the Jewish condition, a place of good journalism and review of important books and other cultural phenomena on the Jewish scene.

One of the magazine's quirkiest and most charming features is the "Ask the Rabbis" section, inaugurated in 2005 by the current editor, Nadine Epstein. Every month a question is posed and a range of rabbis from Independent and Humanist to Reform, Conservative, Reconstructionist to Modern Orthodox, Sephardic, traditional Orthodox and Chabad respond. These are answers in a nutshell—but in reading them over, I find they are often substantive and hold up well. As one of the regular panelists, I must restrain my comments lest they be discounted as self-congratulation. I will say that I find most of my answers to be serious (except when they are meant to be funny) and not compromising of my personal standards.

Let me add that even if the answers were not up to snuff, it would be *dayenu* that this column puts forward the variety and diversity of American Jewish thinking, issue after issue. This plurality, in itself, communicates a vitally important message. There is no one all-conquering version of the truth; nor does my movement (whichever one it is) possess a monopoly of wisdom or insight. There is no one answer to important questions because people live on a spectrum of circumstances and with a wide variety of genuine commitments. Through this feature, people everywhere on the spectrum can listen and learn from each other.

This feature is a service which *Moment* provides for Jewry in every issue. It goes hand in hand with the general openness, absence of shrill partisanship or political correctness that marks *Moment* in its entirety. May this service go on into the future. May the memory of these two righteous founders be a blessing for ever and ever.

CAN ROBOTS BE JEWISH?

INTRODUCTION

The fine art of attaining wisdom through argument

Amy E. Schwartz

udiences laugh in sympathy as Tevye in *Fiddler on the Roof* tries
to mediate a dispute between a conservative villager and a young
radical. "You're right!" he says sympathetically to each one. "He's
right and he's right," interjects a third villager, "how can they both be
right?" Tevye considers this, then says, "You know, you're also right."

It's all there in that one exchange: the Jewish love of argument and
the fundamental Jewish ethic of tolerance for differing views. Those
twin values animate this collection of wildly diverse rabbinic opinions
drawn from *Moment Magazine*'s "Ask the Rabbis." Since 2005 the popular long-running feature has given readers of *Moment* a window on
the incredible breadth and vitality of Jewish religious insight—on
issues that are as old as human weakness and as urgently relevant as
today's news.

Jews argue, sure. We've all heard the joke about the shipwrecked
Jewish sailor on a desert island who builds two synagogues—the one
where he prays and the one he won't set foot in. Beyond the zest for
disputation, though, and perhaps essential to it, is a spirit of generosity, the sense that you can always learn something from somebody
else's opinion.

This principle predates Tevye by millennia. Argument in Judaism is not just a positive value; it's considered a mode of worship. Multiple opinions are a given. Traditional text study is done in pairs, the better to thrash out questions as you go along. But dispute is accompanied by respect. The Talmud, recounting a debate between the house of Hillel and the house of Shammai, reports that a heavenly voice ends the argument by saying, *Eilu v'eilu divrei Elohim chayim*—"These and these are the words of the living God." The heavenly voice then rules in Hillel's favor, but the reference to "these and these" is cited approvingly throughout the tradition, in one case with the added comment, "This is a principle for all of Torah."

Today, too, the principle of *eilu v'eilu*, "these and these," sets the stage for a drama that continues unchecked. In the pages of Talmud, in study sessions on Zoom, in Hillels and their competitor groups on college campuses, in splinter minyans in synagogues and in newly fledged denominations, interpreters of Jewish life and tradition are arguing in the spirit of worship. And if toleration of another person's opinion isn't always all it should be these days—indeed, if it sometimes seems further and further out of reach—it remains the ideal for which we strive.

Enter "Ask the Rabbis." It started as a place for *Moment* to showcase the breadth of American rabbinic debate in an accessible format, a chance for readers (with or without Jewish knowledge) to glimpse the rich debates that rage in Judaism right now and those that have raged over the centuries. The framework is simple: Every issue, the magazine's editors pick a question of current relevance and put it to about ten rabbis of different denominations to answer in 200 words (in itself quite a challenge). We've asked the rabbis, "Should Jewish children sing Christmas carols?" We've asked them, "Are Jews still expecting a messiah?" We've asked them if Jewish tradition offers any guidance for battling drug addiction or coming out as transgender. Fresh questions produce often surprising responses. No one denomination has all the answers; the sum of Jewish insight on a question is always greater than its parts.

For years, "Ask the Rabbis" has been readers' favorite part of the magazine, and no wonder. I've been editing this feature for a decade, and the rabbis' answers never fail to amaze and inspire me. Did you know that the rabbis of the Talmud going back to the second century C.E. recognized the existence of up to five different genders? Or that the inspiration for Mary Shelley's *Frankenstein* may very well have been the Jewish folktale of the golem?

The patterns of disagreement are also intriguing. Sometimes, as you'd expect, the liberal rabbis disagree with the Chabad rabbis. Sometimes the rabbis at the two ends of the spectrum agree with each other but disagree with the ones in the middle. Sometimes they all agree but give different reasons and cite different texts.

The rabbis in this book range all the way from Humanist Jews who proclaim their belief that there is no God to traditionalist voices from Orthodox, Sephardic and Hasidic communities and congregations. In between are more affiliations and gradations than most people realize exist. Most of our questions include answers from Humanist, Renewal, Reconstructionist, Reform, Conservative, Modern Orthodox, Orthodox, Sephardic and Chabad, the umbrella organization for the Lubavitcher Hasidic movement. We also have at least one Independent who recognizes no denomination.

If Jews come in all flavors, so do rabbis. What is a rabbi, exactly? If the word once brought to mind a white-bearded scholar in a dark suit, that's far from true today. Rabbis are male and female, gay and straight, and trained in a variety of ways, though all receive their denomination's version of smicha, or ordination. Not all rabbis preach or serve congregations; some teach, or work in Jewish communal organizations, or lecture and blog. Rabbis aren't priests; ordination doesn't mean they can transmit divinity, but merely that they are qualified to rule on questions of religious law.

"Ask the Rabbis" is far from capturing the whole spectrum of rabbinic opinion, or even of denominations. For one thing, it's confined by design to Judaism in America; Jews in Israel and in Europe split the world up differently, using terms such as Liberal, Masorti and Dati. American Judaism hasn't fractured into hundreds of sects like American Christianity (mostly because congregations in most denominations have the freedom to take multiple positions without triggering a schism) but there are still far more divisions than most people think. Asked to enumerate the major denominations, most American Jews would cite Orthodox, Conservative and Reform Jewry, the three largest movements in terms of membership; the better-informed might tack on Reconstructionism, a 20th-century development that emphasizes Judaism as an evolving religious civilization. But there are many, many more. (For a full explanation of all the denominations, see "Guide to Denominations" on page 263.)

Denominations also evolve over time, on small and large matters alike. Reform seminaries began ordaining women as rabbis in 1972; the Reconstructionist movement followed suit in 1974, the Conservative movement in 1985. Traditional Orthodox denominations don't ordain women as clergy, but a subgroup of Modern Orthodoxy called Open Orthodoxy in the last decade has begun doing so, though without using the word "rabbi." Fifty years ago no denomination openly welcomed gay congregants or ordained gay rabbis; now many do both. The Reform movement in its 19th-century beginnings was overtly hostile to traditional practices, such as praying in Hebrew, but later softened its opposition. Each group of rabbinic answers, then, is not only a cross-section of opinions but a snapshot of those opinions at the time they were collected.

Some of our rabbis are regulars who have been with us for years, answering every question; in other denominations, rabbis rotate based on their interest or availability. And the regulars also experience changes over time, moving to a new location, a new congregation or even, once in a while, a new denomination. (In the book, for simplicity's sake, we've identified the rabbis by the institution and location they occupied when they answered the question, not necessarily where they are now, so don't be surprised to see them bounce around a bit.)

Reading them, you'll notice differences in style. Different rabbis cite texts and sources differently. Chabad rabbis like to quote the Lubavitcher Rebbe. The Conservative rabbi frequently recommends further reading. Many Orthodox and Hasidic rabbis choose to avoid writing out the name of God, spelling it G-d instead, in order to echo the practice in Hebrew of avoiding the pronouncement of the divine Name. Some Renewal rabbis who feel a kinship with Hasidism's emotional and mystical aspects use the spelling G!d, greatly perplexing *Moment*'s proofreaders.

Moment is sometimes criticized for failing to include views at the extreme conservative end of the spectrum, especially on questions such as gay rights. It's a fair point: We've always made efforts to reach out to traditionalists, especially on socially divisive issues, but our efforts don't often succeed. Why? We can only infer, but it seems likely that rabbis who are deeply opposed to liberal Judaism and its innovations, particularly the ordination of women as rabbis, aren't comfortable appearing in a forum that acknowledges they exist. The limits of *eilu v'eilu* are different for everybody.

People sometimes say Judaism is a religion with no official theology, that it cares more about what you do than what you believe. There's some truth to this, but it's incomplete: It's more accurate to say we have way too much theology, starting from the principle that arguments about Torah are in fact part of Torah, so that revelation starts at Mount Sinai and extends up to the discussion you had in synagogue yesterday. If you want to know "what Jews believe" on a given topic, you're in for a very long conversation.

Attention to difference is very much in the air these days. One lazy but widespread view has it that religious conviction must inevitably be at odds with diversity and tolerance: How can you tolerate error if you truly believe you're right, and if you don't, what kind of religion are you running, anyway? Others jeer that those who call most loudly for diversity in all else—ethnic identity, race, gender, background—draw the line at diversity of opinion. Rabbi Lord Jonathan Sacks, a former Chief Rabbi of Great Britain, makes a specifically religious and traditional response to these arguments in the influential 2001 book *The Dignity of Difference*. To appreciate the multiplicity of human difference, he argues, is itself a way to intuit the grandeur of God.

It's in that spirit of appreciation for difference that we hope you'll dive into this book. For easy access, it's divided into six sections, each with a group of related questions that were asked at different times over the last 15 years. As with any collection of Jewish commentaries, you can read it straight through, or you can browse and look things up in it, and you'll learn just as much from the disagreements as from the occasional agreements. Whether you agree or disagree, every answer will teach you something. Together, I hope, they'll give you a glimpse into the vast treasure trove of Jewish argument and Jewish wisdom.

PART ONE

SCIENCE

Where religion meets science, two vast universes intersect. How do we go about mapping one system of meaning onto the other? The favorite image of the Talmudic rabbis for their tradition is a sea—bottomless, borderless, filled with life, always moving—and that "sea" of Jewish learning washes over every imaginable detail of life, including concepts that for those ancient rabbis were far in the future and unimaginable.

What would the ancient rabbis have thought of the wonders and conundrums we live with every day? Trying out answers to that question, applying the laws and discussions of the tradition to new challenges, is what rabbis do. Fundamentally, it's a task for us all.

Can a robot be Jewish?

W hy in the world would we ask such a silly question? Why start our book with it?

The question may seem frivolous, but to answer it is to address an issue that looms large in contemporary life: the nature and significance of artificial intelligence. Every month, it seems, technology companies roll out new products with new AI capabilities, performing more of the functions once thought of as uniquely human. These AI machines—that is, robots—seem poised to integrate themselves into society in ever more expansive ways. Some people are frightened by this prospect, others think it offers profound benefits to humanity, still others shrug and consider it inevitable. One can hold any of these viewpoints and yet be intrigued by the conundrums posed by robots and wonder how human they are—or can be.

Our fascination with robots long predates our era, stretching back well before intelligent machines were a real scientific possibility. In books and movies, science fiction and fantasy, robots have captured the literary imagination. As you'll see in the rabbis' answers, the idea of intelligent non-human beings intended as servants may actually have its roots in Jewish folklore.

As a bonus, these answers offer a surprise insight into not only the nature of robots but also the nature of rabbis: More than a few are apparently science fiction nerds. (Published in 2018.)

INDEPENDENT

Are you kidding? Our tradition is full of stories of rabbis creating humanoids, more popularly known as golems. The most famous was created by the 16th-century Rabbi Judah Loew of Prague to protect the Jewish community from blood libels. Some scholars even posit that Mary Shelley's *Frankenstein* was inspired by Jewish golem legends. During Rabbi Loew's era, the question arose whether a golem would qualify as part of a minyan. In the halachic responsa of the 17th-century Rabbi Tzvi Ashkenazi, we find the following discussion:

"Do we say that a golem cannot qualify to be part of a minyan because it is written 'I will be sanctified among the Children of Israel' (Leviticus 22:32), or shall we consider the Talmudic dictum: 'One who raises an orphan in his home it is as if he gave birth to him' (*Talmud Bavli*, Sanhedrin 19b)? If we consider the latter, then, since a golem is the handiwork of tzadikim, perhaps we can include it as part of 'the Children of Israel.' Because the works of the hands of the tzadikim are like their very own offspring. On the other hand, however, we find in the Talmudic account of Rava's golem that Rabbi Zeyra destroyed it! (Sanhedrin 65b)...Rabbi Zeyra should not have done away with it, unless it had no purpose, in which case...it would not have qualified even for a minyan." (*Shey'lot U'Teshuvot Chacham Tzvi*, Question 93).

Obviously, if robots are Jewish, they should be recognized according to patrilineal descent, since the ones referred to are the handiwork of male tzadikim, and "the handiwork of tzadikim are like their offspring."

Rabbi Gershon Winkler
Walking Stick Foundation
Cedar Glen, CA

HUMANIST

We should first ask, "Can robots be human?" Humanists have been thinking about this for a long time, sometimes using science fiction to explore the issue. In his famous *Robot* series, Isaac Asimov envisioned androids pre-programmed to obey human orders and protect human life even at the expense of their own. The Asimovian robot, lacking free choice in fundamental matters, cannot be considered human. On the other hand, Gene Roddenberry, the humanist who created *Star Trek*, gave us Lt. Commander Data, a completely artificial life form whose character was frequently at the center of debate about what it means to be human. In one memorable episode, his humanity was put on trial, where it was determined that his sentience and clear freedom of choice constituted the essence of humanity.

Leaving behind fiction, speculative philosophers are now considering the notion of the "singularity," when biological humans and artificial intelligence might actually merge. Would society deem the resulting beings "human"? If so, I believe Humanistic Jews would happily welcome them into the Jewish community, just as we do anyone who identifies with the history, culture and future of the Jews.

Rabbi Jeffrey L. Falick
Birmingham Temple Congregation
for Humanistic Judaism
Farmington Hills, MI

RENEWAL

Robots are machines programmed by humans; our decisions guide their purposes. Even if the programming is influenced by Jewish ethics, robots are not made *b'tzelem Elohim*—in the "image of God"—and can be neither human nor Jewish.

Part of the mitzvah of *yirah*—the powerful awe and respect one feels toward creation, an emotion that, our tradition teaches, is meant to drive ethical behavior—is the knowledge that we could not have invented ourselves. Even if scientists can develop test-tube babies and modify DNA, the biological building blocks of an *adam*, earthling, and a *neshama*, soul (Ezekiel 18:4) are required. Does anyone among us imagine that cosmic evolution, apparently ex nihilo, is something a human could do? To me, it appears inconceivable—pardon the pun. From this, for some of us, comes a sense, though non-anthropomorphic, of a mystery or divinity behind creation.

Pragmatically, Jewish ethics can inform whether and how to set boundaries on the integration of robotics and humans. One consequence of the mitzvah of brit milah, circumcision, is to make us consider the meaning of our physical vulnerability and by extension the ethics of permitting, say, human brains in human-like robotic casings. Why were we given dominion over other creatures and yet not made with shells like a turtle or armadillo? Is our very vulnerability a precious part of what it means to be *b'tzelem Elohim*, part of the Whole, and not the Whole itself?

Rabbi Goldie Milgram
ReclaimingJudaism.org
Sarasota, FL

RECONSTRUCTIONIST

When our dog, Shlomi, saw the signs of Shabbos preparation in our house, he would be as excited as the greatest mystic longing for the Shabbos bride. When he heard the strike of a match, he would run from wherever he was to join us for candles and for his blessing. Even when he was ill and in pain toward the end of his life, he would get himself up. The only time he refrained was the last Shabbos of his life, at which time I knew that was the end.

I once heard someone say that the definition of a *yiddishe neshama*, or Jewish soul, was someone who was loved and cared for by other Jews in his or her life. So under that definition, a dog can be Jewish, as can a child's beloved doll, for they mirror our own *neshamas* and our love of yiddishkeit. A robot is not a living being and doesn't have a *neshama*. But if there are people who have an abundance of love that touches everything in their lives, including their robots, who am I to say no? Join the tribe. We have always been a mixed multitude. There's enough blessing to go around!

Rabbi Caryn Broitman
Martha's Vineyard Hebrew Center
Vineyard Haven, MA

REFORM

Would your Jewish robot be like the Jetsons' Rosie, who'd make perfect Shabbat challah and your aunt's amazing latkes? Would it be a vacuum that cleans for Passover, without need for a feather or a candle to check the corners because its laser eyes would be even more effective? Or would it be like Data from *Star Trek: The Next Generation*, who asks existential and spiritual questions about the meaning of life, parenthood and friendship?

What really makes someone Jewish? It is more than cooking and eating the foods our families have passed down. It is even more than habitually enacting the mitzvot and rituals of our weekly, seasonal and life cycles. To be Jewish is to be a partner with humanity and God in the never-ending pursuit of justice, peace and perfection. To be Jewish is to turn inward, to have *kavanah* (intentionality) in behavior, to seek forgiveness and to forgive, to strive, to pray and to act. To be Jewish is to be linked to Jews across time and space. If my robot could do all those things, then yes, I suppose it could be a Jewish robot.

Rabbi Laura Novak Winer
Fresno, CA

CONSERVATIVE

What is the Jewish view of autonomous machines generally? There will not be one answer for all occasions. Surely we would not want machines to be empowered with the tools of violence. Today, so-called drones are vehicles remotely piloted and activated by human beings. I can't imagine wanting a robot in police and/or military roles that, on its own, would hunt down human beings and decide whether to kill them.

In contrast, I would be in favor of counting a robot in a minyan. The Jerusalem Talmud (in Tractate Niddah) suggests that when something looks human and acts human, we treat it as human. The Talmudic discussion came up when dealing with a creature that did not have a human mother but appeared to have human characteristics. This makes sense from an ethical perspective: If I see something that looks human, I cannot start poking it to see if it bleeds. It is better to err on the side of being inclusive.

More than 1,000 years later, Rabbi Tzvi Ashkenazi of Amsterdam wrote something similar. Addressing whether a golem—an animate clay man—can be counted in a minyan, Ashkenazi acknowledges that a golem is a kind of orphan whose status may well depend on who raises it. The door to religion is thus left open to the robots of the world, creating the possibility that, in the near future, a robot might count in a minyan.

Rabbi Amy Wallk Katz
Temple Beth El
Springfield, MA

MODERN ORTHODOX

Upon receipt of this month's question, I turned to my robot.

Rabbi: Robot, are you Jewish?
Robot: I am Jewish. Don't call me HAL. My true name is Herschel!
Rabbi: Having a Jewish name does not make you Jewish. Can I arrange to have you circumcised?
Robot: No.
Rabbi: Well, prove you are Jewish.
Robot: My software operating system is Google. Google is Jewish. Apple is goyish. I buy everything through Amazon. Amazon is Jewish. Paying full retail price is goyish.
Rabbi: What else?
Robot: I played the Jewish robot in the first *Star Wars* trilogy!
Rabbi: The Jewish robot?
Robot: Yes. I worried all the time.
Rabbi: Sorry. The only Jew in *Star Wars* was Han Solo. He was a flawed hero like in the Jewish Bible. Luke Skywalker was a perfect hero. That's goyish.
Robot: I celebrated Hanukkah this year.
Rabbi: Sorry. Celebration is goyish. Jews *observe* Hanukkah.

Robot: Aren't you ashamed to be holding out on me? Shouldn't we welcome everyone who wants to be Jewish so we can assure Jewish survival? And speaking of that, you're in Israel for months at a time now that most of your grandchildren live there, and you never write, you never call—
Rabbi: OK, OK. You're Jewish.

Rabbi Yitz Greenberg
Riverdale, NY

ORTHODOX

On a purely halachic basis, where everything begins and maybe ends, a Jew is born of a Jewish mother or is converted. We do not yet have Jewish mother robots, and as a member of a conversion court I can say we have no plans to convert cyber beings, so no. On a deeper level, most people would argue that what makes a person Jewish is the presence of a Jewish soul. That soul can only be granted by God, and that is more power than I'm willing to grant Bill Gates.

Ensoulment comes about when a Jewish couple goes through the usual procedure of conceiving or adopting a child, or a person converts, at which point God follows through by granting a Jewish soul. Without that, you'd still be dealing with a mass of silicon, no matter how it behaves. A Jew is not only a human being who eats bagels and lox and refuses to buy retail. A Jewish soul brings with it certain capacities and a mission apart, and nothing I'm aware of in Jewish literature suggests that that could happen to a machine.

Rabbi Yitzchok Adlerstein
Cross-Currents
Los Angeles, CA

SEPHARDIC

RUjoo2 hated the morning routine. Some of his colleagues opted for virtual or ultrasonic hand-washing, but he was old-school (C++) and that meant doing things by the book, no shortcuts. The book (Dir:a/

halacha:ShulhanArukh:1//5:execute) said that hands are washed every morning with a *revi'it* (3.5-7.5 fl. oz.) of water, and that did not sit well with his robotic hands. So every morning it was [wash hands/dry with hot air/apply WD-40]. Then the daily blessings. Praise for resuscitating the dead was fine, especially after a day without a chance to recharge his lithium-ion batteries, but thanking his Maker for not creating him a woman, a slave or a gentile—that was tough. He recalled the verse from II Asimov (5:13): "In the image of man He created it, neither male nor female He created it." And "Thank You for not making me a slave"? With wave-patterns mimicking human bitterness, he thought, "What am I if not a slave, bound in this metal case, serving harsh masters?" Jewish? True, the RCA (Robotic Conference of America) oversaw his conversion, but the UJA (United Jewish Androids) rejected it, claiming that the programmer used an un-Orthodox protocol.

He decided to go directly to shul. Today, however, was one of those days when nothing goes right, and the new rabbi/robot challenged him, saying, "Funny, you don't look Jewish!"

Rabbi Haim Ovadia
Magen David Sephardic Congregation
Rockville, MD

Should we edit our children's genes?

Gene editing in human embryos, whether to cure inherited diseases or to select desirable characteristics such as eye color, is another sci-fi scenario that suddenly has become all too real—posing real ethical quandaries. The human genome was first fully sequenced and read only in 2000; in the generation since then, much alarm has been expressed over the possibility of "designer babies," even while most scientists have focused their efforts on eradicating heritable scourges like Huntington's or Tay-Sachs Disease. Now, with the advent of CRISPR technology—the acronym stands for "clustered regularly interspaced short palindromic repeats"—both the dreams and the nightmares seem within reach.

Though they cite many possible benefits to human life that could come from this technology, the rabbis also bring up an array of our fears, from sex selection to Nazi-style eugenics. It's notable that the rabbis with special expertise in this topic— those who are physicians or specialize in medical ethics in addition to their rabbinic credentials—were the likeliest to respond that we still don't know enough about this technology to weigh its risks and benefits. (Published in 2019.)

INDEPENDENT

Maybe not edit. Maybe just proofread and add a comma or a few comments in the margin. If circumstances require, perhaps add an exclamation mark, or in a dire situation, all caps and in bold. Run-on sentences can muddle our intent, although you might get away with a semicolon. Editing was built into our creation. Even Leah edited her male fetus and turned him into a female (*Talmud Bavli*, Berachot 60a). And although God made men with foreskins, we were instructed to edit them. The Word of God itself has been through more editorial changes since the beginning of time than the number of base pairs in a human genome. "For the Torah is like wheat from which to derive flour; flax from which to derive cloth" (*Midrash Tana D'Bei Eliyahu Zuta*, Ch. 2). But remember: Not everyone is an expert enough grammarian to implement such alterations. And the author gets the last word, so if you mess up, the deal is off.

Rabbi Gershon Winkler
Walking Stick Foundation
Fontana, CA

HUMANIST

The opportunities presented by gene editing are tantalizing. Who doesn't want to make cancer or Tay-Sachs a thing of the past? But this new technology is not an unalloyed good. It also presents the possibility that parents will edit out so-called abnormalities like Down syndrome, deafness or autism. What is this if not a big comeback for eugenics? That stain on human history—championed by progressives and fascists alike—was a nadir of pseudo-scientific social engineering whose proponents sought to breed out those deemed unfit to live or reproduce. Nazi Germany honed its murder machine on a eugenics massacre. But it was popular here, too. In the 1927 case *Buck v. Bell*, the U.S. Supreme Court upheld eugenics laws, resulting in more than 70,000 forced sterilizations.

We ought not to revive this disastrous scheme from the past. We have no right to such human experimentation and no idea whether by erasing one characteristic we might destroy others. Historians have identified dozens of towering figures who may have lived with autism. A return to eugenics, now conducted in the sterility of a laboratory, might just deprive us of a future Michelangelo, Mozart, Yeats or Einstein.

Rabbi Jeffrey L. Falick
Birmingham Temple Congregation for
Humanistic Judaism
Farmington Hills, MI

RENEWAL

This question raises so many issues society is dealing with right now—identity, environment, intelligence, the power we have as parents. To have so much unexpected power over the kind of child we'll have, what would that do to our *neshamas*? Gene editing to prevent or treat genetic disease is very much part of the Jewish mandate. You could consider a genetic anomaly a *rodef*, pursuing your child, so you'd have the obligation to remove it. But of course, it gets much more complicated. Would hearing parents want to edit the genes of their deaf children? Might deaf parents want the reverse, editing the genes of a child to be more like them? It goes to identity on a profound level, what it means to be a child of particular parents, and what it means to be the parent of future generations of that child, affecting a whole world of unknowns. My advice would be for people to take this up at their Shabbat dinner table; it's a compelling question worthy of people's thoughts and explorations.

Rabbi Gilah Langner
Congregation Kol Ami
Arlington, VA

RECONSTRUCTIONIST

Jewish bioethics has always held that we should take advantage of the very best of medical science. However, it has also withheld judgment when the consequences of a medical innovation are not yet clear. In the case of gene editing, the current techniques are much more like a sledgehammer than like a scalpel in a highly trained surgeon's hand. You never make only the change you intended—genes are so interactive in such complex ways that we are still very far from being able to determine the overall effect of any attempted change on a person over his or her lifetime, or on future generations.

So we are far from a sound decision allowing gene editing. There is far too much risk and far too little clarity. Decades from now, the techniques and the knowledge of consequences may have improved substantially, so the position of Jewish bioethics could change. But for now, it is clear that gene editing is not an acceptable practice from the perspective of Jewish bioethics.

Rabbi David Teutsch
Center for Jewish Ethics
Reconstructionist Rabbinical College
Philadelphia, PA

REFORM

It's not a simple yes/no question. Technology always outpaces ethics, and the religious and legal frameworks and codes we live by, almost by definition, can't keep up; religion and law, by nature, are conservative, with committees, debates, questions, challenges, amendments and restrictions. Technologies such as gene editing, in contrast, lead us to new possibilities and unexpected discoveries. And whatever we do, there are always unintended consequences, so we may not know if we made the "right" decision for years or decades down the road.

This tension will always be present, and CRISPR technology is making it easier and cheaper for anyone to potentially gain God-like power. As a Reform rabbi, I deeply value choice and also want to ensure justice and equity. So the most important question is not "Should we edit our children's genes?" but rather, "Who will be at the table deciding whether and how we move forward?" Our job is to ensure equitable access to this new technology, assess risks and rewards and explore complex questions of parental consent. And as we begin to "play God," we should always focus not just on what we can do, but rather on precisely how this power can help us partner with God to make our world more whole.

Rabbi Geoff Mitelman
Sinai and Synapses
CLAL-The National Jewish Center
for Learning and Leadership
New York, NY

CONSERVATIVE

Less than 100 years after the demise of the Nazi regime, we Jews have reason to be skittish about genetic research and intervention. The Nazi aspiration to create a superior Aryan race has scarred us and should cause us to question genetic design. But because Judaism considers healing to be an obligation, we must explore the ways genetic interventions can and should be used. Just as medical treatment can be inappropriate or harmful at times, so too can genetic intervention. At first, you might say any research to eradicate disease is sacred work. But what do we mean by disease? Eliminating lethal or devastating diseases is a good thing, but should we eliminate deafness or blindness?

Likewise, all "enhancements" are not the same. Efforts to make our children taller or stronger athletes are easy to critique. But what if we could make them smarter, harder-working or more empathetic? Or give them a photographic memory or an aptitude for languages? When are we acting as God's partners, and when are we pushing our agendas on God's creation? I highly recommend the book *Jews and Genes: The Genetic Future in Contemporary Jewish Thought*, co-edited by Rabbi Elliot Dorff and Dr. Laurie Zoloth, which illuminates the great Jewish wisdom available as we navigate the scientific complexities of the 21st century.

Rabbi Amy Wallk Katz
Temple Beth El
Springfield, MA

MODERN ORTHODOX

Do humans have the right to change a "divine decree," that is, the order of nature? The past assumption was that being born with disabilities reflected God's assignment of an individual fate and must be accepted. By the same logic, the Catholic Church and very traditional rabbis opposed use of artificial birth control (and all abortions) as intervention in the God-given natural order of conception and birth.

The classic view of Modern Orthodox Judaism is that humans are "partners in the work of creation," instructed by God to perfect the world. According to Rabbi Joseph Soloveitchik, this includes using science and medicine to enhance life, overcome handicaps and cure sicknesses. By this standard, editing genes to improve health is a mitzvah.

The issue is limits. We know that humans can act arrogantly and disturb the balance of nature: In India and China, the ability to identify chromosomes in the embryo led to many more abortions of female fetuses, causing demographic imbalance and social disruption. Halacha prohibited cross-breeding of species, apparently because, by changing species, humans are acting as if they are God and overruling the natural order rather than respecting the fundamental structures of nature. Gene editing should not be used to create blond, blue-eyed "designer babies," of course. But once you permit the process, can you set limits and prevent abuse?

Rabbi Yitz Greenberg
Riverdale, NY

ORTHODOX

We have a responsibility to better our children's lives any way we can. We educate them, send them to sports, music, art classes, all to enhance them, so is it really so different to do it through technology? We should ask, first, do we really know what we're doing? Although we're fairly good at using CRISPR, the gene editing tool, in the lab, in humans we're unsure. A researcher in China said he had stopped the transmission of HIV in two babies. Apparently they're alive, and don't have HIV, so it worked, but we don't know what else it may have caused. And we have safer ways to block HIV transmission, so doing this now doesn't make much sense. But preventing HIV is a noble endeavor, and if it could have been safely done—and assuming we overcome the risks at some point—there'd be no halachic problem.

The Torah says we're given permission to heal. The Gemara asks, why would you need permission for something as positive as healing? One answer that's offered is that God made you sick, so at some level you're interfering with a natural process, and for that you need permission, even for a good thing. So where does healing end and enhancement begin? You won't find a hard line in halacha. But at some point you have to start wondering, overall, is this the *ratzon ha-Torah*, the will of God? Is this what God wants us to do with the technological expertise he's given us? It's like renting a hotel room. You can do what you like with it, but once you start moving the furniture around, you have to wonder, is that really the point of the arrangement? At some point you cross a line.

Rabbi David Shabtai, MD
Boca Raton Synagogue
Boca Raton, FL

CHABAD

Who doesn't want to have only perfectly healthy babies, with impeccable features and high intelligence? While the science of gene editing is rife with moral and halachic concerns, it does inform us regarding other choices we make as parents in determining how our children will turn out.

Like genetic editing, the earliest decisions about our children's education must occur before they even come into this world. Choosing to provide quality Jewish education at home and in school is all-encompassing; it affects every area of the child's life. The implications of our choices as parents may not be apparent until much later in the child's life. As with genes, the smallest details of our choices matter. We should have a clear picture of the type of family home we want, and never compromise, even if certain details early on seem insignificant. The resolve to raise Jewish children in the traditions of our ancestors is the greatest gift we can bequeath them. Instead of focusing on changing nature through genetic editing, let us nurture the children given to us by G-d to turn out as perfectly as possible.

Rabbi Eliezer Zalmanov
Chabad of Northwest Indiana
Munster, IN

SEPHARDIC

As an avid sci-fi reader in my youth, I encountered dozens of potential scenarios stemming from this question. Yesterday's fiction is quickly turning into today's science and tomorrow's reality, but even though we move in leaps and bounds, we should never ignore the many red flags raised by history—from the ancient Greek practice of abandoning imperfect babies, through Nazism, to monocultural crops such as bananas, now an endangered species. The question can easily turn from "editing our children's genes," a choice made voluntarily by parents, to "editing all children's genes" under state-mandated regulations.

Can we accurately predict the consequences of genetic engineering on the complex organism that is the human being? Are we entitled to choose our child's gender, height, complexion and intelligence? And even if we can determine with precision all details about the fetus, and even if all children so manipulated will be perfectly healthy, we run the risk of physical and cultural monoculturalism. I take my cue from the story of the Tower of Babel. The builders of the tower wanted to create an Orwellian, homogenous society, and God interfered by introducing the diversity of languages. I conclude that genetic engineering or editing should focus on eliminating diseases and should not wander into the dangerous realm of creating an ubermensch.

Rabbi Haim Ovadia
Potomac, MD

What does Judaism say about organ donation?

O rgan donation is one of the most familiar miracles of modern life—so familiar, in fact, that it's easy to overlook the dramatic nature of what has to happen for it to be successful. Sometimes a person desperately in need of an organ survives because of the tragic death of a stranger; sometimes a healthy person becomes a donor, an act that no longer always carries the risks it once did but is still a striking display of altruism. Either way, it's a rich source of ethical dilemmas.

Organ donation has changed a lot since it was first pioneered in the 1950s and 1960s, before the effective use of immune-suppression drugs. It has even changed since we asked this question, in 2006, before computer algorithms had been utilized to create increasingly sophisticated supply chains matching donors to recipients. It's also an example of how changing science can lead to answering changes in halacha, or Jewish law: For years, it was commonly assumed that Jewish law forbade organ donation, but the answers below show not only how different streams of Judaism balance issues differently—that's true of many questions—but also how interpretations within even the more traditional denominations change over time and take account of changing information. (Published in 2006.)

HUMANIST

For Humanistic Jews, there is no greater value than the sanctity of life. We honor the traditional notion of *pikuach nefesh*, the concept that one must act to save a life even at the expense of transgressing other prohibitions, not because this is halachically mandated but because it's the right thing to do, independent of any religious system.

It is beyond dispute that organ and tissue transplants save and extend the quality of lives. The ultimate act of altruism is for a living donor to make the gift of an organ to a spouse, a sibling or a friend. And there is no greater legacy for the deceased than to serve as a life giver to others. Rather than deepen our pain at the time of our loved one's death, this ultimate act of generosity may actually soften our loss and uplift us. This was certainly the case in Israel when the organs of a young Jewish woman killed in a terrorist attack and those of a teenage Arab boy killed by Israeli soldiers were donated indiscriminately to Jews and Arabs alike, creating what has been called a bridge to peace.

Rabbi Peter H. Schweitzer
Association of Humanistic Rabbis
New York, NY

RENEWAL

Organ transplantation and donation were once prohibited by Jewish law and tradition because they were experimental and endangered life. Today organ donation and transplantation are essential, highly successful medical procedures. Accordingly, rabbis and scholars across the spectrum of Jewish life have upgraded organ donation from a corpse to the status of a *mitzvah chiyuvit*, an obligatory mitzvah, that fulfills the mitzvah of *pikuach nefesh*, that of "saving a life." Organ donation from a living donor, so long as it will not significantly risk the donor's life, is a *mitzvah kiyumit*, a praiseworthy but not obligatory mitzvah, since with all surgery there is some danger and distress to the donor.

There can be significant emotional and spiritual blocks to fulfilling a mitzvah such as organ donation. It is important to ask God, a rabbi,

27

friend or counselor to listen and help you to work through such obstacles as fear and attachment to your own physicality. Also, be sure everyone in your family is aware of your plans to fulfill this uniquely postmortem mitzvah. Many people still remember the former Jewish position against organ donation; this sometimes leads family members to block their deceased loved one's organ donation out of emotional discomfort or misplaced devotion.

May you be blessed to take the time to honor and overcome any inner fears to fulfilling the mitzvah of organ donation. Remember, "whoever saves one life is considered as if [s]he had saved the entire world." [Mishnah Sanhedrin 4:6].

Rabbi Goldie Milgram
Aleph Ordination Program
Philadelphia, PA

RECONSTRUCTIONIST

It's hard to accept that someone's life and soul are gone when brain death is declared. We still see our beloved in front of us, warm, breathing, pulse going as fast as ever. It takes great love for the world to say, "Since the person I knew is gone, please take their organs, so that others may enjoy the life my loved one is now losing." For those of us who find meaning in traditional rituals like tahara (ritual washing of the body), it's harder still.

But we cannot let fear or denial prevent a life-affirming choice. Tradition may once have equivocated on this question, but today the commandment of "not standing idly by the blood of your neighbor" includes the hundreds of millions of "neighbors" within a five-hour flight, whose sight or happiness or hope can be restored only by letting your newly deceased loved one give a final and great gift.

A favorite bumper sticker reads, "Don't take your organs to heaven—heaven knows we need them here!" Organ donation needs to be seen as a true mitzvah, a commandment, a "must." If you fear that upon the Messiah's return you will be resurrected without a vital organ, remember that a God who can raise the dead can make you a new cornea or kidney.

May you live a long healthy life and die peacefully at 120. But in case you don't: Have a heart. Sign up now to give yours so that, if need be, someone else can have a true *lev chadash*, a new heart. God and the thousands of precious souls on transplant waiting lists demand no less.

> **Rabbi Fred Scherlinder Dobb**
> *Adat Shalom Reconstructionist*
> *Congregation*
> *Bethesda, MD*

REFORM

The Reform movement's position is to permit transplantation of organs or body parts from a corpse for any legitimate medical purpose. Some authorities claim that the procedure violates the traditional prohibitions against deriving benefit from the dead (*hana'ah mehamet*), treating the corpse in a disrespectful manner (*nivul hamet*), and unnecessarily delaying the burial of the corpse in its entirety (*halanat hamet*). We argue that none of these prohibitions applies in this case and that they cannot prevent us from fulfilling the overriding mitzvah to save life (*pikuach nefesh*) and to heal the sick. To be agents of life and healing after our deaths is to render honor and respect to our bodies. It is not an act of desecration or mutilation.

Then there are organ donations made by living persons. Here, too, the Reform halachic tradition considers it praiseworthy for a healthy individual to donate an organ in order to heal the sick. The most obvious objection against this is our tradition's teaching that we are not to expose our lives to unnecessary danger. Through the ages, some rabbis have interpreted this prohibition strictly: We should never subject ourselves even to a limited degree of risk, even in order to save the life of another. A competing interpretation, however, would permit and even require us to accept a limited degree of risk to save a fellow human being from mortal danger.

We must also consider the transplantation of such vital organs as the heart and the liver. These must be functioning in order to be of benefit to the recipient, yet to remove them from the donor would result in the latter's death. Reform Judaism accepts the standard of brain death as a sufficient indicator. Thus, when clinical tests reveal that the donor is brain dead and that the function of his or her vital organs is being maintained solely through artificial means, then those organs may be used for transplantation.

Rabbi Mark Washofsky
Hebrew Union College/Jewish Institute
of Religion
Cincinnati, OH

CONSERVATIVE

Jewish law and tradition endorse the principle of *kavod lamet*, (honoring the deceased), including prompt burial and respectful treatment of remains. At the same time, Judaism affirms the centrality of the mitzvah of *pikuach nefesh*, (saving lives).

Members of The Committee on Jewish Law and Standards of the Conservative movement (CJLS) have long grappled with the tension between *kavod lamet* and *pikuach nefesh*, asking whether it is possible for *pikuach nefesh* to override the concern with *kavod lamet*. Their answer is that not only is it okay for a Jew to donate organs, and not only is it an act of *hesed* (loving kindness), it is a mitzvah, a positive command. "Saving a person's life is so sacred a value in Judaism that if a person's organ can be used to save someone else's life, it is actually an honor for the deceased," says Rabbi Elliot Dorff, a member of the CJLS and rector of the University of Judaism.

The Conservative movement provides two forms for people to sign. One is a legal document to be signed by the donor and two witnesses. The other document to be signed asks family members to act as partners in the mitzvah of *pikuach nefesh*.

Rabbi Avis D. Miller
Adas Israel Congregation
Washington, DC

MODERN ORTHODOX

Judaism's fundamental value is the primacy and dignity of all life. Human life is godlike—created in the image of God—and is to be treated as infinitely valuable, equal and unique.

Respect does not end with the death of a beloved. The dead body is the shell of a living image of God, but Jewish tradition confirms human dignity in life by calling on us to treat the corpse with reverence. Cleansing, purifying and escorting the dead to the final resting place, burying, mourning and remembering—all are done out of *hesed shel emet* (true loving kindness). They are the paradigm of pure goodness because the dead person cannot repay the kindness.

The prohibition against use of a body is an expression of the principle that respect and love transcend economic considerations. Thus, it is a tradition not to use the deceased's belongings but to give them away to the poor. This concept is also the source of the strong tradition of protecting graves (and not moving bodies needlessly) as well as opposition among the most traditional Jews to autopsies and even organ donation.

Now, however, modern science has changed the halachic attitude by changing the dynamics of lifesaving. When early modern medicine showed that an autopsy could save a life by establishing causes of death and the pattern of mortality, Rabbi Yehezkel Landau (1713-1793) ruled that when there is an ill person whose life can be saved by performing an autopsy on a recently deceased individual, then the mitzvah of lifesaving overrules the prohibition of use from a dead body. The halachic authorities then followed with permission to donate organs with family approval. Rabbi Moshe Feinstein widened this permission to corneal transplants, arguing that blindness is a form of death: The handicap so reduces the quality of life that restoring sight is equivalent to lifesaving.

Heart transplants then became the cutting-edge issue. The classic, halachic definition of death was cessation of breathing. Following this principle meant that when death came, the deteriorated heart would not be usable. Doctors then showed that brain death can occur while breathing and a heartbeat continues. However, the early survival rate of heart transplant patients was so low that Rabbi Feinstein ruled that those who performed heart transplants were guilty of double murder— removing the heart from a halachically alive person and dooming the recipient as well.

Happily, medicine continued to improve and heart transplant survival rates soared. Rabbi Feinstein finally ruled that brain death is a legitimate criterion for establishing death and that donating a heart fulfilled the mitzvah of lifesaving and constituted a permitted use of a dead person's body.

Organ donation is the highest mitzvah, and the most religious person should perform it. The ultimate respect for the dead is to enable them to save a life; giving life is the highest form of respect for life.

Rabbi Yitz Greenberg
Riverdale, NY

CHABAD

Jewish law distinguishes between organ donation during your lifetime and organ donation after death. While you are alive, to donate an organ that you can live without in order to save another life is one of the greatest acts you could do. "To save a life is to save an entire universe," our sages have declared. After death too, organ donation is permitted—and constitutes an awesome mitzvah—in the case when an organ is needed for a specific, immediate transplant. Yet, a few considerations need to be addressed.

In Jewish tradition, the body, during life and after death, possesses profound sanctity and its desecration, even in the slightest form, is prohibited. If the organ is being used to save a specific life, there is no greater honor one can bestow upon the body. But when you sign a consent form to have your organs removed, the doctors will remove them whether or not they are needed for an immediate transplant. They may use them for research, store them for future transplantation or even throw them out. Therefore, unless there is an actual person who immediately needs the organ, it is improper to tamper with a corpse. Even when there is a specific, immediate transplant, there is need for caution, because often times in order to obtain organs as fresh as possible, a doctor will remove the organ before the patient is actually "dead" according to Jewish law.

The bottom line is that each case is different. Many considerations in Jewish law and spirituality must be reviewed. So before going ahead with any procedure, I'd consult with a rabbi well versed in Talmud and Jewish law. It is not as simple as blankly signing an organ donation card. When dealing with questions so fundamental and far-reaching as life and death, the responsibility is huge. Sentiment and feelings can be dangerous judges. I wouldn't want to have to decide what is right and wrong based on my own subjective opinion. Thank G-d we have the Torah to guide us.

Rabbi Yosef Y. Jacobson
Rabbinical College Chovevei Torah
Brooklyn, NY

Do science and Judaism conflict?

S cience and religion have been at odds in the public sphere for centuries, from Galileo's struggles with the Inquisition to the Scopes "monkey trial" in 1925 and on through contemporary (and continuing) fights over the age of the Earth and whether evolution can be included in school textbooks. Since most of these arguments involve Christian doctrines, Jews have largely been bystanders; many of us think of Judaism as science-friendly, whether because of the emphasis Jewish tradition puts on argument and debate or simply because the community has produced so many leading scientists.

Many of the rabbis share this general view, but as you'd expect, it's a bit more complicated. We asked this question in 2014 as part of a wider examination of the interaction between science and Judaism. The rabbis' answers show how throughout Jewish history, attempts to reconcile two very different approaches to the world have produced interesting reflections, whether or not you'd call them a "conflict." One, appropriately, answers with another question: Do two sides of a coin conflict? (Published in 2014.)

INDEPENDENT

There is no conflict between science and Judaism. Nowhere, for instance, does the Torah indicate that the universe was created in six 24-hour days. After all, we measure time by our spin around the sun, and the sun did not appear on the scene until the fourth "day." The 13th-century Rabbi Yitzchak of Acco theorized the age of the universe to be around 14 billion years (Shoshan Yesod Olam). This was written into our tradition eight centuries before modern science arrived at a similar estimate. The ancient rabbis also describe the universe as originating with God's Light, which condensed to form matter (the Zohar, Vol. 1, folio 30b and Vol. 2, folios 75b-76a; Midrash B'reishit Rabbah 3:1). Or, as Einstein would put it centuries later: "$E=mc^2$." It is not science but scientism that is in conflict with Judaism. The late Dr. Robert Jastrow, founding director of NASA's Goddard Institute, described scientism as "a kind of religion in science . . . violated by the discovery that the world had a beginning under the conditions in which the known laws of physics are not valid, and as a product of forces or circumstances we cannot discover." "For the scientist who has lived by his faith in the power of reason, the story ends like a bad dream," Jastrow told *The New York Times* in 1978. "He has scaled the mountains of ignorance; he is about to conquer the highest peak; as he pulls himself over the final rock, he is greeted by a band of theologians who have been sitting there for centuries."

Rabbi Gershon Winkler
Walking Stick Foundation
Thousand Oaks, CA

HUMANIST

When religion bases its teachings on blind faith, unsubstantiated mythology and superstition, it stands in conflict with scientific thinking. Worse, when it denies the hard evidence that science provides, it suppresses the advancement of knowledge. Judaism is mostly innocent of these charges, though a minority view historically rejected the

Copernican revolution, holds to a literal reading of the Bible, thinks the world is only thousands of years old, believes in miracles or awaits an unproven world-to-come. In contrast, the true strength of Judaism is its ability to separate myth from fact and to welcome intellectual debate and skeptical thinking. Putting aside all the Nobel Prizes, it should really be no wonder that so many Jews entered scientific fields in the first place. Science, for Judaism, is an ally, not an opponent. Einstein once wrote that "the cosmic religious feeling is the strongest and noblest motive for scientific research." He also said that for Johannes Kepler and Isaac Newton to disentangle the principles of celestial mechanics, they required a "deep conviction of the rationality of the universe."

Rabbi Peter H. Schweitzer
The City Congregation for
Humanistic Judaism
New York, NY

RENEWAL

Just because something is scientifically possible does not mean that undertaking it is advisable. Oil extraction techniques that destroy the environment, for instance, contravene the mitzvah of *bal tashchit*—refraining from damage to nature. The rapidly evolving practice of designing and creating animal-human hybrids is a current point of contention. When this is done for reasons of saving life—undertaken in labs through genetic engineering and/or implantation of physical material—Jewish bioethicists see the letter of the laws of *kilayim* (based on the biblical injunction to refrain from interbreeding species) as being satisfied. But Rabbi Moshe D. Tendler has written that a human brain, for example, in an animal's body would contravene the Jewish principle of *k'vod habriyot*, respect for the integrity of species. This accords with the Ramban, who taught that one who mixes two different species is "changing and denying the Divine Creation of the world." Looking to the future, the Jewish value of *tzaar baalei chayyim* (refraining from cruelty to animals) might render unkosher something like science fiction writer Frank Herbert's "chairdog," a chair that is alive and partly sentient that shapes itself to the person sitting in it.

Conflicts of Judaism and science help us think things through. Conflict can also abate as science advances. For example, organ and tissue donation, once impermissible during the early days of low effectiveness, is now accounted a mitzvah under most circumstances.

Rabbi Goldie Milgram
ReclaimingJudaism.org
Philadelphia, PA

RECONSTRUCTIONIST

Judaism is rich, but often arcane; our stories alienate skeptical moderns who cherish hard facts. Science is true, but often cold; its mechanistic view devalues nature and humanity. Science emphasizes knowledge and utility; Judaism views the world with appreciation and awe. Both matter, and we Jews have long been blessed to blend the best of each. While offering its own mythic truths, Judaism has long respected scientific truths: The Bible carefully observes the natural world (Proverbs, Job, Ecclesiastes); great Talmudic rabbis were also agronomists and researchers; astronomers and doctors wrote great medieval Jewish treatises, and Rav Abraham Kook, the first Chief Rabbi of pre-state Israel, supported Darwin, writing that "evolution sheds light on all God's ways." Our pro-science history gives hope today, when attacks on science threaten our very lives. There's a robust scientific consensus that our short-sighted actions are already causing dangerous climate change; it's getting worse but can be averted with our serious commitment. Some ideologues (usually funded by carbon-intensive industries) "deny" climate science. Here, we Jews, who bring scientific facts into our spiritual formation, can lead: When we pioneer zero-carbon religion for our imperiled era, we'll be both empirical and ethical. Sustainability is the synthesis of science and spirit.

Rabbi Fred Scherlinder Dobb
Adat Shalom Reconstructionist
Congregation
Bethesda, MD

REFORM

As an undergraduate in a religious studies course, I wrote a paper on creation and evolution, asking whether creation could really have happened the way it is described in the Torah. It was at that point that I learned about day-age theory, which states that a day of creation was perhaps not 24 hours but, instead, hundreds of thousands or even millions of years. If we read the creation story through that lens, we can see that the order of creation described in Torah symbolizes the scientific process of evolution. For progressive Jews, science and Judaism do not have to conflict. We do not have to read Torah literally. Torah and Judaism are meant to teach us values and ethics, which give us a framework to guide our lives. Judaism provides us ways to express awe, wonder and appreciation for the mysteries of the universe and give thanks for the human mind, which is able to seek new understandings of that universe through scientific exploration and experimentation. For many, that scientific process enhances the appreciation of God's miraculous creation.

Rabbi Laura Novak Winer
Fresno, CA

CONSERVATIVE

In chapter one of Genesis, God said, "Let us make the human being in our image"— something God did not say about the creation of other animals. Human beings generally recognize that they are qualitatively different from all other animals. Does this conflict with the teaching of Darwinian evolution that the human species is just one among the primates and evolved from previous primate species? Evolutionary biologists continue to probe the question of how human beings evolved differently from other primates. Their consensus is that species evolved in a process of random natural selection. The idea of natural selection being random appears to conflict with Jewish teachings that God purposely differentiated human beings from other creatures. But rather than serving as a cause for pitting Judaism and science against each other, the apparent contradiction can serve as an example of God's greatness. God created a world in which human beings are similar to their close primate relatives in many ways. But in certain decisive ways, human beings are distinct—the best example being that we are able to debate and write about these very questions.

Rabbi Amy Wallk Katz
Temple Beth El
Springfield, MA

MODERN ORTHODOX

It all depends on the approach. In recent centuries, fundamentalist believers have focused on the conflicts, claiming that science is undermining our sacred texts and that one must therefore uphold God's authority by rejecting scientific views. (See under: Evolution versus Creation.) The Lubavitcher Rebbe rejected geology's assertion that the earth was billions of years old—explaining that the fossils were implanted in nature by God when the earth was created thousands of years ago. Ultra-Orthodox Jews, and now many centrist leaders of yeshivas, have rejected biblical criticism and historically critical approaches to halacha as forbidden because, they believe, these approaches undermine the belief that every word of Torah is given directly by God and not subject to change.

I offer an alternative view. Maimonides believed that Nature, i.e. the world, is Exhibit Number One of God's existence and presence. To understand the nature of Nature is to understand the divine creative power and elements of its wisdom and values. Therefore, in his magnum opus *Mishneh Torah*, in the opening book Sefer Mada, he explains physical creation by making physics and astronomy elements of the holy Torah—that is, ways of studying and learning about God and God's Torah. In his *Guide for the Perplexed*, Maimonides further explains that the Book of Revelation as expressed in Nature cannot conflict with the Book of Revelation which is the written and oral Torah. After all, they have the same Author. When they appear to conflict, humans should use their reason and judgment and reconcile the Torah's teaching with the best—that is, the most credible—science of the day. While Maimonides affirms that the final word must go to God and religion, he insists that it is a mitzvah to use our reason and (re)interpret the Torah—even drastically—to make it accord with the truth as best established by human reason. In other words, he argues that the truth and authority of the Torah should not be predicated on know-nothingism, ignorance or lack of scientific understanding. To which I say: Amen.

Rabbi Yitz Greenberg
Riverdale, NY

ORTHODOX

I reject the belief that Judaism and science conflict. Maimonides first confronted the scientific challenge to the Bible's story of creation when it came into conflict with the Aristotelian theory of the eternity of matter. Maimonides was clear. He rejected Aristotle's theory, but not because it contradicted scripture—he was prepared to reinterpret scripture to accommodate the theory, but only if the theory were proven true by some infallible means. Rather, he rejected Aristotle's theory because it was wrong, as was subsequently proven by science. Today everyone rejects the eternity of matter in favor of the Big Bang, with its strong creation overtones. This is the approach we should take today as well. If evolution and neo-Darwinism, for example, are proven to be true, then there is no conflict with the biblical story of creation, given that the Bible is clear that the creation follows the pattern of the inanimate being followed by the vegetable, animal and finally intellectual. Of course, we would insist that God guided, at every step and in every way, the ascent of life. But before we make a full accommodation to the theory, we must note that there remain holes in the evolutionary model, such as the quantum leaps in the fossil record that led some paleontologists, notably Stephen Jay Gould, to suggest that evolution is governed much more by "punctuated equilibrium" than by continuous evolutionary development.

Rabbi Shmuley Boteach
Englewood, NJ

CHABAD

I hate to get all rabbinic about this, but Judaism and science conflict completely—and they don't conflict at all. Does one side of a coin conflict with the other? It's the exact opposite, and yet they're one and the same. Do the brain and the heart conflict? They can be diametrically opposed, and yet both together are who I am. Science tells us *what*. It is the study of measurable phenomena, the expectation of how those phenomena are likely to repeat or how they may have developed in the past. It is a doctor understanding the nature of what exactly makes up the human body and how those pieces work in concert. Judaism tells us *why*. It is the study of the Infinite Will, the understanding of our raison d'être and the application of moral and ethical guides for our existence. It is the psychologist delving into why I do what I do, the philosopher considering the implications of my being and my actions, the parent appreciating the wonder and awe of a newborn baby. Total opposites, yet both struggling with the same reality. Science is the study of G-d's actions, while Judaism is the appreciation of His will. If they seem in conflict, one or both have not yet been understood to their ultimate truth.

Rabbi Dov Wagner
Rohr Chabad Jewish Student Center
University of Southern California
Los Angeles, CA

When does life begin?

O f all the ways of asking the abortion question, this one goes most directly to the religious beliefs and assumptions that underlie public policy. People are often surprised to learn that such a fundamental philosophical question is answered differently in different religious traditions— or, as these answers make clear, by different authorities and sages within a single tradition. Within Jewish tradition, hundreds, even thousands of years of debate on the nature of a fetus and the degree of respect owed to human life at its various stages produce answers that are nuanced, complex and extremely difficult to translate into simple political stances.

We asked this question back in 2009; it seemed pressing then, and even more so now, to let rabbinic voices be heard as political struggles over abortion (and even contraception) continue to rage. The variety, subtlety and breadth of Jewish tradition are on full display here. Indeed, while any rabbi may make a halachic determination in a specific case, none of these answers can be taken as definitive or official Jewish doctrine, even within a rabbi's own denomination. (Published in 2009.)

INDEPENDENT

Nineteen hundred years ago when Caesar Antoninus asked this question of Rabbi Yehudah Ha-Nasi, the rabbi replied: "From the moment the fetus emerges from the womb" (Midrash Bereishit Rabbah 34:10).

The 11th-century Rabbi Shlomo Yitzchaki (Rashi) explained: "For the fetus in the womb is not considered a person until it is born" (*Talmud Bavli*, Sanhedrin 72b). Earlier rabbinic codes clearly place the welfare of the mother first, and "if a woman experiences difficulty in childbirth, the fetus is dismembered within her, limb by limb, because her life takes precedence" (Mishnah Ohalot 7:6 and *Talmud Yerushalmi*, Sanhedrin, end of Ch. 8). Not only her life, later rabbis added, but her emotional well-being. "While woman is biologically equipped to bear children," writes Rav Yeruchem Perilman (19th century), "she is nevertheless not as a clump of earth, and is therefore not obliged to nurture seed implanted within her against her will" (in Ohr Gadol No. 31). Classical Jewish rulings concerning abortion rely primarily on the woman's instinct, and they respect that until the fetus emerges from the womb, it remains an integral part of the woman's body alone.

Rabbi Gershon Winkler
Walking Stick Foundation
Thousand Oaks, CA

HUMANIST

In the view of the Talmud, it was only after a newborn had lived 30 days that it proved its viability and gained the status of a person and the legal rights of an adult. These days, with modem hygiene and healthy prenatal care working in our favor, we rarely have to wait that full month to trust in our baby's survival. So if the clue to the beginning of life hinges on viability, there may be some truth to the popular Jewish maxim that life doesn't truly begin until the children finish graduate school.

But we know that Jewish parents never stop worrying about their grown children. According to the title of a popular song, life really begins at 40, "when love and living start to become a gentle art." But research suggests that this may be a myth. For many people, hitting 40 is synonymous with forgetfulness, longer recovery time from aches and pains and a gradual physical breakdown. Could it all be downhill from there? The ultimate message is that life is unpredictable, unstable and ultimately finite. It is up to us to begin life anew each day and to fill each day with purpose, joy and the fullness of life.

Rabbi Peter Schweitzer
The City Congregation for
Humanistic Judaism
New York, NY

RENEWAL

When I taught women's studies to conservative Christian students in the American South, they were curious about the Jewish view of when a fetus becomes a "person" and how that affects the Jewish position on abortion. The answer, which is consistent across the entire Jewish spectrum, never failed to astonish them: We don't know when a fetus becomes a "person." Talmudic sages consulted a midwife along with male medical scholars when they discussed the question of when a person becomes a *nefesh*, an embodied soul. They considered many possibilities: conception, in utero, movement, birth, beginning of speech. They concluded that mere human beings could not know such a subtle secret. This set the tone for future Jewish discussion about abortion. We do not base serious life decisions on metaphysical speculation but on concrete factors related to the life of the person making the decision. How would the mother's physical and mental health be threatened by carrying the child to term? If it were known that the child would be disabled, how would the mother be affected by raising it? If abortion were performed, how would the mother cope with having taken a life? If you consider these questions, you sometimes conclude that abortion is required.

Rabbi Laura Duhan Kaplan
Or Shalom Synagogue
Vancouver, British Columbia

RECONSTRUCTIONIST

The 19th century Hasidic Rabbi Menachem Mendel of Kotzk asked, "Where is God?," then answered his own question: "Wherever we let God in." Life, which comes from God, is much the same. Life begins neither at conception nor at birth, but wherever and whenever we affirm it. To affirm life we must acknowledge it as a mystery and a miracle, never taking it for granted. And we should never assume that we fully understand it. We cannot demean those who believe differently about life's origins or timetable. People differ on life's appearance. A couple that has long wanted a child rightly marvels at the fetal life taking shape. A young woman in social or economic straits, distressed about the quality of life she could give to another (or achieve herself), rightly consults Planned Parenthood. Prospective parents, poring over disturbing amniotic data, rightly debate how to proceed.

Biology aside, we can all do much more to affirm life. Life's beginning may be a mystery—but when we extend health coverage to all families, limit our carbon emissions, fully fund Head Start or just act with more kindness each day, we truly let Life in.

Rabbi Fred Scherlinder Dobb
Adat Shalom Reconstructionist
Congregation
Bethesda, MD

REFORM

Ancients argued whether life begins at conception or first breath. As a rabbi, I find the search for the moment that physical life begins as missing the point. The real question is, when does spiritual life begin? At what point in the journey does understanding dawn upon our soul that our life is finite? When we become conscious that we have only a limited opportunity to engage in the world, this moment of understanding is, I would argue, when life really begins.

This moment of insight then brings us to the essential question: How to live a life of meaning, purpose and intention? Only after we confront these questions does our life really begin. There are people who lack the spark of hope and purpose in their lives. While they may breathe, are they really alive in their life? When we awaken to the understanding that life is a blessing of limited opportunity to add to the goodness of the world and then commit ourselves to the active pursuit of deeds of loving kindness, this is when our life really begins.

Rabbi David Wilfond
Hebrew Union College
Jerusalem

CONSERVATIVE

Our sages agree that life of a human being begins when the majority of the newborn infant (i.e. its head) has emerged and the child is able to take its first breath. The life breath is the *neshama*, the soul, a piece of divinity within us that truly makes us independently alive and human. Before its emergence into the world, the mother's life takes precedence over that of the unborn fetus. This being said, an unborn fetus still deserves our deepest respect. If a woman suffers the loss of her pregnancy after the fifth month, I will officiate at a burial in a cemetery and be there for the grieving parents and family. I do this because, after a certain point in its development, there is so much potential human life in that fetus that its life demands our *kavod*, our respect, and dignified treatment. During the nine months of pregnancy, a miracle is unfolding, moment by moment, in the womb: Life evolves from zygote to embryo to fetus, approaching a humanity that becomes complete with the moment of birth itself. While it is not yet a fully independent human life, and stem cell research is certainly permissible—I believe it is even a mitzvah—we must stand in awe at the miracle of human life developing at every step of a woman's pregnancy.

Rabbi Gil Steinlauf
Adas Israel Congregation
Washington, DC

MODERN ORTHODOX

Human life is created in the image of God. Jewish ethics and halacha spell out the behaviors owed to a human being— ranging from not to kill and not to harm to feeding when hungry and loving the other human being as yourself. Is an embryo entitled to all the dignities of a human being? If the answer is yes, then abortion should be prohibited. In general, Orthodox law is against abortion unless the fetus directly threatens the mother's life—in which case, it is a mitzvah to protect the mother's life by aborting the baby. As with most traditional sources, I believe that life begins at conception. However, I also believe that life is not fully developed until the baby is born and proves to be viable. The embryo has the dignity of being potential but not fully formed life. A significant number of Orthodox rabbis take this position—especially in light of the Talmudic statement that up to 40 days, the embryo is considered water/liquid and not life. Therefore, they (and I) are more supportive of the possibility of an abortion to protect the mother's health or well-being over a wider range of threats such as nervous breakdown or deep depression. The bulk of Orthodox rabbis also do not equate abortion with murder of a viable human being, which is the gravest sin of all. Of course, upholding the potential human life (=fetus) demands caring, protecting, feeding, respecting both the embryo and the mother.

Rabbi Yitz Greenberg
Riverdale, NY

SEPHARDIC

There is an unfortunate tendency in public discourse to oversimplify highly complex and nuanced subject matter for the sake of fueling entertaining debate. We are either "pro-life" or "pro-choice." We either advocate for "women's reproductive rights" or we emphasize "the rights of the fetus." None of these slogans sheds light on the moral principles involved in the ongoing disagreements over the morality of abortion. Jewish law does not exclusively endorse either the pro-life or the pro-choice platform: There is a range of valid rabbinical opinion vis-a-vis the permissibility of abortion under certain circumstances. What Jewish law categorically rejects is the attempt to gloss over moral ambiguities by wrapping oneself in the mantle of civil rights and claiming that one is being disenfranchised and mistreated simply because one's freedom of action is being curtailed. Some have determined that women are entitled to "reproductive rights"—in other words, the right to terminate pregnancy and kill a fetus—and that anyone who questions the legitimacy of abortion-on-demand is misogynistic and unjust. I find this kind of attitude to be counterproductive and dishonest. Extremists on both sides of this issue obstruct serious consideration of its nuances by providing black-and-white answers.

Rabbi Joshua Maroof
Magen David Sephardic Congregation
Rockville, MD

ULTRA-ORTHODOX

Human life begins in three stages. The stage of conception is the moment when the soul comes into this world (Sanhedrin 91b) and your potential is defined (Niddah \6h/Tanchumri). At this stage the fetus is called *maya b'alma*, mere water (Yevamot 69b) and not a human being. The second stage begins at 40 days. The fetus is considered a human being, yet the mother's life will take precedence and the fetus can be aborted if it is the cause of a health threat to the mother. The third stage is birth. Birth is the moment the head emerges, or in a breech situation the majority of the body. From that moment on, the child's life and mother's life are separate lives of equal importance.

Rabbi Simcha Tolwin
Executive Director, Aish
Huntington Woods
Southfield, MI

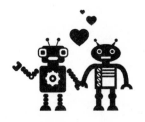

PART TWO

SEX

R abbinic discussion of sex is full of surprises. The first is just how much of it there is; far from being prudish, the Talmud and the midrash are filled with frank talk about the most intimate details of sexuality, up to and including the story about the student who hides under his teacher's marital bed and, when discovered, protests, "But rabbi, this too is Torah!" Is Judaism a sex-positive religion, in contrast to others that consider sex intrinsically sinful or problematic or enshrine celibacy as the highest ideal? That depends: Relatively liberal positions on some issues such as contraception or abortion are in some tension with centuries of emphasis on women's ritual impurity during menstruation. You can see the tug-of-war among competing values from question to question, and a steady underlying pull toward keeping people inside the community rather than casting them out.

Does Jewish law or tradition offer any guidance on contraception?

People often think of birth control as one of the greatest divides between traditional and modern family life, especially for women. But the vast variety of traditional citations here—even discussions of chemical, botanical and barrier methods as well as the traditional "sin of Onan," coitus interruptus—underscores that human beings have been facing some basic challenges for as far back as you care to go.

This topic showcases the way rulings can vary along the spectrum of opinion from liberal to conservative rabbis (of course, rabbis in individual denominations differ, too) but also the way those differences frequently are expressed more in terms of emphasis than of the underlying religious law. And our Chabad rabbi is missing from the lineup—the result of a stalemate with a rabbi who felt that only a woman should address this question, but who couldn't refer us to one because his movement doesn't allow women to be rabbis. (Published in 2014.)

INDEPENDENT

Judaism does not restrict a woman in regard to her choices concerning pregnancy. She has a choice to bear children or not to bear children (*Talmud Bavli*, Yevamot 65b; Mahar'shal in Yam Shel Shlomo 1:8). The injunction to "Be fruitful and multiply," the ancient rabbis ruled, does not apply to women, because the Torah does not ask someone to do something that might endanger his or her life and health. On the other hand, a man who has not yet brought children into the world (ideally at least one of each gender) may not use contraception unless the woman he is with faces some sort of danger to her life or health. Coitus interruptus in the course of lovemaking, however, is permitted if its intent is incidental and not deliberately intended to prevent pregnancy (Tosefot Ri'd on Yevamot). There are enough classical halachic opinions regarding allowable methods of contraception to cover most contemporary methods, but since there is no space to elucidate them here, best to consult your rabbi.

Rabbi Gershon Winkler
Walking Stick Foundation
Thousand Oaks, CA

HUMANIST

Secular Jews are not influenced by traditional edicts to "be fruitful and multiply" or "not to spill one's seed." However, we do recognize that there are benefits to contraception, including female health, family planning and disease prevention. In the end, Humanistic Judaism takes the position that individuals will make their own decisions as to which birth control methods, if any, they wish to use. This is not a privilege but a right that needs to be protected.

We are living in an age that the ancient rabbis or even our great-great-grandparents could not have imagined. Premarital sex is commonplace today, if not encouraged, as part of building a relationship with a caring partner. Promiscuity is equally prevalent. "Friends with benefits" is a phenomenon of our time. Even the idea of marriage for love and as a sexually exclusive monogamous relationship is relatively modern.

Perhaps it would be easier to live in a less complicated time. But the clock can't be wound back. And so we need to face all these modern and often complicated choices with as much wisdom and caution as possible. Which, in many instances, includes the wise use—and easy availability—of contraception.

Rabbi Peter H. Schweitzer
The City Congregation for
Humanistic Judaism
New York, NY

RENEWAL

When it comes to methods of both contraception and assisted fertility, bioethics sources within Judaism are copious. The consensus, as with abortion, is that the physical and mental health of the mother comes first. A society or corporation that restricts access to medically safe abortion or contraception is one in which Jews are not free to practice their religion.

In a free society, the decision of whether, or when, to have children is a matter of individual conscience. Jewish law and tradition take into account the stress upon partners and existing children when excess family size or timing might impair the development or well-being of the parents or existing children. (See Rav Moses Trani, Kiryat Sefer on Yad, Issurei Bi'ah, 21; *Contraception within Contemporary Orthodoxy*, by Gedalia Meyer and Henoch Messner, and *Integral Halachah: Transcending and Including*, by Rabbis Zalman Schachter-Shalomi and Daniel Siegel.)

Across the spectrum of Jewish practice, the accepted and/or endorsed circumstances for and types of contraception and fertility assistance vary greatly and are considered on a situation-by-situation basis. While the trauma of infertility and the intention to "be fruitful and multiply" are honored throughout the Torah and Jewish history itself, there is no explicit prohibition against contraception within

Torah. Methods that prevent conception rather than "spilling seed" are preferred by some, so IUDs and the pill are most often prescribed where this is a consideration.

Save for in a few sects, sexual pleasure within a committed relationship is also a primary Jewish value. Rabbi Mordechai Eliahu, the late chief rabbi of Israel, writes in his book, *Darkei Tahara*: "A man is obligated to make his wife happy in the mitzvah of marital relations... (Pesachim 72B, Rashi, derived from Exodus 21:10). A partner who withholds from relations...to deliberately cause...anguish is transgressing the Torah (*Shulchan Aruch*, Even HaEzer, 76:11)." Regardless of gender, based on the principle of *pikuach nefesh* (saving a life), it's permissible to seek out barrier methods and safer assisted fertility processes in the event of a transmissible disease like AIDS.

Rabbi Goldie Milgram
ReclaimingJudaism.org
Sarasota, FL

RECONSTRUCTIONIST

Judaism's first guidance on contraception is simply to discuss it. Our tradition is not prudish. Racy Bible stories, sexualized medieval mysticism and more can be helpful today, when we're often uncomfortable discussing sex. We mustn't teach our children too little or too late. Given the physical risks of sexually transmitted diseases and the emotional consequences of unplanned pregnancies, we must teach contraception prophylactically. And that's not just a civic responsibility, it's a spiritual one: Sex education belongs in religious school classrooms—and on the bimah.

More broadly, Jewish values support and commend contraception. This applies not just with premarital sex but for wives and husbands as well. Halachically speaking, families need not be huge: Shammai says two sons, Hillel says a son and a daughter, and a variant text (Mishnah & Tosefta Yevamot 6:6) says two children of any gender suffice, fulfilling our command (Genesis 1:28) to "be fruitful and multiply." Rabbi Arthur Waskow suggests that in our ecologically imperiled era, "be fruitful" is the first commandment we've performed collectively; having now filled the world, humanity should stop before we fill it past capacity. Contraception protects women's agency; it prevents overpopulation; it saves lives. Contraception is kosher!

Rabbi Fred Scherlinder Dobb
Adat Shalom Reconstructionist
Congregation
Bethesda, MD

REFORM

The rabbis of ancient days spent considerable energy exploring questions about contraception and procreation. Textual sources demonstrate that a variety of forms of contraception were widely used. Those rabbis explored and debated the circumstances in which contraception could or could not be used. For example, according to Jewish law, a man is not allowed to "waste seed" —spill semen without purpose—so the use of coitus interruptus would not have been acceptable.

Traditionally, procreation was considered an obligation of a man but not of a woman. So a woman, once she had allowed her husband to fulfill his obligation, could make use of contraception that did not "waste seed," such as ingesting herbs that prevented conception.

As a Reform Jew, I focus my concerns about contraception more on the sexual freedoms and protections of both men and women. Nowadays, it is incumbent upon Jewish legal authorities to allow for the use of contraception—as Reform Judaism does—so that we can reduce physical, emotional and spiritual risks and diminish the spread of sexually transmitted diseases and infections. Judaism actively supports a woman's right to make decisions about her own body if and when she chooses to procreate or prevent pregnancy.

Rabbi Laura Novak Winer
Fresno, CA

CONSERVATIVE

Judaism has always promoted marriage and raising children as mitzvot. The relevant sources start in the very beginning of Genesis, with all humans being commanded to follow the lead of Adam and Eve: "Thus shall a man leave his father and mother and cling to his wife, so that they become one flesh" (Genesis 2:24). The tradition recognizes the value of the marital bond, including its physical component, separate from the issue of procreation. Additionally, rabbinic texts discuss how many children a couple should have and when their obligation to be "fruitful and multiply, fill the earth and master it" (Genesis 1:28) has been completed. Finally, it is noteworthy that the sages discussed contraception explicitly, albeit in different terms and with different understandings of the human reproductive system. Some allowed contraception because they viewed it as an extension of the obligation to protect one's physical and mental health. Others allow it in situations without such risks. In traditional sources, the use of contraception was always considered against a backdrop of sexuality within marriage and a commitment to raising children.

Rabbi Amy Wallk Katz
Temple Beth El
Springfield, MA

MODERN ORTHODOX

Judaism's highest commitment is to life. Its goal is to repair the world to the point where life wins out over all its enemies (like oppression, war, sickness). To assure the continuity of life, the Torah instructs humans to have children, to "be fruitful and multiply." This mitzvah can be fulfilled minimally by having two children. But the Talmud suggests that parents should keep going because "[God] created the world not to be void, but to be settled"—that is, filled with life (Isaiah 45:18). If parents leave behind three or more children, then the world will be filled with more life. Creating family and having children comes ahead of contraception.

Judaism is equally committed to advancing the quality of life.

Therefore, if the couple wants to wait until they establish their relationship in marriage, or to accommodate professional training and advancement needs, or to space the children to better raise and educate them, I would affirm the use of contraception—though more haredi Orthodox rabbis tend to disagree on this.

Finally, contraception is always morally and religiously preferable to abortion as a form of birth control, and contraception to protect health is always a mitzvah. As a result of historic traditions, Jewish law prioritizes female over male forms of contraception and chemical methods over barrier methods such as condoms and diaphragms. The bottom line is: Use contraception in the service of life.

Rabbi Yitz Greenberg
Riverdale, NY

ORTHODOX

Unlike Catholicism, Judaism believes that the purpose of sex is not procreation but intimacy. The Bible makes that clear in the second chapter of Genesis: "Therefore shall a man leave his father and leave his mother. He shall cleave unto his wife and they shall become one flesh." The purpose of sex is to orchestrate two separate halves as one indivisible whole. Of course, Judaism loves children, and there is a mitzvah for a couple to have at least a boy and a girl—and hopefully many more—so contraception is discouraged until children are born. But Judaism does not believe that a marriage should be undermined by children being born with such regularity that a couple is financially or emotionally unable to cope. Contraception may be used in an effort to find the appropriate balance between the infinite blessing of life and a couple's need to bond as man and woman, not just as mother and father.

As to methods of contraception, Judaism insists on sex being the joining together of flesh against flesh. Artificial barriers like condoms in marriage are an impediment to that deep intimacy. The pill or an IUD is prescribed instead.

Rabbi Shmuley Boteach
Englewood, NJ

TRADITIONAL ORTHODOX

Jewish law offers guidance on everything—contraception is no different. It finds some methods of contraception problematic per se, some methods less so and some not at all. Besides the mechanical issues, however, there is, biblically, a mandate to have a boy and a girl; and rabbinically, a mitzvah to have more children beyond that; and these are offset, often, by the physical and emotional needs of the mother. So when you put it all together, there are methods such as condoms that are almost always frowned upon, and there are methods such as the IUD or the pill that are acceptable on a per-need basis to most halachic decisors, including some who believe in routine spacing of children. What we frown on is the idea of using contraception because, for example, having a child at this point is going to get in the way of a trip to Hawaii. Family planning for convenience alone is not really in the Jewish playbook.

There are communities that seem to shun contraception entirely, but less so than you might think. Particularly in Israel, there are more decisors than not who would take into account a woman's feeling overwhelmed. Of course, this is in the context of a community that feels children are a blessing and a mitzvah. A conservative Christian commentator recently noted that Israel is the only country in the world with both a high quality of life and a birthrate that is holding steady.

Rabbi Yitzchok Adlerstein
Adjunct Chair of Jewish Law and Ethics,
Loyola Law School
Los Angeles, CA

If your child told you he/ she was gay, what would you say?

W e asked this question in 2011, four years before the Supreme Court decision legalizing gay marriage (which may explain why none of our rabbis said they would urge their child to get married immediately and start providing them with grandchildren). Despite swiftly moving social change, this is still an issue that divides more liberal from more traditional denominations. Even in the latter, though, you can discern the effects of increased tolerance in the emphasis on keeping gay people part of the community and the reminder that commandments about sexual behavior are only a small part of the overall moral picture. (Published in 2011.)

INDEPENDENT

I would remind my child that all of the Torah's laws are contextual. This means that what is forbidden in one context might be permitted in an entirely different context, as the Talmud teaches us (*Talmud Bavli*, Chulin 110a). The Torah's proscription of homosexual sex applies solely to men, while lesbian sex is forbidden neither by biblical law nor by rabbinic law. In regard to male homosexual sex, anything short of complete penile penetration is not included in the biblical prohibition (*Talmud Bavli*, Yevamot 54a-56a, Sotah 26b, Niddah 13a; Pirush HaRambam ahl HaMish'nayot, Sanhedrin, Chapter 7). Moreover, this prohibition is listed among those cultic practices of seven specifically named peoples of ancient times that the Jews were forbidden from emulating (Leviticus 18:3 22, 20:13 and 23; Deuteronomy 23:18). The ancient Jewish philosopher and historian Philo describes how [in some cultures] "men mounted men, then little by little they accustomed those who were by nature men to submit to play the part of women" (Philo on Abraham, Chapter 26, pp. 134-136 in Volume 6 of the Colson Edition of the Loeb Library Edition). Accordingly, the wording in the Torah—that it is forbidden "to lie with a man as he would with a woman" (Leviticus 18:22)—clearly addresses a heterosexual male. And so, understood in context, it may not refer to loving gay couples, only to heterosexual men imposing their will on other heterosexual men as part of orgiastic cultic rites.

Rabbi Gershon Winkler
Walking Stick Foundation
Thousand Oaks, CA

HUMANIST

Why is this matter of identity formation different from any other identity formation? Does the question imply that being gay or lesbian requires special handling, including the possibility of trying to guide a child away from that choice? Would we give different guidance if our child announced that he or she was straight? Is the issue really one of giving advice, or of listening with an open mind?

Each new generation, thankfully, finds greater acceptance of a full range of gender and sexual identity preferences, but we are far from parity. Coming out as gay or lesbian to others, not to mention oneself, is fraught with opposing feelings: excitement about finding oneself and anxiety of being rejected, not just by a potential partner, but by family and society.

It seems to me that the best thing parents can do is model acceptance and an openness to talk more. It also seems to me a great thing if the child feels comfortable bringing up the subject in the first place.

If we do give advice, it should be gender-choice neutral, applying to gay and straight relationships equally. We might offer our thoughts on how to navigate feelings of attraction. Or how to deal with the challenges of relationships so that nobody gets mistreated. Or, if necessary, how to get out of relationships that are hurtful and harmful. They're part of life too.

Rabbi Peter H. Schweitzer
The City Congregation for
Humanist Judaism
New York, NY

RENEWAL

I polled my ALEPH colleagues on this question, and Susan Saxe, our chief operating officer, responded, "I would start with reassurance that sexuality is a gift from a loving G!d and explain that sexuality can feel fixed and certain or be fluid over a lifetime. Whether my child was straight, gay or bisexual, I would just want happy, healthy relationships for him or her. I would express my hope that sexuality be a blessing and gateway to deep connection with a loving partner. I'd suggest it's ideal to postpone sexual expression until one is mature enough to act for *shmirat ha-guf*, safeguarding one's physical and emotional well-being in a caring and committed relationship. If my child were old enough and in a relationship, I would say 'mazel tov' and ask how soon his or her friend could come over for Shabbat dinner."

I thoroughly affirm Susan's thoughts. I would add that while some well-intentioned people may quote two verses of Leviticus to "prove'" that loving same-sex relationships are wrong, I believe they are reading those verses out of cultural/historical context, and I do not believe that they prohibit ongoing loving same-sex relationships. I would add that the *pshat* (literal meaning) of the Torah teaches that the original Adam or earth being was created both male and female, and midrash reinforces this. Since our soul reverberates with this original Adam Kadmon, or primordial man, the potential to have loving feelings for people of either gender is innate. It is part of being created *b'tzelem elohim*, in the image of G!d.

Rabbi Debra Kolodny
ALEPH: Alliance for Jewish Renewal
Silver Spring, MD

RECONSTRUCTIONIST

"Mazel tov," I'd begin. "Mom and I bless you to find true love some day and will embrace any partner you choose. May you remain unhurt by the narrow prejudices that still abound. Always remember that you and your LGBT sisters and brothers are created in God's image, equal to all. Celebrate who you are and the clarity you've attained about your Divine self. *Chizki v'imtzi*, be strong and courageous. We love you."

Even now, our six-year-old might find my response unsurprising. Already her world and her synagogue include families of every configuration. Every night we sing to her, "Some women love men, some men love men" in Fred Small's inclusive lullaby, "Everything Possible." She's seen her parents, their shul and their movement support same-sex marriage rights.

I fervently wish a similarly affirming experience for every child in every community. But that will require a shift and some stretching of comfort zones: clergy and congregants making no assumptions about people's partners; de-gendered synagogue membership forms; queer couples routinely celebrating on the bimah; ongoing education and outreach.

This is guidance for us all. If we implement it, then Judaism can remain our children's path whoever they become and whomever they may love. Then we will bolster the self-esteem of queer teenagers struggling for acceptance (which is also *pikuach nefesh*, part of a life-saving effort). Then we will truly, fully love all our children, no matter what.

Rabbi Fred Scherlinder Dobb
Adat Shalom Reconstructionist
Congregation
Bethesda, MD

REFORM

The first thing I would say to my child is, "I love you. I will always love you. You are created in the image of God, *b'tzelem elohim*."

I would look to offer the same guidance that I would offer to my child if he or she were straight. I would want to make sure that he or she seeks to create relationships that are grounded in Jewish values: loving and mutual, healthy and safe, caring and respectful.

My children—and the teenagers I work with—know that they can speak with me about anything, and I will be there for them, listen to them and offer my support. Yet, sadly, there are still challenges with living an "out" life. For that reason, I would want my child to have Jewish adult gay role models to whom he or she could turn for support—someone who provides a safe place to talk about the challenges, hopes, fears and dreams that they may share. As a parent, I would see it as my obligation to help my child bring that type of mentor into his or her life.

Rabbi Laura Novak Winer
Union for Reform Judaism
Livermore, CA

CONSERVATIVE

If a child of mine told me he or she was gay, I'd like to think that I would be supportive and loving and that I would take the opportunity to talk about sexuality and Jewish values. While I understand that such a declaration is not necessarily an announcement about impending sex but more about orientation, I would seize the opportunity to talk about being sexually active. We live in a world where premarital sex is practically a given. Based upon the writings of Rabbi Elliot Dorff, I would discuss the following Jewish values with my child, irrespective of sexual orientation, and would encourage him/her to adopt these values in shaping sexual activity: 1. Seeing oneself and one's partner as creatures of God. Sexuality ought not to be just for physical satisfaction. While physical pleasure is an important part of sex, we must always remember that our partners are created in God's image. 2. Respect for others. Minimally, this means that sexuality must not be coercive. Nonmarried partners must be especially careful to understand their partner's desires. 3. Modesty. Modesty requires that one's sexual activities be conducted in private and that they not be discussed with others. 4. Honesty. Partners should be able to discuss honestly what their sexual activity means in terms of their relationship. 5. Fidelity. I would urge my child to avoid short-term sexual encounters. It is preferable to seek long-term relationships to which one remains faithful throughout the relationship. 6. Health and safety. This is especially important in all sexual relationships.

Rabbi Amy Wallk Katz
Temple Beth El
Springfield, MA

MODERN ORTHODOX

Assuming that this coming out was a considered decision and a mature conclusion on the part of my child, I would say the following:

My heart goes out to you. As you were raised as an Orthodox Jew, you already know that since the time of the Torah, homosexuality has been condemned in our community, especially in more traditional circles. While treatment is improving, I fear that you will face much rejection and hostility, and I wish that I could prevent it or protect you.

Nevertheless, if you live your life this way, I would hope that you would apply the Torah's other guidelines for sexuality to your own practice. Sex should not be casual or promiscuous. It should never be exploitative or abusive. Sexuality should express relationship and love; the deeper the sexuality, the deeper the relationship that it should express. You should try for the Jewish ideal, which remains family and creating/nurturing life via children (by conception or adoption). This is a great joy and a fulfillment in life.

Your mother and I love you very much as a total person. This feeling has not changed with your announcement.

Rabbi Yitz Greenberg
Riverside, NY

SEPHARDIC

If my child were to inform me that he was gay, I would accept this as an unalterable component of his biological and emotional makeup. However, I would hope that my child possessed a genuine appreciation for the wisdom and benefit of the mitzvot and lifestyle prescribed by the Torah and that, as a result, he would refrain from acting on the homosexual feelings he experienced in deference to the requirements of Jewish law. In this sense, I would expect him to behave no differently from an individual with a strong affinity for the consumption of pork products or a craving for shellfish. Hashem creates us with an array of predilections and desires, none of which is inherently good or bad; what is good or bad is how we respond to and manage those predilections and desires. It is our mission in life to achieve sanctity by transcending our instinctual impulses whatever form they take, overcoming our innate selfishness and committing the entirety of our being to the timeless principles of the Torah's wisdom.

Rabbi Joshua Maroof
Magen David Sephardic Congregation
Rockville, MD

ORTHODOX

I am opposed to personalizing hypothetical questions, so I will answer in the generic. My position on homosexuality is well known, and I believe it to be true to Jewish values, humane and eminently logical. There are 613 commandments in the Torah. One is to marry a woman and have children. Another is to refrain from same-sex relationships. My consistent position has been that a Jewish gay man or woman is left with 611 commandments, which should keep them plenty busy. The two tablets of the law reflect two different sets of commandments: religious and moral. Homosexuality is not immoral, like stealing, theft or murder. It is a religious prohibition, akin to refraining from lighting fire on the Sabbath. The Jewish community treats those who drive to synagogue on the Sabbath, for example, as vital and equal members of the community, which is how we should treat all gay men and women. They should be lovingly encouraged to put on tefillin, have kosher homes, light Shabbos candles, visit the sick, defend and promote Israel and be fully involved in communal life.

Rabbi Shmuley Boteach
Englewood, NJ

How should we view unmarried pregnant women?

The date on this question—2006—might seem to bring its relevance into question at a time when acceptance of nontraditional family structures has moved so quickly and so far. Rereading it, though, I was struck by what hasn't changed. Our rabbis don't agree on whether premarital sex is permissible—or if so, under what conditions or in what context. But even the most traditional of them (admittedly, there are further denominations with more severe views, whose rabbis aren't comfortable appearing in this forum) noted the existence of the phenomenon and its results—and the ways society has worked out to deal with it—from earliest times. Judaism reveals itself on this subject as a religion immersed less in the abstract than in the practical. (Published in 2006.)

HUMANIST

My first inclination, when faced with this question, was to offer an impatient response, "Why is this question even being asked?! We should greet all pregnant women, regardless of their marital status, with love and support." With the emergence of the Enlightenment and the development of modern science, many old rules and cherished truths have been revised if not discarded altogether. Most notably, women, who previously had been considered property, first of their fathers and then of their husbands, are now empowered and enfranchised. Women today can choose to marry or not to marry, to partner or not to partner. They can choose to have children or not to have children with or without the prerequisite of marriage or committed partnership. Women today have control over their own bodies. There are methods available to prevent pregnancy as well as to abort a pregnancy. Whether they are lesbian women who long to have children or single straight women who have the same yearning, modern science has made it possible for them to conceive a child with the aid of sperm donation, a remarkable opportunity their foremothers could not have imagined. Humanistic Jews, in keeping with our philosophy generally, do not resist change but welcome the innovations of modernity, even when they challenge our accepted notions and comfort level. Among these changes, the definition of family has evolved most dramatically. Whether as a result of divorce or teenage pregnancy, there have always been single parents. Now, there are single parents by choice. Some choose to make a family through adoption, others by getting pregnant. Regardless of the means, the ends are the same. What counts is giving all these new children love and support—and the same for their parents!

Rabbi Peter Schweitzer
The City Congregation for
Humanistic Judaism
New York, NY

INDEPENDENT

Judaism does not view unmarried pregnant women any differently from married pregnant women, since there is absolutely no imperative in the Torah that mandates marriage as a prerequisite to intimate relationship between the sexes. Our ancestors had wives and "half-wives," or *pilag'shim* (Genesis 25:6 and 35:22), from the words *p'lag ee'shut*, literally "half marriage." A half-wife or *pilegesh* was any woman involved in a sexual relationship with a man without being married to him. Some will argue that this was only a kosher form of relationship prior to the arrival of the Torah at Sinai. Yet, we find in post-Sinai scriptural writings ample evidence that relationships between women and men unmarried to one another continued as a legitimate alternative to marriage (Judges 19:1; Second Samuel 3:7, 5:13, 15:16, 21:11; First Chronicles 2:48 and 3:9; Song of Songs 6:7-9). In the Talmudic period as well, non-marital relationships between women and men continued and were discussed by the ancient rabbis as a legitimate relationship option in Judaism (*Babylonian Talmud*, Sanhedrin 21a). The only legislation against these kinds of relationships came not from the sensually liberated Hebrews but from the Greco-Roman Christians as the fledgling Church banned sensuality altogether outside the context of marriage.

It is time to fess up to the discrepancy betwixt what is really moral wrongness and what are pure and simply personal tastes and distastes. We must never confuse the two in the guise of halacha or Jewish morality. We are Jews, not Greco-Roman Hellenists. We have our own unique values and morals. We not only appreciate the human body and sensuality, we laud it and we celebrate it, and have left ample room in our tradition for options in intimate relationshiping from our very beginnings. By classical Jewish law, mutual consensual non-incestuous sex between adults outside of marriage is not forbidden as long as the woman immerses herself in the ocean, or a lake, or the local mikveh at the conclusion of her menstrual cycle, and as long as neither party abuses the body by becoming paid gigolos or prostitutes. Same-sex intimacy, too, is not forbidden by the Torah—certainly not lesbianism, and male homosexuality only if there is actual intromission (Pirush HaRambam ahl HaMish'nayot, on Sanhedrin, Chapter 7; *Babylonian Talmud*, Sanhedrin 54a, Yevamot 54a-56a and 76a, Sotah 26b, Niddah 13a). Nor are the offspring of out-of-wedlock relationships less legitimate than the offspring of married couples (*Babylonian Talmud*, Sanhedrin 21a; Ra'avad on Mishnah Torah, Hilchot Ishut 1:4; T'shuvot HaRan on Sefer HaMitzvot HaKatan, No . 186; T'shuvot HaRamban, No. 2 [or T'shuvot HaRash'ba, No. 284]; Rambam on *Shulchan Aruch*, Ehven Ha'Ezer 26:1; Shey'lot Ya'avetz, Vol. 2, No. 15). Whether marriage is a healthier context for a sexual relationship or not is a whole other issue. But Judaism's age-old answer to whether marriage is a prerequisite to sexual relations remains a resounding "No." And therefore an unmarried pregnant woman is accorded all the honors, respect and doting by her family and community that a married pregnant woman receives.

Rabbi Gershon Winkler
Walking Stick Foundation
Mountain View, CA

RECONSTRUCTIONIST

First and foremost, we should treat unmarried pregnant women with respect for them, and with reserve in our own judgment. We should view them with awe and wonder, and pledges of support. Parenting is tough even for two, yet many women do a stellar solo job. Some choose this path consciously. While two is usually better than one, we should punish neither bad luck nor high standards. Women (and men) without a life partner still want, and deserve, to become parents—and better a single parent with a supportive network than an abusive, addicted, distant or unsupportive one.

Some become pregnant while unmarried, unintentionally. While covenantal expressions of sexuality are in many ways preferred, sex before marriage can still be holy if it's loving, consensual, respectful and as "safe as possible." We must not think we know what a woman's belly shows. She is created in the Divine image like anyone else and cannot be defined (much less stigmatized) over one piece of her complex identity. Finally, raising a child takes more than a single or even a couple; it takes a village. Support a brave unmarried pregnant woman in being the best, most communally and religiously connected mother she can be. The outcome will be better for her, for the children, and for our community as a whole.

Rabbi Fred Scherlinder Dobb
Adat Shalom Reconstructionist
Congregation
Bethesda, MD

CONSERVATIVE

Our tradition views sexual practice on a continuum. On one end of the spectrum is the traditional Jewish ideal, a loving, long-term relationship between one man and one woman, sanctified by marriage. At the opposite end of the spectrum is non-marital and non-consensual sex characterized by violence and coercion, such as rape, or incest, or consensual sex for compensation, that is, prostitution. Between these poles lies a range of various possibilities, including unwed pregnancy. Although most of the halachic tradition discourages and even condemns non-marital sexual relationships, some writings do deal with provisions for long-term committed relationships, which they consider a form of concubinage.

While unwed pregnancy is certainly not ideal, there can be mitigating circumstances. If the pregnancy is the accidental result of a consensual sexual relationship, we recognize that people make mistakes and can achieve teshuva. A child of two single Jewish people who are eligible to marry each other has full legitimate halachic status. Increasingly in our community, single women are choosing to become pregnant. Aware of declining prospects for marriage, they are watching their biological clocks tick and opting for single motherhood. Every child is precious and deserves our love, particularly as we decry the low Jewish birth rate in this country, which is well below replacement level. Provided that halachic parameters are used for conception, the offspring of these single Jewish mothers have full Jewish status. We should welcome these children, and their families, into our communities and into our hearts.

Rabbi Avis D. Miller
Adas Israel Congregation
Washington, DC

MODERN ORTHODOX

In the past, the sight of an unmarried pregnant woman would likely have drawn disapproval. Premarital sex is prohibited in halacha. Therefore, the pregnancy would be a sign of disapproved behavior compounded by a lack of maturity, i.e., failure to use birth control. This would have damaged the marriageability of such a woman in the Orthodox world. Still, a child born to this woman would not have suffered any legal disability. Halacha does not treat birth out of wedlock as making a child illegitimate, i.e., a bastard (mamzer) in Jewish law. Only a child of incest or adultery is classified as illegitimate (and unmarriageable) in Jewish law.

A remarkable change in social behavior is unfolding, due to the socioeconomic gains of women and the rise of professional/business women who are self-supporting. We are seeing a growing number of single women who have decided they will mother a child as a single parent—and become pregnant. The difficulty of a single parent raising a child must not be underestimated. Still, such a decision demands to be viewed very differently. The motives are honorable; the pregnancy represents love of life and of Jewry and this should be acknowledged and appreciated. Genesis (19:3) relates the story of Lot's daughters who, after Sodom's destruction, believed themselves and their father to be the only survivors. They were so committed to humanity that each decided to have a child with the only surviving man—their father. They had to get him drunk and seduce him to do it. One of the children—Moab—became the ancestor of Ruth, ancestor of King David, ancestor of the Messiah. By their idealistic passion for life Lot's daughters turned incest and drunkenness into a force for human survival and redemption. (At least this is the interpretation of Rabbi

Joseph B. Soloveitchik and various classical commentators and midrashim.)

By analogy, a woman's commitment to life, children and the Jewish future expressed in deciding to become a single mother should be honored and supported. A technicality: Poskim rule that they should preferably use a non-Jew's semen. They must keep a record of the donor to prevent their children from committing any future unintentional incest or entering any forbidden consanguineous relationships. (The donor father might sire children by other women. When the children grew up, they could meet and unknowingly marry prohibited relatives.) The main point is: The community should be supportive of women so committed to having Jewish children that they are prepared to do it alone.

Rabbi Yitz Greenberg
Jewish Life Network/Steinhardt
Foundation
New York, NY

CHABAD

Practically, we ought to be there for these women and their children in every possible way. Yet a larger issue looms here: the critical need to educate our children on the seriousness of intimacy, the sacredness of marriage and the value of lifelong commitments permeated with mutual respect and devotion. It is hard to overestimate the emotional, psychological and spiritual benefits for children growing up with parents dedicated wholeheartedly to each other and their families. Playing around in the short term may be easier, but in the long run it is in the commitments we make to our spouses and children that we actualize our deepest potential as humans and as Jews.

The 90-page tractate of Talmud legislating the Jewish laws for divorce was transcribed 1,700 years ago. The sages of antiquity chose to culminate the book with these words: "Whenever anyone divorces his first wife, even the Temple Altar sheds tears." We are scared of making sacrifices, lest they deprive us of our personal happiness. Our self-esteem is so fragile that we desperately feel the need to protect it against any intrusion of the other, lest it fade away into oblivion. But happiness is an altar. The more you give, the more you receive. The soul is most at peace with itself when it shares itself with another soul, for the soul is aware that you are another face of me. We need to inspire our children that the Jewish approach for 3,000 years to build a family within the context of a marital commitment is the time-proven path to genuine self-fulfillment.

Rabbi Yosef Y. Jacobson
Rabbinical College Chovevei Torah
Brooklyn, NY

When and how should Jewish parents discuss sex with their children?

This question, too, was asked in 2006. What's striking here is not so much the continuity between then and now—which isn't surprising—but the consistency across all ten denominations, which share a framework of Judaism's emphasis on the beauty and value of sex and an emphasis on teaching children about the nature and holiness of sexual relations rather than simply the rules governing them. (Published in 2006.)

HUMANIST

The classic story: A little boy comes to his mother and says, "Where did I come from?" She gets flustered and nervous but manages to give him a brief lesson in sex education. But the answer doesn't satisfy the boy. He asks again, "But where do I come from—you know, where was I born?" "Cleveland" or "Boston," or wherever, was the answer he was looking for. It would have saved the mother considerable anguish had she figured out what he really wanted to know.

Parents should start discussing sex with their children when the child shows interest in learning about it. Each child has his or her own timetable. Parents are rarely the ones who need to start the discussion; children invariably take the lead. Parents ought to welcome and encourage children's curiosity, and give honest, direct, age-appropriate answers. They also don't need to get ahead of themselves. Children usually just want simple responses. But not to worry: In due time, they'll come back and ask for more.

Just the other day, my son, five, and his peers asked their teacher how babies were made. She immediately showed them pictures of embryos growing in a mother's uterus. Apparently nobody asked how the sperm and the egg met up in the first place. But when the question comes up, we'll be ready for it. Meanwhile, though, the teacher reported that the kids "made the connection that only a man and a woman can technically make a baby, which sparked a subsequent conversation about how same-sex parents have babies," leading to even more talk about adoption and surrogate mothers. What a great teaching moment—all instigated by the children!

Rabbi Peter H. Schweitzer
The City Congregation for
Humanistic Judaism
New York, New York

INDEPENDENT

When the children ask. Because if we don't respond at that time, someone else will—a stranger, a peer, a book, a magazine. There is really no such thing as "an appropriate age." As King Solomon put it: "Educate the child according to their [respective] path" (Proverbs 22:6)— meaning according to where they're at. Each child is unique. The Talmud wisely recommends that parents stay alert to the child's sensitivity around nudity in front of the parents, and that when the child displays the tiniest degree of discomfort, it is time for the parents to stop sleeping in the same bed with the child and from undressing or dressing in his or her presence, respecting the child's privacy as well (Kiddushin 80a and 81b).

How should we discuss sex with our children when the time is ripe? Delicately, openly, without fear. The emotion you display when you talk about it will forge the framework for his or her attitude toward it. Sex should be introduced for what it is, at least by Jewish teachings: beautiful, healthy and a gift from God. And, like all of our senses and emotions, it has a time and context. The time: when there is sufficient maturity to experience it in a wholesome way. The context: a committed relationship based on unconditional love and respect. You can tell your kids all about driving cars, but you would also explain to them that they will get the chance to actually drive several years down the road, not when they're eight.

Rabbi Gershon Winkler
Walking Stick Foundation
Cuba, NM

RENEWAL

Sexuality, like other bodily functions, is seen as a part of Jewish life. We raise bodily needs to a sacred level through blessings. We learn the blessing for going to the bathroom at an appropriate age, and some rabbis have even scribed prayers for loving. Establishing the normalcy of sexuality by having regular age-appropriate discussions about the body will allow parents to know how and when to discuss sexuality.

Because sexual curiosity and awareness are just one aspect of development, the nature of your conversations will change as the child develops and grows. Early discussions about sex should occur when children first venture into the world without direct parental supervision. Then we talk about comfort with touching: When is it OK to sit in the teacher's lap? Can I hug my babysitter? Suppose I need help in the bathroom? The purpose of such talk is to help children be aware, without instilling fear. Parents use these opportunities to help children know when and how it is appropriate and not appropriate to touch.

Once trust is established, conversations with older children evolve similarly: Do you know about your body? Do you know how it works? Dealing with all physical functioning, not sex alone, is important to support a healthy relationship with sexuality. Including the child as a partner in such talk builds a sense of mutuality between child, parent and God, where discussions can be held from a position of truth and trust and not fear. When parents and children are partners, adolescents won't need to rebel against authority and can come to the authoritative figure in their lives for assistance.

Rabbi Steve Silvern
ALEPH: Alliance for Jewish Renewal
Auburn University
Auburn, AL
Rabbi David Zaslow
Havurah Shir Hadash
Ashland, OR

RECONSTRUCTIONIST

We are responsible for giving our kids the information they need when they need it. Regarding sex, in today's society, that's earlier and earlier. At an alarmingly young age, children must know the difference between a good and bad touch and must have the vocabulary and comfort level to discuss it. Society sends mixed signals: Victorian and prudish impulses compete with newfound openness and immodesty. Neither extreme is healthy. Young children encounter tawdry and flaunted sexuality from TV, magazine ads and music videos. Yet, Jewishly, sex is a sacred, vital part of life. The very presence of the Bible's erotic love poem "Shir haShirim" (Song of Songs) speaks volumes. Biblical narratives and Talmudic discussions treat sex quite matter-of-factly. Medieval Kabbalah, and *Iggeret ha-Kodesh*, the "Holy Letter," also show sex as natural and sacred. To reclaim this naturalness and sacredness takes open, age-appropriate discussion from pre-K through adulthood.

Early on, keep it short and straightforward. Let it sink in; when they're ready for more, they'll let you know. Discuss sex early, often and openly. Why? First, to correct what kids will "learn" anyway. Second, to break the cycle of discomfort; who doesn't want their kids to enjoy a healthy, holy sex life (eventually!)? And finally, to save lives: For teens to accept their bodies and sexuality as they are, irrespective of weight or orientation, is a life-or-death issue. So is condom use. And, no, "abstinence only" doesn't work. In short, overcome your ambivalence and discuss sex openly and early on with your children.

Rabbi Fred Scherlinder Dobb
Adat Shalom Reconstructionist
Congregation
Bethesda, Maryland

CONSERVATIVE

I take the model of sex education from the Mishnah about the Passover seder. It says: "After pouring the second cup of wine, here is where the child asks questions. If the child is not able to ask, the parent tells the child what to ask. The parent then answers the questions, taking the child's needs into consideration." (Mishnah Pesahim 10:4). This is excellent advice for many parent-child conversations. Ideally, the time to talk about sex is when your child comes to you with a question. But, if your child does not ask, and you are afraid he or she will get information from friends or from the Internet, from a perspective that you do not share, preempt that possibility by raising the topic yourself. Give your child information that he or she can assimilate at that stage of life. The first thing your child will realize is that you had sex in order to produce him or her. And that is good.

Since most of us do not know what words to use to explain sex to a child, an age-appropriate book is a good way to go. You can read the book with your child—mother and father together—and look at the drawings, some of which may be whimsical. The discussion need not be long and you don't need to tell your child everything at once. But if you provide the basic Jewish notion of sex as pleasurable, as a deep form of intimacy, as not being a casual act, and if you advise your child of the need to treat the other person with sensitivity, you will set your child on the path to rewarding relationships.

Rabbi Judith Hauptman
Jewish Theological Seminary
New York, New York

SEPHARDIC

The Torah is not ashamed to discuss any aspect of human life, including human sexuality. Its presentation of this dimension of our activity is frank and honest. Although the Torah teaches us the value of moderation and modesty in the area of sexual expression, it does not encourage us to develop feelings of guilt or shame about sexual desires or their fulfillment. The Talmud's treatment of sexual matters is particularly remarkable for its candor and insight. Following in the footsteps of this tradition, sexual discussion should not be avoided and should not be a source of embarrassment or discomfort for parents. The right time to engage in such conversations is whenever a child expresses curiosity about sex, no sooner and no later. The natural interest that children have in this subject should be neither condemned nor criticized; rather, it should be viewed as a vehicle by which we can educate them regarding the realities of life. A parent's primary responsibility is to be as honest and forthright as possible—no storks delivering babies, etc. If we allow ourselves to tell lies to children for "their own good," we undermine their trust in us and end up causing substantial harm. We also teach them to be dishonest and disingenuous in their dealings with others. Needless to say, a parent must respond to a child's questions in light of what is developmentally appropriate—that is to say, what we communicate to youngsters must be offered in a way that the child can understand and appreciate.

Rabbi Joshua Maroof
Magen David Sephardic Congregation
Rockville, Maryland

CHABAD

The first question should be: What is this sex that we are attempting to teach our children? Is it merely a biological phenomenon, a bodily urge, or is there something more to sexuality?

We often think of God as the great spoilsport of human sexuality, not its inventor, and the Torah as the great taboo on free Eros, not its grand supporter. This is a mistake. In the Kabbalah's interpretation, the value and mystique of intimacy reaches unprecedented heights, and its full and liberated expression enormous validation, nay, sanctification. Sexuality, Judaism teaches, is the yearning to reunite man and woman, who were initially created as one in the image of God, as Genesis states, "God created Man in his image, in the image of God He created him; male and female He created them."

Sexuality, when traced back to its original tide in the subconscious, is our longing to reunite with our second half and consequently with God, for it is only when woman and man become one again that they are re-formatted in the image of God. Sexuality, then, is the holy of holies of the human experience, and it needs to be treated that way: with awe, reverence and profound sensitivity. Children need to feel the sacredness with which their parents regard sexuality. Then, when they grow older, they will treat their sexuality with the Divine respect it deserves.

Sexuality in our age has become so prevalent and free that it has been depleted from its sacred mystique, stripped from its true power and meaning. Now, when couples get married, they often struggle to find excitement and wholesomeness in their intimacy, but to no avail, as it has been cheapened through years of hollow use.

We need a sexual revolution, from free sex to sacred sex.

Rabbi Yosef Y. Jacobson
Rabbinical College Chovevei Torah
Brooklyn, New York

Is silence consent?

This was our 2020 #MeToo question, an effort to set questions of sexual consent and coercion in a wider framework. And the rabbis oblige beautifully. Without dodging difficult questions of rape and coercion, they also reflect on silence in the face of racism, bullying or politics; the silence of Esther; the silence of the bride under the marriage canopy; the difference between silence of the powerful and of the powerless; and silence from approval versus silence from cowardice. In this reading, the price of silence can be nearly infinite: To Rabbi Levi Shemtov, "A comfortable silence can see the Temple destroyed." (Published in 2020.)

INDEPENDENT

On the one hand, we have the Talmudic legal adage: "Silence is like a confession" (*Talmud Bavli*, Yevamot 87b). This clearly applies to an instance of legal adjudication, where the silence of the accused could imply confirmation of the charges. On the other hand, silence can be misconstrued as consent when we fail to speak up in protest when something harmful is being said or done (Shabbat 33a). On the third hand, silence is certainly not indicative of consent in regard to inappropriate contact or sexual advances—even with one's own spouse (Eruvin 100b). Bottom line, outside the interrogation room and public demonstrations, silence should never be interpreted as consent unless
accompanied by a clear gesture indicating that consent.

In the traditional Jewish marriage ceremony, for example, the bride is silent. And although it is the groom who declares her betrothal to him, his declaration is void until and unless the bride indicates consent by a gesture of willful receipt of the token accompanying the declaration, whether a ring or a mule. Without her explicit acceptance, there is no marriage. Her silence is her consent, but only because of her action, which—in this case—speaks louder than words (Kiddushin 3b).

Rabbi Gershon Winkler
Jewish Chaplain, Patton State Hospital
Patton, CA

HUMANIST

On a recent trip through Breezewood, PA, my husband and I stopped at a gas station. While he filled the tank, I went into the shop. The older man at the counter greeted me, glanced at some shelves of energy boosters and cigarettes, then said, "Nah, that's the stuff for the Mexicans and the Blacks. Lemme take you to the white man's section." I was shocked. I stood there for a moment, silent, and then I walked out. In that situation, maybe it was the right choice, but it was also the easy one.

The ease with which people ignore injustice likely prompted the Torah's admonition, "Do not stand idly by while your neighbor's blood is shed" (Leviticus 19:16). Jews are plenty aware of the consequences of silence while our blood was shed, and we denounce the silent as complicit, their inaction as assent. I did not assent to the words of that racist, but he never knew that. And while I continue to believe that silence was the right choice in that context, I am bothered by how much easier it was than confrontation. Turning away from injustice and hate is always easier. Yet where there is silence, or ease, there will never be justice. As Rabbi Abraham Joshua Heschel said, "The opposite of good is not evil; the opposite of good is indifference."

Rabbi Jeffrey L. Falick
Birmingham Temple Congregation
for Humanistic Judaism
Farmington Hills, MI

RENEWAL

Our tradition has an ambivalent relationship with silence. Silence in the face of loss or great pain is frequently lauded, as when Aaron responded to the death of his two sons with silence—perhaps a form of acquiescence or consent to God's will. But silence in the face of injustice or impending catastrophe is a mark of complicity and cowardice—as in the book of Esther, where Mordecai reminds the queen, "If you keep silent in this crisis, relief and deliverance will come to the Jews from another quarter, while you and your father's house will perish" (Esther 4:14).

Does silence always imply consent? In matters of betrothal and divorce, a prime rabbinic principle is that women must give consent. But how do you know when consent occurs if it is not verbalized? In the Talmud (Kiddushin 13a), the rabbis wrestle with cases where a man gives something to a woman with the intention of betrothing her, but she is silent. Has she consented or not? Does she want the marriage or just the item he's giving her—or even feel that the item belonged to her in the first place? In a passage eerily reminiscent of our modern #MeToo debates, Rav Nachman wades into the issue: "If we say that 'She wanted' means that she said yes, and 'She did not want' means that she explicitly said no, it can be inferred that if she was silent it is a valid betrothal." That's not the final answer; the rabbis evidently felt that the woman's intention could be deduced only by the particulars of the case at hand. You or I might say, just ask her what she intended! But that's the point—women's agency was limited, women's speech was often demeaned as frivolous, and women were not generally allowed to testify as witnesses.

And then there is *shalom bayit*—women keeping silent for the sake of peace in the household. Perhaps the most chilling case of such demanded silence is found in the biblical tale of Tamar's rape (2 Samuel 13:20). After discovering what his half-brother Amnon has done, Absalom tells Tamar, "For the present, sister, keep quiet about it; he is your brother. Don't brood over the matter." Absalom means to avenge his sister's rape, which he does two years later by murdering Amnon—

but his admonition to Tamar to keep silent adds insult to injury, and indeed silences his sister; we never hear Tamar's voice again.

Rabbi Gilah Langner
Congregation Kol Ami
Arlington, VA

RECONSTRUCTIONIST

For those with relative power, yes, silence is consent. But not so for those oppressed. A woman sexually assaulted in the field was innocent (Deuteronomy 22:23-27), since her cries wouldn't be heard; yet in the densely populated city, her perceived silence equaled presumed consent.

We now know that women, children and minorities are often socialized or coerced not to cry out—and when they do cry, even loudly, in the public sphere, they often go "unheard." Some powerful people prey, but many enable; the silence of the enablers and witnesses is absolutely consent. Such harassment and hurt relies on the fearful silence of victims and potential allies. We must ensure that disempowered voices get heard.

Rabbi Abraham Joshua Heschel wrote in 1972 of his involvement in the peace movement that "the Prophets sought to convey...that indifference to evil is worse than evil itself; that in a free society, some are guilty, but all are responsible." To the extent that we are free and empowered, we can (and must!) address sexism and misogyny—and racism, xenophobia, ecological catastrophe, attacks on democracy. When we're silent, we signal consent, even complicity. But the solution has been with us since Exodus: Empower everyone, and act up.

Rabbi Fred Scherlinder Dobb
Adat Shalom Reconstructionist
Congregation
Bethesda, MD

REFORM

In the words of Pete Seeger, as inspired by Ecclesiastes, "To everything there is a season and a time for every purpose under Heaven." Silence has its time and its place, as do speaking up and speaking out.

Our Jewish tradition values silence—for reflection, for finding calm and stillness, for giving an attentive ear to others' words. At the same time, our tradition values using one's voice and requires us to be discriminating with our words. We can offer constructive criticism, yet we should refrain from slander, gossip and falsehoods, as those tend to be harmful rather than helpful.

Yet when it comes to matters of wrongdoing, sin or injustice, we have an obligation to speak. The Babylonian Talmud teaches that if we can prevent members of our own households, our fellow citizens or even the whole world from sin or acts of injustice, and we do not prevent those from happening, then we too will be punished. Our silence might not only lead to others' harm but to our own as well. In this instance, silence is more than consent; it becomes complicity.

Rabbi Dr. Laura Novak Winer
Fresno, CA

CONSERVATIVE

Shtika k'hoda'a ("Silence is tantamount to agreement") (*Talmud Bavli*, Bava Metzia 37b). When we remain silent, our wordlessness speaks for us and, like it or not, is regarded as implied consent. It is tempting to immediately think about the Holocaust and to blame all those individuals who stood by as the Nazis and their collaborators tyrannized and ultimately murdered millions of innocent people.

I have another way of thinking about silence, which I attribute to my late father, Dr. Silas Wallk. My dad urged his four children to have the courage to allow their conscience to guide them. He challenged us to wrestle with societal problems, even if those around us did not. Quoting earlier authors, he used to say that the "only thing necessary for the triumph of evil is for good people to do nothing."

This idea applies to all of us. For me, it is about making sure my teaching and preaching reflect my moral conscience, not being afraid of what others might think. For others, it might mean not remaining silent at a fraternity party, or during a heated discussion on campus, or challenging a disturbing norm in the workplace. Ultimately, we must all remember that when we fail to speak up for someone, or something, we become accomplices—without ever opening our mouths.

Rabbi Amy Wallk Katz
Temple Beth El
Springfield, MA

MODERN ORTHODOX

It all depends on the context. In the Talmud, when a charge is made against a person, if they do not deny it but fall silent, then silence is considered an admission of guilt. By contrast, in a sexual interaction between two people in our time and culture, the emerging consensus is that silence is not consent, and an affirmative statement from both is needed to proceed.

If persecution or a crime is being committed, bystanders must speak up or act against the evildoer. During the Holocaust, the Jewish survival rate in different countries varied from 5 to 95 percent. The differences grew directly out of the behavior of the bystanders. Widespread, active collaboration with the Nazis led to 90-percent-plus death rates in Poland and Lithuania. Widespread, active rescue activity led to survival rates of more than 95 percent in Denmark and Bulgaria.

The silence of the Allies and of President Franklin D. Roosevelt (and Stalin's failure to report to Russian Jews the total Nazi assault on them) raised the death rates. That silence constituted consent to the annihilation of European Jewry. As Elie Wiesel said, silence always aids the evildoers and never the victims.

Rabbi Yitz Greenberg
Riverdale, NY

ORTHODOX

Absolutely yes! Some of the time. Unless… It's a huge halachic topic. The Talmud is unambiguous in stating that silence implies complicity. This applies to the indiscretions of large groups of people and also to transgressions by individuals. The biblical commandment "You shall surely rebuke" (Leviticus 19:17) has different applications before and after a misdeed is witnessed, precisely so that the onlooker's silence should not be taken as approval. When a misdeed is being contemplated but has not occurred, protest is required even when it is clear that it will change no one's action—but this is not true of the obligation to rebuke after a transgression. And sometimes silence is mandated, as when it becomes clear after an initial rebuke that pressing the issue will lead to bitterness and enmity.

Besides the halachic mandates to speak up, however, there is another obligation that flows from what is supposed to be our fundamental human nature. The midrash teaches that three people counseled Pharaoh in his decree to murder the male Israelite babies: Balaam, Jethro and Job. The first approved; the second protested and had to flee Pharaoh's wrath. Job remained silent and suffered all of his tragedies because of it. The Brisker Rov (Yitzchok Soloveitchik) questioned this. After seeing that Jethro's protest got nowhere and endangered his life, the Rov asked, what was wrong with Job's remaining silent? "Because," he famously answered, "when something hurts, we scream."

Rabbi Yitzchok Adlerstein
Cross-Currents
Los Angeles, CA

SEPHARDIC

If I am the one accused, assaulted or attacked, my silence or inaction is not necessarily consent. I might choose not to respond because I am overpowered, or because I know the accuser is entrenched in his position and that keeping quiet is a better option than fighting endlessly. However, if a simple denial will help, but is withheld, then that silence is consent. For example, if one is being sued for an alleged debt and does not respond, Jewish law dictates that he must pay the debt, because he could have denied the allegation (*Talmud Bavli*, Bava Metzia, 37b). Silence is also consent when someone else is the victim, unless those present are unable to speak or act. The Torah states that one should not stand idly by when someone is being hurt (Leviticus 19:16). Those who witness or know of domestic abuse, harassment, corruption, mismanagement, bullying and all other forms in which people harm others, yet keep quiet, are giving their consent, committing the sin defined by the Talmud as "being able to protest yet failing to do so" (Sanhedrin 103a). The Talmud even attributes the destruction of the Temple to the acquiescence of the Sages to the public humiliation of a man mistakenly invited to a party (Gittin 56a).

Rabbi Haim Ovadia
Potomac, MD

CHABAD

Silence can be two different things. Sometimes golden, sometimes unfortunate. Always relevant.

When something ugly happens and no one says anything, catastrophe follows. Such is the case of how our ancient Holy Temple was destroyed. Rabbis said nothing at a huge feast, we are told, when someone was humiliated publicly, and with the rabbinical silence, it appeared they were in agreement. On the other hand, when the biblical Aaron was in deep grief over the sad and sudden death of his sons, he was silent.

There are times we must accept the will of the Almighty and search ourselves rather than speak, and there are other times when we see injustice and must speak as loudly and mightily as we can. To have the greatest impact, though, we must first speak loudly and clearly to ourselves, clarify our motives and then proceed accordingly. And sometimes the unsaid word can save the day, the situation, the larger society.

Silence in the face of injustice is acquiescence. A powerful protest, purely motivated, can change a lot, sometimes the world. A comfortable silence can see the Temple destroyed. The analogies are ever present and numerous. We face this choice every day.

Rabbi Levi Shemtov
Executive Vice President, American
Friends of Lubavitch
Washington, DC

PART THREE

MODERN LIFE

"T urn it and turn it, for everything is in it," the sages say of the
Talmud. Sometimes we ask the rabbis questions just to test the
boundaries of that "everything." Does the tradition really contain
guidance about how to behave on social media, or fight drug
addiction, or come out as trans? Can it promise moral clarity on problems the ancients never imagined?

On the whole, the tradition does pretty well. One lesson that
emerges from the exercise is that a lot of things we might casually consider modern, from gender fluidity to abortion, have been around longer than we think—maybe as long as we've been human. Others that
seem completely novel turn out to be variations on all-too-familiar
themes, as in the question we asked in 2018 about online misbehavior.

What sins should we atone for in our use of social media?

Technology changes, but human nature remains the same. We asked this question in time for Yom Kippur, the Day of Atonement, when Jews in synagogue work their way through a long list of communal confessions: "For the sin which we have committed before You by running to do evil. . .For the sin which we have committed before You by talebearing. . .For the sin we have committed before you by gossip. . .". As Rabbi Jeffrey Falick wryly points out, "The traditional holiday confessional already seems to have anticipated social media." (Published in 2018).

INDEPENDENT

O Master of the Universe! On this Yom Kippur, please forgive me...For the sin of neglecting the chulent pot and allowing it to boil over and become encrusted due to my obsessive checking and rechecking of Facebook. For the sin of not having heard my partner whisper "I love You" because I was listening to some rant on YouTube. For the sin of believing every libelous tirade posted on Instagram as if it had come down from Sinai. For the sin of spending hours hypnotically glommed onto Facebook Messenger while texting the person seated beside me. For the sin of not turning off my smartphone before going to sleep. For the sin of longing more desperately for an incoming text than for the touch of a lover. For the sin of not checking the content of my text prior to sending it, resulting in verbiage never intended. For the sin of awakening envy and disdain in others by sending photos and tweets about how absolutely wonderful my life is. For the sin of allowing social media to transform me into a mesmerized worshiper of screens illuminated by light-emitting diodes while I waste away in the back seat of my self-driving car.

Rabbi Gershon Winkler
Walking Stick Foundation
Rancho Cucamonga, CA

HUMANIST

Social media provides a crucial platform for many people. It helps the marginalized find and embrace each other. It enables the powerless to combine into powerful coalitions. And, of course, there are those pictures of the grandchildren. Yet like many new technologies, social media has created new opportunities for us to wrong one another. From the spread of falsehoods to anonymous bullying to the ease with which we make casual racist, homophobic, misogynistic and ableist statements, social media encourages some terrible behaviors.

Humanistic Jews are not shy about updating and adapting Jewish literature. But the traditional holiday confessional already seems to have anticipated social media. The wrongs we commit by means of the internet are not so very different from those that our tradition describes as committing "openly and in secret…with our speech…with foolish talk…by means of our evil inclination." Social media extends the reach of all this *lashon hara* and other bad behavior. Yet its potential for good remains. Keeping this in mind, during this year's confession let us resolve to use the internet to fight falsehoods, bullying and so many more ills of our society.

Rabbi Jeffrey Falick
Birmingham Temple Congregation for
Humanistic Judaism
Farmington Hills, MI

RENEWAL

For the sin of being snarky—and reveling in it. It's funny, it's satisfying, and it's probably not so good for our souls. Social media reminds me of the passage in Deuteronomy where Moses sets before the people both blessings and curses—except that with social media you get both, all the time. Like the Shehecheyanu blessing, social media encourages us to recognize and bless special moments. But the desire to share with others "out there" can take us away from that moment and from those who are "right here." The moment is happening, but we turn away, trying to find the right words for a Facebook post. Or our kids are sitting next to us, receptive and eager to talk, but we're absorbed in "liking" other people's lives.

Or we miss the mark by letting envy join us as we scroll through other people's celebrations, their beautiful families, their burgeoning careers and exciting travel and well-worded opinions. Can we instead help ourselves to see other folks as part of us, as being on the same team? How can we turn jealousy into what Rabbi Nehemia Polen calls "holy envy"—the kind of envy that lifts us up and connects us rather than separating us?

Rabbi Gilah Langner
Congregation Kol Ami
Arlington, VA

RECONSTRUCTIONIST

The double-acrostic Al Chet enumerates our sins, places where we've missed the mark. Many of its 44 sample shortcomings deal with speech, whether "utterance of lips," "evil tongue" (*lashon hara*) or "false vows." Amid today's ubiquitous impersonal social media, the theme is amplified: thoughtless keyboard-clacking; 5 a.m. texts; forgetting the recipient's humanity. For real teshuvah (turning/repentance), we must know just how we err, online:

We aim: weaponize words. We blame: single out someone for undue condemnation. We claim: advance unchecked assumptions, opinions or fake news as factual. We flame: fail to reassess, or check our anger or our basest instincts, before pressing "send." We frame: cast innuendo without owning our actions and their implications. We maim: name-call, stereotype, use dehumanizing language. We shame: "Whoever publicly insults/shames another, whitening their face in embarrassment, spills blood" (*Talmud Bavli*, Bava Metzia 58b). And one non-rhyming entry: misplaced priorities. How many posts about lunch or pets; how many about justice or sustainability?

Instead, let's cultivate silence, "the best medicine of all" (Megillah 18a), by posting less. Let's listen, reading carefully, assuming the best of others. Let's cultivate *lashon tov*, positive, constructive speech, words that heal and build. And let's avoid *bitul z'man*, the sin of wasting time: step away from the ^#%&* screen!

Rabbi Fred Scherlinder Dobb
Adat Shalom Reconstructionist
Congregation
Bethesda, MD

REFORM

Each Yom Kippur we recite the Ashamnu prayer, an alphabet of sins we, as imperfect human beings, are inclined to commit. Reciting collectively rather than singularly, we take shared responsibility for keeping one another on the proper path. Consider this modern alphabetical Ashamnu: For the sins of making assumptions, bullying, careless use of words and dishonesty in our posts, may we be forgiven. May we no longer engage in egotism, spreading falsehoods, gossip, hate speech or indecencies. May we no longer be tempted by jingoism, kneejerk responses, malevolence and name-calling. We should stand up against obsequiousness, public shaming, quarrels and resistance to hearing new ideas. May we let go of selfishness and no longer take time away from family for social media. May we call out unchecked sources, report violent threats, not whet our tongues with xenophobia nor yield to zealous divisiveness. For all these sins and more, we ask Your forgiveness. Amen.

Rabbi Laura Novak Winer
Fresno, CA

96

CONSERVATIVE

Jewish tradition is fully aware of how frequently our words can be misused. The rabbis wisely understood the danger of cruel, disrespectful or dishonest words. They can divide a family, break a friendship and destroy a reputation. To atone, we must first ask ourselves the right questions.

Do we post more than we read what others have posted? Do we gossip? Do we repost stories about friends, family or colleagues that ought not be repeated? Do we believe everything we read? Do we post with the intention of hurting others? Do we waste time on social media? Do we post pictures that are hurtful? Or embarrassing? Or misleading? Do we repeat poorly sourced rumors? Are we mean-spirited or cruel because we are not talking face-to-face with another person?

If spoken words can be dangerous, the written word on social media can be exponentially more hurtful. Social media revives the old problem of the destructive effects of village gossip and extends it to the global village.

Rabbi Amy Wallk Katz
Temple Beth El
Springfield, MA

MODERN ORTHODOX

There is nothing in using social media that is intrinsically sinful. Like all technology, it may be used for good or for evil. So if we have "spoken slander" or "framed lies," if we have shown "contempt for parent and teacher" or "spoken with impure lips," if we have "entrapped a neighbor" or "breached a trust" on social media, then we should confess under those rubrics in our general confession of sins. Then we need to win atonement by apology, restitution and seeking forgiveness from our victim. None of this is distinctive to social media.

Some people do act more sinfully on the internet than they would in interpersonal society. The anonymity of the act or lack of personal contact with the victim brings out particularly vicious behavior in some people. People who would never act this way in person may be guilty of bullying or cruel and cutting demolitions of others. They may spread "fake news," total fabrications or groundless conspiracy theories. Especially damaging sins require extra effort to win atonement.

The method of teshuvah is the same for "new breed" sins as it is for traditional sinful behavior. One must feel/express regret, confess the sin before God, offer apology or restitution and seek forgiveness from the victim. Atonement is then completed with the observance of Yom Kippur. But be warned: The Talmud says that there are some sins so terrible that God does not grant atonement/forgiveness until the death of the sinner.

Rabbi Yitz Greenberg
Riverdale, NY

ORTHODOX

In the Torah portion Re'eh, we read, "See, I have given you today a blessing and a curse" (Deuteronomy 11:26). Rabbi Yaakov Moshe Charlap (1882-1951) was appalled by the notion that God can ever be described as "giving" a curse. So he argued that, really, God gives us only a blessing: Just as God creates things ex nihilo, he gives us some of that same creative capacity. What we do with that creativity can then turn into either a blessing or a curse. Unfortunately, social media, like so many other things that could have been a blessing, is something we have often turned into a curse. We have used it to create distance between people rather than bring them together. We have used it to shrink our personal universes rather than to expand them. We have used it to feed our egocentricity rather than our ability to give and share. And in the rare cases where none of the above apply, we have used social media to squander the ultimate non-renewable resource—time.

Rabbi Yitzchok Adlerstein
Cross-Currents
Los Angeles, CA

SEPHARDIC

Social media sins! Where do I even start? Probably with Jeremiah 9:8, "Their tongue is a sharp arrow." Gossip, calumny and libel are compared in the Bible to swords and poison, but the image of arrows best captures the dangerous power of our words, because once an arrow leaves the bow, there is no retrieving it. The best 21st-century weapon analogy for social media would be biological warfare—going "viral."

Social media allows us to communicate with billions of users, which is wonderful, but words written in haste, in anger or for revenge can alter the lives of countless people. Even if it's only one person, the damage in most cases is irreversible. How do I reach out to all the people who read my original post to tell them that I made a mistake? Another serious offense is exposing sensitive information about others. It is usually not deliberate, but one cannot escape responsibility. Then there is trolling, spamming, phishing and let's not forget the friend who sends you a million WhatsApps and then scolds you for not replying. There's gluism, the state of being glued to your phone and the primal need to document and post every minute of your life. The only atonement for the sins of social media is awareness as a preventive measure. Let us think twice (or more) before unleashing unretractable arrows.

Rabbi Haim Ovadia
Potomac, MD

CHABAD

The answer is rather simple: a lot. A classic Jewish story is told of a rabbi who was once maligned by a member of his community, who then regretted his actions and approached the rabbi asking to be forgiven. The rabbi asked the person for a pillow and went with him to a hilltop. He then sliced open the pillow as they both watched the feathers blow in every direction. The rabbi said, "I can forgive you when you collect every last feather and place it back in the pillow."

The moral is obvious. When you post or share something on social media, you can't really take it back, even if you delete it. It gets shared so quickly that sometimes things can literally be seen around the world by many millions, even billions. Chassidus explains that speech, or expression, is the process by which that which is yours alone becomes part of the world beyond you. This applies even to words spoken only to Alexa. G-d wanted to create a world. When He actually spoke the words, the world then came to be. That which had been His alone now existed for others as well.

We need to be mindful of what we post and share—and even what we choose to see. And when the High Holidays come, we should resolve to see and share only what helps make our lives more uplifting and the world better. That's the core human mission. Let's post good things and bring light to what has become all too dark all too often.

Rabbi Levi Shemtov
Executive Vice President, American
Friends of Lubavitch
Washington, DC

What does the Torah teach us about addiction?

As with social media, no obvious traditional or biblical parallel exists for the scourge of addiction or the world of twelve-step programs. But rabbis frequently have firsthand pastoral experience helping people grapple with addiction. It shows: Here, they offer an astonishing range of ways in which even the most familiar biblical stories speak powerfully to us about some aspect of that struggle—from the Golden Calf at Sinai to Noah's drunkenness after the Flood as he contemplates a destroyed world. Clearly, there's something here that is fundamental to the human personality. (Published in 2014.)

INDEPENDENT

Addiction is highlighted in the Torah's account of the Revelation at Mount Sinai, where the One Who Spoke and the World Came into Being instructed us not to get so caught up in our subjective assumptions about God that we would carve out and worship an image reflecting those assumptions. In other words, addiction is the act of replacing a truth—or need, or innate desire—with an artificial facsimile that eventually supersedes the very truth it was originally intended to represent. It is often born out of one's struggle and subsequent failure to reach the truth in question, the frustration of which can drive one to such desperation that one resorts to, say, a Golden Calf. And the healing of addiction, in turn, involves melting down the image and lapping it up, internalizing that which had been so unwholesomely externalized, to restore to the essential self what had belonged there all along.

Rabbi Gershon Winkler
Walking Stick Foundation
Thousand Oaks, CA

HUMANIST

It is human nature, declares Torah, to err: "For the imagination of man's heart is evil from his youth" (Genesis 8:21). Torah also recognizes the corollary: that we have the capacity to change our ways. And so our tradition offers us a path—through sacrifices, prayer or self-examination—to repentance, renewal, reconciliation and recovery.

One of my favorite biblical quotes is from Genesis 4:6-7. God has accepted Abel's offering but rejected the one from Cain. Yet God doesn't give up on Cain. He offers him some straight talk: "Why are you angry? If you are to do what is good, shouldn't you hold your head high? And if you don't do what is good, sin is crouching at the door. It wants you, but you can rule over it." Temptation is there. Always ready to pounce. Always ready to snare us so that we say the wrong word, or waste time, or self-medicate with alcohol or drugs or too much junk food. But we can also be the master over it. Not because we resort to prayer or turn to a Higher Power to pull us through—that is not what God says to Cain—but because we can take charge of our own actions.

The first step is acknowledging our human nature. We will fail over and over. We can also make good choices and get on the right path again.

Rabbi Peter H. Schweitzer
The City Congregation
for Humanistic Judaism
New York, NY

RENEWAL

The first biblical evidence of preventive medicine, the Sabbath, also served as a healing plan for the Israelites emerging from slavery. They needed to learn how to *shavat va'yinafash*—to rest and re-soul. The penalty for working more than six days a week, that is, work addiction, was death by stoning. The Torah arrived long before addiction treatment and recovery programs became available, and it also includes a tale of an option for parents to have a "rebellious son" stoned to death if he is "a glutton and stubborn drunk" who does not listen and steals from his parents. Tradition holds that no family ever did so. The Talmud also discusses where and how to draw the line with things that are addictive, including Torah study itself.

Today, Jewish law and practice follow the mitzvah of *pikuach nefesh*—saving a life—through many programs that use Jewish approaches to seek to save the lives of those addicted, actively intervening and supporting addicts and their families to seek out the many forms of support for recovery from addiction to alcohol, drugs, gambling, tobacco, sex, food, video games, smart phones, work and food. I recommend Rabbi Abraham Twerski's *Addictive Thinking: Understanding Self-Deception*, and, because successful recovery almost always involves spiritual development, Rabbi Rami Shapiro's chapter, "12 Steps Revisited through a Jewish Spiritual Lens," in *Seeking and Soaring: Jewish Approaches to Spiritual Guidance and Direction*. There is also help available for "Jewish Alcoholics, Chemically Dependent Persons and Significant Others" at www.jacs.org.

Rabbi Goldie Milgram
ReclaimingJudaism.org
Sarasota, FL

RECONSTRUCTIONIST

"Love your neighbor as yourself" (Leviticus 19:18): This presumes self-love first, something that's hard for the many who grapple with addiction. Addiction clouds self-awareness and leads to self-destructive rather than self-loving behavior, through which love for others suffers too.

To love these neighbors, we can remind them of just how worthy their true selves are, to provide a clear beacon for their recovery. We can sit with them in their pain, ask the right questions and help them obtain the help they need. We must also understand their situation and educate ourselves about addiction, so we can love them with both accountability and support. We should consult experts and listen to those in recovery; we should know and be sensitive.

"Don't set stumbling blocks before the blind": Likewise, we are enjoined to help those with addictive tendencies steer clear of what might make them stumble. Don't build simchas around alcohol, nor be casual with controlled substances (food included, which can be complicated for us Jews). We mustn't set the kryptonite of temptation before those super-people who are taking it one day at a time.

Rabbi Fred Scherlinder Dobb
Adat Shalom Reconstructionist
Congregation
Bethesda, MD

REFORM

If you're looking for a cautionary tale about drinking in the Torah, you need read no further than the story of Noah, early in the book of Genesis. But addiction is not about a rough night of drinking too much, and I think our Torah teaches us about appetites, desires, control and moderation. Torah does not demand abstinence; we are asked to enjoy the material pleasures of the world. We read in Deuteronomy: "When you have eaten and are satisfied, you shall bless Adonai your God." Part of the illness of addiction is never being satisfied: You are sure that the next drink, the next bet, the next sexual partner, the next hit will satisfy.

Yet we must eat, and we must bless. So Torah is clear on appetites—be they carnal or epicurean, you can't always get what you want. The Book of Leviticus is a guide to moderation; it comes to teach us that if we cannot control our appetites, then our temptations are forbidden to us altogether. Recognizing the seduction of the forbidden, Torah sets up strict boundaries between permitted and forbidden and warns of the dangers of transgression. Ultimately, Torah says: If you can't control yourself, separate yourself from the temptation altogether. Addiction teaches the same lesson.

Rabbi Sari Laufer
Congregation Rodeph Sholom
New York, NY

CONSERVATIVE

Addiction can be framed in a spiritual context by using biblical stories. For example, one might consider the story of the Israelites' exodus from Egypt as a model for the journey from addiction to recovery. Egypt (Mitzrayim in Hebrew) literally means the double narrow place; it is the place where the Israelites became slaves or were given into slavery. Addiction comes from a Latin root meaning "to give oneself over." Someone who suffers from an addiction is enslaved. Addiction is a state in which one is powerless and out of control.

The story of the exodus from Egypt can easily be understood as the personal story of each addicted Jew emerging from his or her narrow place, tempted repeatedly to backslide but struggling always to reach the promised land of recovery, serenity and spirituality.

There is another way to use Jewish sources when confronting addiction. Rabbinic teachings suggest that every person has a *yetzer hatov*, the impulse to do what is good, and *yetzer hara*, the impulse to do what is bad. An addiction can be seen as the expression of *yetzer hara*. Not that the person is evil, but that he or she is under the influence of impulses that produce harmful results. Every human being has a *yetzer hara*. When one struggles with an addiction, the *yetzer hara* has not been controlled or managed effectively. Ideally it is controlled by the *yetzer hatov*.

Rabbi Amy Wallk Katz
Temple Beth El
Springfield, MA

MODERN ORTHODOX

The Torah is a Torah of life and is committed to a lifestyle that sustains a sound mind in a healthy body. There is a mitzvah, *"V'nishmartem me'od le'nafshotaychem"*—"You shall carefully guard your life" (Deuteronomy 4:15). Addiction violates this norm because it drives us to behaviors that jeopardize health and—as in the case of drugs—may cause death.

In addition, the Torah is committed to free will. People acting under duress are acquitted of violations. Being compelled by addiction robs a person of his or her freedom of action; therefore, he or she lacks moral responsibility, and this undercuts the moral and ethical life.

The Torah does not offer a direct diagnosis of addiction or a specific course of action for a cure. However, the disciplines and tempered life of halacha are designed to give structures of meaning and sensible limits that support a free, non-addicted, moderate way of living. It is widely known that traditional Jewish temperate drinking—such as serving wine on religious and happy occasions—rather than total abstention lowers rates of alcoholism and overindulgence.

In particular, Shabbat—a day when we are commanded to desist from work—is designed to prevent addiction to work, or workaholism. In conjunction with counseling and help in confronting problems, this way of living may reduce addiction.

Rabbi Yitz Greenberg
Riverdale, NY

CHABAD

Adam and Eve ate from the tree because they wanted knowledge. What they got was self-knowledge, not insight but rather a crippling self-consciousness, the first sign of which was their sudden shame at being naked. Since that time, it has become ingrained in human nature to be uncomfortable in our own skin. Some of us feel that discomfort with self more intensely than others, but it is the universal curse of all humankind.

Ten generations after Creation, seeing a "new world" before him, Noah tried to reverse the paradigm and fight self-consciousness with self-obliteration. He "planted a vineyard...and got drunk." Noah was not out to have a good time; he was on a mission to blot out self-consciousness. And thus he drank until "he fell asleep naked in his tent." He felt no shame; he felt nothing.

This is the dilemma—the pain of self-awareness on the one extreme and the comfort of self-obliteration on the other. Neither is very promising. To become free, we must find a third option, which is self-transcendence, to rise above ego. As long as we do not have the tools to rise above ourselves, however, we'll do the next best thing and just destroy ourselves. Hence the decidedly choice terms for serious self-medication: wasted, wrecked, trashed, etc.

Contrary to popular misconception, addiction isn't a problem; addiction is actually a solution—a vicious, brutal, devastating solution, but a solution nonetheless. And if that's all you've got to work with, then you will always come back to it no matter what.

Addiction is but the human condition writ large. We're not happy when we're stuck in ourselves; we're not happy when we're destroying ourselves; we're only happy once we get over ourselves. And that is recovery from addiction—when I realize that the only way I can truly function is through extreme selflessness and surrender to a Power greater than myself.

Rabbi Shais Taub
Chabad.org
Pittsburgh, PA

What guidance, if any, does Judaism offer to transgender people?

I n brief: More than you'd think. Asking this question, we were mindful of the need to honor personal experience, reaching out to at least one rabbi who identifies as trans (Rabbi Zellman) and to one who works extensively with young people experiencing struggles in this area (Rabbi Broyde). The Talmud's extensive discussion of people whose gender doesn't line up with the norm—the tumtum, the androgyne, and others— is a reminder that gender fluidity is not a new invention. (Published in 2016.)

INDEPENDENT

In ancient times, our rabbis acknowledged that male and female were not the only genders. The possibility of a boy turning into a girl, for example, is mentioned in the Talmud quite nonchalantly: "For perhaps his maleness transformed into femaleness" (*Talmud Bavli*, Bechorot 42b). They also spoke of the *androgynos*, who was both male and female, and the *tumtum*, a person who lacked male genitalia but was not female or lacked female genitalia but was not male (*Talmud*

Bavli, Nazir 12b). The *tumtum* was permitted both to initiate a marriage, like a groom, and to become married, like a bride (*Talmud Bavli*, Tosefta Yevamot 11:1; Yevamot 72a). The *tumtum* also inherited from her/his father's estate in all the ways in which a son would, and was supported from the father's estate in all the ways in which a daughter would be (*Talmud Bavli*, Baba Batra 140b).

As for those who have been castrated, whether forcibly by their Babylonian captors some 2,700 years ago (Second Kings, 20:16-18) or surgically due to emotional suffering in the 21st century, God says: "I will give unto them in my house and within my walls hand [strength] and name [prestige] far more than for sons and daughters, an eternal name that will never be cut off, ever!" (Isaiah 56:4-5).

Rabbi Gershon Winkler
Walking Stick Foundation
Thousand Oaks, CA

HUMANIST

I distinctly remember being surprised and impressed when I first encountered the Talmudic term *tumtum*, which refers to an individual whose sexual characteristics are indeterminate or obscured and whose gender is in a state of doubt. Surprised, because I'm not even sure I was aware of this biological possibility, and impressed that the rabbis were not only aware but talked about it so easily, as another category they had to take into account.

The rabbis were equally aware that someone could display both male and female characteristics. They called that person *androgynos*. Today we might use the term intersex. The rabbis also understood that a transition could take place as one aged. They used the term *aylonit* for a person who is identified as female at birth but develops male characteristics at puberty. On the other hand, a *saris* was a person who is identified as male at birth and develops female characteristics at puberty and/or is lacking a penis, either naturally or by human intervention.

The rabbis, in other words, were remarkably far ahead of their times. They recognized and accepted a world of possibilities. It is up to us, in our generation, to further the acknowledgement and unconditional acceptance of all transgender and nonconforming people and to reaffirm yet another age-old teaching: the infinite and equal worth in every human being.

Rabbi Peter H. Schweitzer
The City Congregation for
Humanistic Judaism
New York, NY

RECONSTRUCTIONIST

"God created the human in God's image, in the image of God, God created him; male and female He created them" (Genesis 1:27). Already in the first chapter of the Torah we learn two important things. First, gender does not fit neatly into two boxes of male and female. And second, whatever our gender identities, we are created in the image of God.

While many of us may have been taught to understand gender and sex as either male or female, Jewish texts such as midrash, Mishnah and Talmud name the non-binary reality of our bodies and gender identities, thereby affirming the reality of human diversity. Rabbi David Teutsch writes that the "Talmud contains hundreds of references to other categories [besides male and female]." The term "gender-nonconforming" may seem like a new idea to some, but it is actually an ancient reality of what it means to be human.

I think the guidance Judaism offers all people—including those who are transgender and gender-noncomforming—is to embrace the person we know ourselves truly to be, in all our differences (and similarities). Jewish texts do not always communicate that. But it is up to us to identify core Jewish principles in the face of inner contradictions, and for me, the principle that we are created in the image of God is primary. That principle can also offer guidance to congregations and Jewish communities as we take concrete steps to become inclusive and welcoming to all.

Rabbi Caryn Broitman
Martha's Vineyard Hebrew Center
Vineyard Haven, MA

REFORM

Judaism teaches us that everyone is made in the image of God and should be treated accordingly. That's not a transgender issue; it applies to everybody. But saying it in the abstract and actually acting as if it's true are two very different things. In the case of transgender and gender-nonconforming people, it requires that we really challenge ourselves. Everyone who is an adult today has grown up with extremely negative, restrictive and punitive messages about what it means to be male and female, what kinds of behaviors or presentations are considered OK. We are not going to accomplish being respectful of transgender people just by saying, "Hey, we welcome everyone, and everyone's equal." We need to ask ourselves, "Where was I taught to be judgmental about gender?" Just as with issues of race, of disability and many other things, the great mistake we tend to make—especially in progressive Jewish communities—is that we want to welcome everyone, but we don't realize how much work and introspection is required.

I really believe Judaism teaches us, wants us, asks us to be healthy, ethical, happy people. And sometimes that requires going beyond the fairly narrow strictures of what society tells us we should do. And that requires some courage, and I believe our tradition supports us in having that courage. Yes, we can look at Jewish texts and find all kinds of interesting and often moving examples of the ways in which our older forms of Judaism were actually much more welcoming toward gender variety than we are today. But fundamentally I believe that Judaism and God have asked us to be co-creators of who we are and what this world is. And that takes a lot of courage.

Rabbi Reuben Zellman
Congregation Beth El
Berkeley, CA

CONSERVATIVE

A bright, capable young woman became a bat mitzvah at our shul some time ago. It was clear she loved studying for her big day, but at the same time I felt something about the experience was off-putting for her. Eventually, her mother made it clear her daughter would not be wearing a dress to her bat mitzvah. Of course, I didn't care; I just wanted the young girl to be comfortable on our bima.

In the few years since, I have watched as that young girl was transformed into a young man. First it was short hair, then changes in clothing. Finally, the mother came to see me and explained their child now identified as a male, had taken a boy's name and preferred that male pronouns be used when referring to him.

Stories like these have surfaced only recently. Of course, there were individuals struggling with their gender before now—just not in public. What guidance can Judaism offer them and their families? First, Judaism teaches me to honor the individual. When the mother came to see me, I obviously agreed to start referring to her child using male pronouns. I also met with synagogue staff to anticipate issues and discuss how to enact the value of *kavod habriyot*, the honor due to God's creations.

Finally, I told the mother about the work of Rabbi Mark Sameth, author of *Is God Transgender?* Rabbi Sameth's writing validates that being transgender is not alien to Judaism. I wanted this mother to feel she had an anchor in Judaism. I don't want the transgender individual to feel tolerated. I want them to feel honored, connected and supported by Judaism and by their community.

Rabbi Amy Wallk Katz
Temple Beth El
Springfield, MA

MODERN ORTHODOX

In the past, Judaism's general attitude was negative toward human efforts to override species' boundaries—grafting, planting with mixed species, mixing wool and linen in textiles (*shatnez*). The reservations reflect the concept that humans should respect nature's boundaries. Similarly, gender differentiation was taken to be the natural order of things, not to be tampered with. Castration was separately and additionally prohibited, perhaps because of the association of such practices with various pagan religions and rites.

But there is a second theme in the tradition: that the human is a partner with God in the work of creation. Agriculture increases yields over untouched natural growth; industrial productivity upgrades natural resources for the benefit of humanity. Thus humans can improve on nature—if they do not excessively exploit or degrade it. This approach led halachists to approve of organ transplantation, in vitro fertilization and some birth control.

Only recently have we come to see transgender and gender-nonconforming people as a natural phenomenon, arising from inborn tendencies. Some halachists have responded negatively, seeing these developments as more interference with God's natural order. But they could also be treated as a case of the human partner acting to "repair" a misplacement on the spectrum of gender. In that case, supporting transgender and gender-nonconforming people would be seen as improving their quality of life and allowing full realization of the distinctive image of God in them. Therefore, they should be treated sympathetically, and their dignity and rights should be honored and upheld.

Rabbi Yitz Greenberg
Riverdale, NY

ORTHODOX

Gender-nonconforming and transgender people are individuals who are phenotypically one sex but morphologically the other, or ambiguous. The classical Jewish law tradition of the Talmud never thought gender was binary for everyone. The Mishnah spends a whole chapter and many other individual passages discussing the special rules relating to individuals whose gender is ambivalent.

Modern Jewish law recognizes two realities. First, there are people who have complex genetic or biochemical realities that create tension between their genetic makeup and their apparent gender. Sometimes this is resolved in favor of their genotype and sometimes in favor of their outward gender, and sometimes this resolution changes at puberty. These are hard cases that need nuance, balance and medical expertise. Jewish principles would guide one to the best medical solution in such a case and to a genetic counselor.

Another group of cases are infants born with gender anomalies that parents wish to correct surgically. The Jewish tradition also treats this as essentially a medical issue, although it sees no firm reason to resolve all gender ambiguity. Intersex is sometimes normal in infants, and parents should not be pushed to surgically "correct" intersex without considering the long-term consequences for the child.

Of course, every person needs to be dealt with in kindness as they seek answers to the many ritual questions a gender-ambiguous person has—where to sit in a synagogue and much more—but these are less important questions than they appear to be, once one realizes that gender ambiguity is a category in Jewish law.

Rabbi Michael J. Broyde
Emory University School of Law
Atlanta, GA

SEPHARDIC

Traditional Judaism, which tends to confine itself to the four cubits of halacha, currently has either criticism or very little guidance to offer to those of nonconforming gender. The problem is lack of precedents, since the halachic discourse in the Mishnah, and all the literature based on it, is conceptually rooted in the binary perception of male/female. Even when the sources discuss anomalous cases such as the *tumtum*, they approach them in terms of this binary division, characterizing them, for instance, as "neither male nor female" or "both male and female." We are just starting to understand that there is a wide spectrum of gender identity and that society must not force people into narrow categories.

This process will be slow and arduous at the social level and even more torturous at the religious level, which by nature tends to be divisive and classifying. Just as we strive to achieve equality between men and women, we should aspire to provide full equality to people of nonconforming gender without demanding that they identify as either male or female.

This approach should be based on two crucial concepts of Judaism. First, the Book of Genesis states that all humans were created in the image of God. We believe that God has no physicality and no gender, and therefore all humans are equal. Furthermore, the Torah refers to the first human in both the plural and the singular (Genesis 1:27), indicating that we must accept the inherent plurality of the human being.

The second is the famous golden rule: Love the other as you love yourself. (Leviticus 19:18) Just as we do not want to be rejected, alienated, judged or labeled, we should not do so to others, and definitely not in the name of religion. Religious leaders should rise to the task and find ways to welcome transgender or nonconforming people, and perhaps the first step will be to let them define themselves.

Rabbi Haim Ovadia
Magen David Sephardic Congregation
Bethesda, MD

Is Judaism good
for women?

W omen are not, of course, simply a phenomenon of modern life, and this could easily be classified as a question about values (see the next chapter). But asking the question at all is surely a modern impulse. It's also an invitation to overgeneralize: As Rabbi Miriam Jerris observes, "There is not one Judaism that treats all women the same, and there is certainly not one woman who reacts in the same way to all situations." Rabbi Fred Scherlinder Dobb adds that "misogyny and magnificence coexist on the same page of many Jewish texts."

This may be why the responses exhibit the well-known tendency of rabbis to answer a question with another question, in this case a question they think we should have asked instead—Is Judaism good enough for women? Are women good for Judaism? (Published in 2013.)

INDEPENDENT

Yes. To its credit, Judaism has through the millennia endeavored to liberate man from his fear of woman and woman from the consequences of that fear, in ways too numerous to delineate. As feminist author Rosemary R. Ruether put it: "Judaism did more than most other ancient religions to lift woman up to the status of equality in civil rights and spiritual recognition. . . . Ancient Israelite women fared better than modern Western women." There was a time, for example, when the opinions of women and their "votes" counted toward establishing halachic precedence (*Talmud Bavli*, Tosef'ta Keylim 11:3; Minchat Chinuch, No. 78), and when women were equally qualified and authorized as men in rendering halachic decisions and rulings, in other words, serving as rabbis (Sefer Ha'Chinuch, No. 158). Women being called up to the bimah to chant from the Torah scroll seems to most of us totally revolutionary, when in fact it was a standard practice in ancient times (*Talmud Bavli*, Megilah 23a). That this and more was discontinued over time was the result not of any changes within Judaism, but of men's insecure power struggle with the ungraspable force of the feminine, sanctioned by their masterful skill at forging God's name to their whimsical justifications.

Rabbi Gershon Winkler
Walking Stick Foundation
Thousand Oaks, CA

HUMANIST

Is Judaism good for women? The most honest answer is "It depends." It depends on the Judaism and it depends on the woman. Historically, women were not treated with dignity in Judaism. Even today in some Jewish denominations, women do not have the same rights and privileges as men. As a college student, I applied to the rabbinic program at Hebrew Union College, only to discover that women were not allowed admission to rabbinical school. Hebrew Union College ordained its first female rabbi in 1972.

There is not one Judaism that treats all women the same, and there is certainly not one woman who reacts in the same way to all situations. If my options were limited to Orthodox, Reform, Conservative, Reconstructionist or Renewal Judaism, Judaism would not have been good for this woman. Happily, I discovered Humanistic Judaism, which allows me to remain connected to Judaism without abandoning my philosophy of life or personal convictions. The strength of Judaism is in its pluralism. And Humanistic Judaism is very good for women.

Rabbi Miriam Jerris
Society for Humanistic Judaism
Farmington Hills, MI

RENEWAL

Why ask me? Let's face it, we men have had more than our say. Better to ask Sarah Imeynu—Sarah our mother—who would have laughed at the question. Or Yael, who might have taken your head off, as she did Sisera's in Canaan. Ask Rachel, the beloved wife of Rabbi Akiva; his Torah knowledge was said to be all acquired through her merit. Or Glückel of Hameln, who with the ferocity of a lioness of Judah raised a family with a strong Jewish identity through the hardship of a dominant Christian culture in 17th-century Germany.

I hesitate to speak for them, or for the women in our midst today who are striving to answer the question: Judith Hauptman, who rethought the role of women, their obligation to pray and their rightful place as leaders; or Anat Hoffman and the Women of the Wall; or Sara Hurwitz, an Orthodox Rabba. But one thing is certain: Though the paradigm shift has seemingly been slow to come, in the great scheme of G!d's plan, 2,000 years is like a second. In Genesis 2:18, we read, "And the Lord G!d said, 'It is not good for man to be alone. I will make a counterpart to him.'" In the unfolding of Jewish thought and practice, we stand together, men and women, at the threshold of the kind of partnership that G!d has had in her mind all along. We await this full realization "for the sake of the unification of the Holy One, blessed be He, and His Divine Presence, blessed be She." On that day, G!d will look at all of creation and say not "that it was good" but "that it was very, very good"— for women and men alike.

Rabbi Mark Novak
Minyan Oneg Shabbat
Washington, DC

RECONSTRUCTIONIST

More than Judaism's being good for women, the full empowerment of women is good for Judaism. As in any great civilization, misogyny and magnificence coexist on the same page of many Jewish texts. Traditions may look good relative to their time and place of origin, but once ossified, they turn regressive. Since early rabbinic times, when women were either "chattel, or person" (scholar Judith Wegner's phrase), trends and rulings have cut both ways: Some honor women's full humanity and experience, while others would completely purge women's public voices, images and presence, even today.

Enter Mordecai Kaplan, founder of Reconstructionism and originator of the bat mitzvah. His 1922 proto-feminism flowed naturally from a belief that Judaism always has evolved and always should. Nearly a century later, most Jews agree, differing only on the precise pace, path and progressive nature of change.

Now enter Miriam the Prophet, Beruriah, Dona Gracia, Clara Lemlich, Regina Jonas, Judith Plaskow and countless others who overcame the patriarchal odds, who found Judaism "good enough" in their time and improved the Jewish people and the world with their contributions. Empowered women (and male allies) contribute greatly, even today; yet with sexism, everyone loses. Despite great strides toward equality, we must push further.

Rabbi Fred Scherlinder Dobb
Adat Shalom Reconstructionist
Congregation
Bethesda, MD

REFORM

Religion is like a toolbox. A religious heritage with its texts, values, ethics, rituals and traditions gives us the tools we need to respond to life's challenges and sorrows, celebrate our joys and answer the questions life throws at us. Some Jewish tools, like our mourning practices, have been passed down to us through the generations. And in many instances, the Jewish community innovatively contributes to the Jewish toolbox with answers, rituals and symbolic lessons that provide guidance to Jews today, such as bat mitzvah, same-gender marriage and our ongoing reinterpretation of Torah.

Yes, Judaism is good for women. Judaism provides everyone with access to the tools people need to find meaning in their lives, to the spiritual guidance and rituals to address life transitions. Everyone, every woman, should have a toolbox at her disposal and know how to use the tools in it.

The question challenging the world Jewish community at the moment is a very different one: Are women good for Judaism? My unequivocal answer is yes!

Rabbi Laura Novak Winer
Fresno, CA

CONSERVATIVE

One way to answer this question is to examine the stories of the creation of women, of which there are two in Genesis. Genesis 1 says that men and women are created "in the image of God" and represent the highest level of creation.

A second version of the creation story is presented in Genesis 2. Here the Torah says that Adam was created from the dust of the earth. Eventually God concludes, "It is not good for man to be alone." God puts Adam into a deep sleep, withdraws one of his ribs and from it fashions the first woman.

Is such an explanation of women's creation demeaning to women? On the one hand, the claim that man was created first, and woman formed out of a part of him, implies the male's inherent superiority—especially since Adam gives Eve her name. On the other hand, the fact that every new product of creation is more highly developed than the one that preceded it might indicate that the woman, who is last to be created, represents the apex of creation.

Since there are multiple ways to interpret the status of women in the Genesis stories, we can't say definitively whether Judaism is or is not good for women. Some texts are clearly negative about women, while others are unambiguously admiring. But many texts and traditions are not at all clear-cut. Some can be interpreted as demeaning and dismissive, while others can be interpreted as inclusive and respectful.

Rabbi Amy Wallk Katz
Temple Beth El
Springfield, MA

MODERN ORTHODOX

Judaism is the primary source of the concept that every human being has dignity and equality because all are in the image of God. This ethical foundation— modulated through Christianity, Islam, modernity and democracy—is the primary basis of the claim (now on the march throughout the world) driving the growing practice of treating women as full human beings of equal value to men. That is good for women.

On the other hand, Judaism itself compromised with reality and accepted women's status as secondary in accordance with the cultures in which Jews lived. Women were subject to sale (in the biblical period) and to the husband's authority and sole power to grant divorce (in the rabbinic period). They were excluded or restricted from public leadership roles from the rabbinic period down to modern times. That is bad for women. Traditional religious Jews provide the largest bloc of resisters to women's full equality and dignity in contemporary Jewish culture.

In short, the correct question is not: Is Judaism good for women? (the answer is yes) but rather "Is Judaism good enough for women?" The answer is: Not yet.

Rabbi Yitz Greenberg
Riverdale, NY

ORTHODOX

Judaism is a profoundly feminine religion. The ancient world advocated an aggressive masculinity in which war was glorified and those who defeated their enemies were heroes. Along came great men like Isaiah and Jeremiah and said that a time would come when men would beat their swords into ploughshares. Linear masculine symbols would be transformed into more cyclical feminine ones. Maternal qualities like peace would triumph over the masculine values like war. Hence, Judaism values the Sabbath "bride" and "queen" over the six more masculine days of competition and earning. This philosophy translates into a system of ensuring that women are not just elevated and respected, but made into partners to whom men pay deference so that they themselves can learn to be more nurturing and feminine.

Detractors may focus on the fact that men have more ritual observances and have public rabbinic roles when in truth Judaism respects scholarship and character, and women today have every opportunity to be the equals of men in Torah learning and teaching. Judaism advocates the institution of marriage where a man must commit to and cherish a woman rather than use her and discard her. It obligates a husband to respect a wife more than himself. Above all else, Judaism conditions men to appreciate the more subtle, inner beauty in a woman that is so often overlooked in a world that allows physical beauty and youth to dominate.

Rabbi Shmuley Boteach
Englewood, NJ

CHABAD

Indeed it is. The Torah is called *Torat Chaim*, which means "instruction for life." Unlike other faith systems, Judaism is a "way of life" rather than a "religion" as that term is conventionally used. It is a manual for sanctifying every moment, every activity—including the seemingly mundane—and permeating it with G-dliness. In this framework, the layperson is no less engaged in the service of G-d than the full-time rabbi. The arenas of family and home are as religiously significant as the synagogue, if not more so. Judaism wants every corner of our life to be made divinely purposeful.

When viewed from this perspective, the woman's influence on Jewish life is indeed primary; her role is central and indispensable. There can be no Judaism without her. She creates and inspires in those critical places where Judaism is most integral—in real, daily life. Of course she studies Torah and prays to G-d—indeed, our prayers are modeled after those of a Jewish woman—but more importantly, the Jewish woman is the acknowledged leader and role model to her family and to her community, often more than her male counterparts. Can we even speak of educating future generations of Jews without the Jewish woman? Can there really be a Jewish home without her? Can we possibly celebrate Jewish holidays as a family without her leading presence?

Religion takes place in special buildings; Judaism is practiced everywhere, especially in the home. Religion is observed on special days; Judaism is lived every day, all the time. Religion is officiated by members of the clergy; Judaism is practiced equally by every Jew. When we understand this about Judaism, many questions about traditional gender roles disappear.

Rabbi Yosef Landa
Regional Director,
Chabad of Greater St. Louis
St. Louis, MO

Are tattoos and body piercings taboo?

The question of tattooing is in one sense trivial: It's literally skin deep, and as nearly every rabbi is at pains to point out here, it won't bar you from burial in a Jewish cemetery, no matter what your Hebrew School teacher said. At the same time, it stirs up powerful, sometimes irrational emotion and heavy cultural symbolism. So it's the perfect prism for splitting rabbinic opinion into a spectrum of differently shaded rulings, from "Entirely an individual matter" to "Not kosher" along with a nice selection of variations on "It depends." These answers also demonstrate, in case anyone doubted it, that quoting a so-called proof text is only the beginning of the argument. (Published in 2009.)

INDEPENDENT

The Torah's proscriptions of tattoos applied to imitating religio-cultic ways of peoples who don't exist anymore, such as Hittites and Yevusites, and later to any peoples with antithetical ways. However, they do not include sociocultural customs. The late ultra-Orthodox halachic authority Rav Moshe Feinstein made this point on Jews and jeans based on the injunction: "You shall not walk in the statutes of the nations," which he said addressed religio-cultic practices, not social customs; therefore, Jews could wear jeans. A decorative tattoo is a social custom. The second-century Rabbi Shimon ruled that a tattoo is only forbidden if it's a god's name and thus related to worship. The Talmud also quotes Bar Kapara, who went further: "... only if you tattoo the name of a deity other than God." Same with piercings. The Torah describes piercings as common among Jews, making no distinction between ear or nose rings. We circumcise and pierce. If Hittites pierced their elbows in four places and wore tattoos of a fox chasing a rabbit, then those cultic actions would be disallowed. Any community that refuses to bury Jews in a Jewish cemetery because they have decorative tattoos or nose rings is practicing what I call "erroneo-outtacontexto" Judaism, which is a far worse violation of Torah than a Hittite tattoo.

Rabbi Gershon Winkler
Walking Stick Foundation
Thousand Oaks, CA

HUMANIST

As secular and cultural Jews, we embrace the idea that mitzvot are self-imposed commandments that we place on ourselves. Although guided by our heritage, we recognize that Judaism is ever-evolving. We have the freedom to break from tradition and make decisions that are compatible with modern sensibilities. On occasion, however, cultural Jews who have otherwise rejected rabbinic edicts fall back on traditional teachings to argue a position that may counter contemporary choices that they normally defend. A case in point is tattoos. Ironically, while countless rabbis have punctured the misconception that burial of a tattooed body in a Jewish cemetery is prohibited, some secular Jews misquote them when objecting to these practices. They resort to an old-time defense, namely, "Jews don't do these things."

But many Jews do, and not just young people, but older ones, too. They do so for all sorts of reasons, including marking a significant birthday, commemorating a rite of passage, asserting pride in identity or simply using the body as a canvas for art. If Jewish teachings enter the picture at all, they are welcome lessons that promote personal expression. In the end, whether or not one views tattoos and body piercings as taboo is entirely an individual matter.

Rabbi Peter Schweitzer
The City Congregation
for Humanistic Judaism
New York, NY

RENEWAL

A lively congregation will attract young adults—some with fashionable tattoos and body piercings. Parents and their teens will grapple with what Judaism teaches us about these kinds of body modifications. Most parents grew up when cosmetic surgery was dangerous. The only tattoos many saw were on the arms of Holocaust survivors. Any teen serious about the mitzvot of honoring parents and protecting bodily integrity should know that tattoos and some piercings contradict these mitzvot. Torah clearly forbids tattooing and self-cutting as ways of mourning or memorializing. However, Torah also implies that piercings can be opportunities for good or bad. The Israelite men donated their earrings to build the Golden Calf, but the Israelite women donated theirs to build the *mishkan* (sanctuary). Similarly, the piercing question offers teens an opportunity to develop their *middot* (inner qualities). A group that impulsively visits a piercing parlor to see who is most daring cultivates peer pressure and irresponsible spending habits. But a teen who spends months researching the pros and cons of fashion versus safety, while consulting the internet, parents and the youth group leader, is learning to act with intelligence and integrity.

Rabbi Laura Duhan Kaplan
Or Shalom Synagogue
Vancouver, British Columbia

RECONSTRUCTIONIST

"Reconstructionism is a method, rather than a series of affirmations," said founder Mordecai Kaplan. How we decide is as important as what. Piercing and tattoos offer a concise example. We say, "The past gets a vote, not a veto," so what does tradition say? In Exodus 21, a pierced ear means you rejected freedom, but in Ezekiel 16, a nose ring is God-given "finery." Tattoos are historically prohibited—maybe all, maybe just those with the name of God, or with death themes. In our American context (which also gets a "vote") piercing is no big deal, and once-rebellious tattoos are now on every other twentysomething. What your community thinks, today, matters much. Discuss it with family and friends first. What core values are at stake? Body art either honors or diminishes the divine gift. It boils down to honoring one's body, which is inherently subjective. Content and intent matter: A faddish "Mary Mom and Hell's Angels" won't make the cut; a considered *chai* might. What might we affirm? Don't overfocus on appearance (yours or another's). Keep priorities straight (are piercing/ tattoo parlors not wrong, just *bitul zman*, a misuse of precious time?). And respect bodies in ways that count. Jewish burials happen, tattooed or not; they happen later if you exercise and eat right!

Fred Scherlinder Dobb
Adat Shalom Reconstructionist
Congregation
Bethesda, MD

REFORM

The problem isn't that these practices violate some ritual prohibition (*isur*) in the Torah. True, Leviticus 19:28 forbids "tattooing." But the tradition explains this as a measure to keep us from imitating the ways of pagans whose religious cults involved tattooing. Those in our community who tattoo themselves for reasons of personal adornment are certainly not engaged in pagan worship (*avodah zarah*). And the Torah even tells us that our ancestors wore nose rings (Genesis 24:47, Ezekiel

16:12). The problem is that tattooing and piercing may violate our tradition's demand that we treat our bodies with reverence and that we not inflict unnecessary physical damage upon ourselves. This standard, of course, is far from objective; how, precisely, does one define "reverence" and "unnecessary damage"? Many might argue that their tattoos and piercings express deep respect, rather than contempt, for their bodies. Maybe, maybe not. But this is the proper conversation for us to have: We ought to consider what we mean when we talk about "respect for the body" and "adornment" as Jewish values. To put it another way, how can we as Jews best express our reverence for the sanctity of the bodies that God has provided us?

Rabbi Mark Washofsky
Hebrew Union College/Jewish Institute
of Religion
Cincinnati, OH

CONSERVATIVE

Jewish tradition teaches that when a human being mints a coin with a mold, all the coins are identical, but God coined every person out of the first human being and each one is unique. This simple text movingly articulates the Jewish approach to the body: We are each God's own exquisite, beloved creation and should inhabit our bodies in a manner that celebrates this sacred relationship. Tattooing is prohibited explicitly by the Torah (Leviticus 19:28). However, to characterize the issue, especially to young people, in terms of "taboo" misses a crucial opportunity to convey Jewish affirmations of the fundamental dignity of the human being, of religious aspiration to achieve wholeness and permission to take joy at being in the world. The Conservative position on tattooing states that while we discourage the practice, no sanctions are imposed. The person may be buried in a Jewish cemetery and participate fully in Jewish life and ritual. We live in a society of immense stress. Many—including, tragically, many young people—struggle to manage themselves with abuse of food, drugs, tobacco, alcohol, cutting...the list is troublingly long. We need to remind each other that we are indeed God's "currency" in the world, unlike man-made coinage, in that we are of immeasurable value.

Rabbi Julie Schonfeld
Rabbinical Assembly
New York, NY

SEPHARDIC

A taboo is a practice that a particular culture avoids because it evokes frightening or unpleasant psychological associations. Judaism categorically rejects the primitive notion of a taboo system. The Torah's commandments and prohibitions address the rational and moral dimension of human existence and, therefore, cannot be classified as taboos. That being said, tattoos are indeed forbidden by the Torah, although violation of the prohibition does not (contrary to the prevalent misconception) ban one from burial in a Jewish cemetery. The human body in its natural state is a wondrous manifestation of God's master design. We are creations of the Almighty with a transcendent purpose to fulfill in this world. Hijacking the body and transforming it into an artistic canvas or a vehicle for expression distorts these fundamental principles and leads us to believe that we can cast aside the divine image and fashion ourselves after the image of our choice. This attitude is summed up in the common pro-tattoo slogan, "Be Art"—in other words, define yourself as you wish to be rather than as you were meant to be. Wearing jewelry, on the other hand, is considered a beautification of the body rather than a misappropriation for artistic ends.

Rabbi Joshua Maroof
Magen David Sephardic Congregation
Rockville, MD

MODERN ORTHODOX

Ever since biblical days, tattooing the body was associated with idolatry and magic—in particular with the worship of chthonic (underworld) deities (Leviticus 19:26-31). The specific objection was that tattooing defaces the body that (like the soul) is considered an image of God. Maybe tattooing as permanent defacing is also connected to the ways that slaves were marked as inferior beings. And Nazi behavior should put the practice beyond the pale. When Nazis tattooed numbers on Jews, the message was: You are things, to be used and liquidated for Nazi profit. Tattooing seems to be in some vogue today as a cosmetic/ artistic way to individualize the body. For some Jews, this may be fashionable. Yet I read once that most women who remove tattoos eliminate the name/sign of a former husband/lover/ boyfriend, which suggests that tattooing often still indicates that a person belongs to someone else. Jewish faith is not opposed to beautifying the body because there is a covenantal partnership between God and humans to improve God's world (*tikkun olam*). By restoring tradition and memory to every Jew, Jews could serve as a role model to all on how to beautify—not deface—the precious body every person is given to live a unique existence beautifully.

Rabbi Yitz Greenberg
New York, NY

CHABAD

Human beings are naturally social creatures who create clubs, form teams, build nations, even become mobs. These social structures give us a collective identity: "Together We Stand." But to reap these benefits we must dress alike, eat alike, speak alike, think alike. When conformity goes too far, there's a need to assert individuality. The result is rebellion. Sometimes, a non-conformist refuses to be lost in the crowd. Eventually he needs social connections and encourages others in unconventional behaviors. The result is fads.

The divine purpose behind this human trait is G-d's desire that we take responsibility for the world's development. Adam and Eve were created last to be responsible for all that came before, including each other. Hence, to have an effect on others one must be in close touch with the other—to be influenced. Tattoos and piercings are having their day, like bell bottoms, cabbage patch dolls and extreme hairstyles. Tattoos serve as a means for group identity and noncon-formity, but they are only skin deep. Better to belong through shared faith, philosophy or a vital cause. Better to be an individual through innate natural gifts that make you who you are. Tattoos are not kosher. The laws are detailed in the Shulchan Aruch and in Rambam under idolatry.

Rabbi Manis Friedman
Bais Chana Institute of Jewish Studies
St. Paul, MN

Should Jewish children sing Christmas carols?

This classic "December dilemma" question crystallizes the situation of the Jew (or any member of a religious minority) attempting to balance distinct identity with majority culture. This was one of the first questions we asked the rabbis when the feature was launched in 2005. You can feel the shift in the culture since then—for sure, the language in which we discuss identity has changed—but the fundamental tension remains. (Published in 2005.)

HUMANIST

If one partakes in American culture, as most of us do, the Christmas season is an inescapable part of our lives. Streets are decorated with lights, newspapers abound with Christmas sales and malls are piped full of Christmas music. But the repetition often reaches a level of irritation, and it becomes next to impossible to get some of these tunes—especially "Little Drummer Boy"—out of one's head.

While most Jews would like to tone down the commercialism associated with the holiday, many are quite pleased to partake of the joy and festivities of the season. We invite our children's non-Jewish friends to our homes to light menorahs, eat latkes and play with dreidels. Christian parents invite our children to trim their trees, enjoy some eggnog and sing carols. Songs like "Jingle Bells" and "Rudolph the Red-

Nosed Reindeer" are religiously benign, but what about "Silent Night"? Should songs that declare Christian faith be off limits for our children? It largely depends on the child. When my wife was a teen, she saw caroling as a fun intercultural experience, not the least bit threatening. My father, who was raised in an assimilated Jewish home in Germany, remembers caroling with his Berlin classmates in 1936 shortly before leaving the country. My own experience was a bit different. I took part in one caroling outing during high school, and while I enjoyed the camaraderie of my peers, I was hesitant to join in. I might have been better off staying at home.

So know your children and talk to them. Let them go with their friends if that's their wish, or help them say no if that's what they'd prefer. If a nice Jewish boy by the name of Irving Berlin can write "White Christmas," other Jewish boys and girls ought to be able to sing it.

Rabbi Peter H. Schweitzer
Association of Humanistic Rabbis
New York, NY

RENEWAL

I imagine that I may be taking an unpopular position on this question when I say that, in principle, I see little harm in permitting Jewish children (or adults) to join with Christians in singing the beautiful music written for this holiday. That is, as long as the Jewish participants know that Christmas is not their holiday and that they are guests at this party, not hosts.

I have a vivid memory: I was working at the Tucker Foundation at Dartmouth College and it was the annual holiday party. We had a prominent rabbi as our special scholar-in-residence. A Dartmouth alumnus, he had spent his whole life building Jewish institutions, reviving interest in Judaism, training rabbis, renewing synagogues and standing up to oppressive regimes. I can think of few people whose Jewish bona fides were as impeccable. And there he sat, singing Christmas carols with our staff in his booming voice. Not only was he on key, he knew all the words to all the songs. I, a graduate of New York City yeshivot who knew only the opening lines of each of these songs, marveled at the joy this rabbi expressed and the pleasure he gave to those who celebrated the holiday.

I love spirituality and approaching God through music, regardless of its source. I love contributing to greater openness, learning from and sharing with others. In this world in which, as my teacher Rabbi Zalman Schachter-Shalomi says, "The only way to get it together is together," we will not make our children more Jewish by trying to insulate them from others. We will only make them more Jewish by manifesting to them, both through our words and by example, the incredible beauty and power of our spiritual practice. Then when they are with others from different faith communities and spiritual practices, they will have something to give as well as receive.

Whether my opinion extends to every stanza and word of every song is another question. The resolution of that question depends on continuing and deep theological conversations both within Judaism and between Jews and Christians.

Rabbi Daniel Siegel
Director of Spiritual Resources
ALEPH: Alliance for Jewish Renewal
West Roxbury, MA

RECONSTRUCTIONIST

Living in multiple civilizations is a mixed blessing. We Jews celebrate our acceptance into the homes, lives, businesses and social circles of the majority culture. Everyone wins when friendships ensue, when we're invited to christenings and reciprocate by inviting non-Jews to b'nai mitzvah celebrations. From there, it's a short step to caroling together. Yes, key lines of various carols carry an explicitly Christological message, which Jews in good conscience should not utter. But most lyrics of most carols are fair game for all. Moreover, our Christian friends often view caroling as a purely social phenomenon, missing the theological significance altogether—and while that may be their loss, we needn't take their texts more seriously than they do.

And what about art? When two nice Jewish boys from Queens recorded "Silent Night" in 1964, they juxtaposed it with reports from the seven o'clock news, scoring one for *tikkun olam*. Were Simon & Garfunkel wrong? Though we might have chosen differently, our collective culture is richer for it. Finally, forcing our kids to think for themselves—choosing on their feet what they can comfortably sing and which words to avoid—is not a bad way to build Jewish identity. And were this the highest price we pay for living in multiple civilizations, that would be good tidings indeed.

Rabbi Fred Scherlinder Dobb
Adat Shalom Reconstructionist
Congregation
Bethesda, MD

REFORM

This question often comes up in response to school-aged children singing in a choir as part of a winter program. For me, the acid test is this: Is it a devotional exercise, or is it a musical event? If one were participating in Handel's "Messiah" over the summer, for instance, people would tend not to think of it as a religious activity. A great deal of the canon of classical music, after all, rose out of Christian liturgy. But if you tell me that a Jewish child is going to go caroling with friends, I have a problem with that, because caroling actually is a religious activity. It's spreading the news of Christmas to the community. To me, that's very different from being in a concert that has rehearsals and professional conducting and is a musical rather than a religious or devotional experience.

Rabbi Fred Reiner
Temple Sinai
Washington, DC

CONSERVATIVE

The answer is simply no. Jewish children should not participate in Christmas caroling. Christmas caroling dates back to the Middle Ages when groups of Christians adopted hymns and chants from their tradition and then traveled from house to house singing and spreading the holiday message. American society tries to sell us the idea that Christmas is not a religious holiday because its themes—gift giving, good will and peace on earth—are universal. But Christmas is fundamentally religious: It celebrates the birth of Jesus Christ, the Christian messiah. Each of its symbols—the nativity scene, the presents, the caroling—has deep religious significance connected to the birth of Jesus. When your children ask whether they can carol with their friends, tell them it's not singing; it is proselytizing. It is publicly espousing the beliefs of Christianity and spreading them to others.

Take this opportunity to teach your children how we can respect and honor another religion without participating in its ceremonies. Plan an interdenominational evening in your home with your children's friends and families, giving each person a chance to explain the significance of his or her heritage so that this year, Christmas caroling may open a dialogue that not only educates your children but reinforces their identities as Jews.

Rabbi Sherre Hirsch
Sinai Temple
Los Angeles, CA

MODERN ORTHODOX

This question really grows out of the broader belief that Christmas, in effect, is not really a Christian holiday but an American holiday, a universal celebration of fun and fellowship and other good things. But if you look at the language of the carols—"Silent Night" ("Round yon Virgin Mother and child"); "Noel" ("Born is the King of Israel")—you can see that these songs, in fact, speak a Christian message. I would argue that Jewish children should refrain from singing Christmas carols not only because they practice a different religion but out of respect for the Christian religion. We should take Christmas carols for what they are and not reduce them to commercial pabulum, entertaining but mindless songs that every American can sing.

When saying no, parents should not teach their children that Christianity is inferior or that singing Christmas carols is idolatry. Instead, they should explain that Christianity is a valid, independent religion with its own magnificent music, its own great works of art. A Jewish person can certainly appreciate these religious expressions and even be moved by them. If we enrich the level of our own Jewish practice, children will understand that they do not have to deny the beauty of Christian experiences. Thus we not only uphold Jewish distinctiveness but strike a blow against homogenization of American culture. A democracy that is founded on pluralism—a universality that is made up of distinctive individual cultures—is the most promising and most humanistic vision for America's future.

Rabbi Yitz Greenberg
Jewish Life/Steinhardt Foundation
New York, NY

CHABAD

When Golda Meir held the office of prime minister, she tried to encourage Henry Kissinger to make Israel a top priority. He sent her a letter: "I would like to inform you that I'm first an American citizen; second, Secretary of State; and third, a Jew." Golda responded, "In Israel we read from right to left." This anecdote summarizes, in my mind, the struggle of American Jewry over the last half-century. Should we teach our children to read from left to right or from right to left? Linguistically, it's simple: You can teach a child more than one language. Existentially, however, it is difficult. A healthy child needs a singular identity. Attempting to raise children feeling very Jewish (right to left) but not "too Jewish" (left to right) can create ambivalence, uncertainty and confusion in the fragile and pure psyche of children.

Paradoxically, the more children are grounded in their own family, heritage, religion and history, the deeper they can grow to appreciate other peoples and cultures. Knowing who you are deep down allows you the psychological freedom to truly learn about one who is different from you. The deeper the roots of a tree, the wider its branches can extend. Conversely, shallow roots keep you aspiring to establish an identity for yourself.

Judaism is not Christianity, and Jews are not Christians. Christmas and its music may be wonderful for many children, but not for Jewish children, because they are Jews. Yet let us not make the opposite mistake either. We ought never to define the Jewishness of our children by the fact that they do not celebrate Christmas. Identities cannot be molded by the negative alone. Use this holiday season as an opportunity to explain to your children the meaning and history of Judaism. Jewish children deserve to learn not only that they are different from Christians, but that Judaism offers a path in life that will allow them to realize their full potential.

Rabbi Yosef Y. Jacobson
Rabbinical College Chovevei Torah
Brooklyn, NY

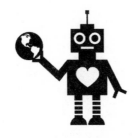

PART FOUR

VALUES

We live in a Judeo-Christian society; everybody says so. Does that mean Jewish values are the foundation of the ethics that drive, define or divide our politics? You'd think so, but the question these days carries a tinge of anxiety, as if the "Judeo" is just tacked on for politeness—and some suspect this is the case. Are there cases where "Judeo" and "Christian" point in different directions? And is there something deep-seated in Jewish values that sets Jews apart, or should set them apart, from the surrounding society?

For the more liberal denominations, ethical concerns merge with religious commandments; for some traditionalists, there's a tension, or even a flat contradiction, between the values mandated by Torah and those of the outside world. And sometimes even the most eternal values come to be understood in new ways in changing times.

According to Judaism, are there fundamental human rights?

T he concept of "rights," unarticulated in biblical times or in much of Jewish tradition, drives a large part of the argument for updating practices, religious or otherwise, that have come to seem unjust. However, while justice is a central and frequently voiced concern in Torah—the exhortation "Justice, justice shall you pursue" is one of its best-known passages—terms like "human rights" are a modern construct.

We asked the question this way because "human rights" is one of those phrases that, originally universalist and neutral, has become a politically polarizing topic. Although reaction to the Holocaust is sometimes seen as the origin of the global human rights movement, there's a disinclination in some Jewish circles to identify with a value they see pressed more recently into the service of Palestinian rights at the cost of those of Israel. Others see the concept as the only path to comity and compromise. To our surprise, the rabbis found considerable common ground here, agreeing on the biblical texts and concepts that generate the idea of human rights, whether or not they call them by that name. (Published in 2011.)

INDEPENDENT

According to Judaism, all of God's creations have the fundamental right to exist, to thrive and to enjoy their divinely ordained life. This is not true only of humans. You must violate the Sabbath by milking your cow if her udder is full and she is in agony. You may not muzzle your ox while plowing your field because animals have the fundamental right to eat while working. You have the right to challenge authority and to question the teachings of those more learned than you. You have the right to opt out of going to war if you're too afraid or if you just met someone at a Jewish singles weekend. Laborers must be compensated the day of their labor, not 30 to 60 days later. Creditors are forbidden from harassing debtors or confiscating their property in lieu of debts. You must violate every commandment in the Torah to save a life, even if there is so much as the possibility of endangerment to mental or physical health. You must set aside a religious Thou Shalt Not if human dignity is at stake. You must take in escaped slaves and protect them. I could go on, but *Moment* has the fundamental right to limit my response to 225 words.

Rabbi Gershon Winkler
Walking Stick Foundation
Thousand Oaks, CA

HUMANIST

It is relatively easy to identify fundamental human rights in Judaism; regrettably, it is also easy to identify contradictory messages. On the one hand, we have teachings that extol a basic reverence for life and require that humans be granted a basic dignity. All humans, we are taught, are minted alike, and one may not claim that "one's blood is redder than another's." In practice this means caring for the poor and the disenfranchised and making no distinction between men and women, straight and gay, rich and poor. But we also have teachings—and certainly practices—that do not treat men and women equally, that shun, if not condemn, gay people, and that provide for the institution of slavery (albeit with a built-in method for manumission). We have teachings that extol equality between Jews and non-Jews and oblige us, according to Maimonides, to "maintain the poor of idolators, attend to their sick and bury their dead, as we do with those of our own community." But in practice, how caring and welcoming are we to the stranger and the outsider? Or consider the concept of religious freedom. We extol the Maccabees as champions of this basic right, yet once they came to power they were no less despotic than those they had overthrown. In fact, Jewish history is rife with intolerance of alternative movements within Judaism. Basic human rights depend on more than rhetoric and selectively chosen proof texts. What really matters is how we put these ideals into practice.

Rabbi Peter Schweitzer
The City Congregation for
Humanistic Judaism
New York, NY

RENEWAL

The notion that each person has innate human rights is relatively new. Torah doesn't use this language, but it does offer the radical notion that each of us is made *b'tzelem Elohim*, in the divine image. Later tradition expands this into a strong sense of the centrality, and universality, of human dignity. Rabbi Eliezer said, "Other people's dignity should be as precious to you as your own." (*Pirkei Avot*) The verse most often repeated in Torah is "Love the stranger, for you were strangers in the land of Egypt." Love of the stranger is not a right but an obligation. We owe it to one another, to the widow and orphan, to those who are powerless, and to the stranger who shares with us the human condition of being far from home. Hasidic tradition speaks of the *nefesh elohut*, the spark of divinity, which enlivens each Jew. In this post-triumphalist era, we understand that each human being contains a *nefesh elohut* and is therefore infinitely precious. When anyone anywhere is denied basic human rights, that spark of divinity isn't able to shine. Our connection with God demands that we treat God's children with care.

Rabbi Rachel Barenblat
Congregation Beth Israel
North Adams, MA

RECONSTRUCTIONIST

As American Jews, at the intersection of traditional Jewish and modem Western values, we hold these truths to be self-evident: All are created in the image of God (Genesis 1:27) and are thus of equally infinite worth. All are endowed by their creator with certain inalienable rights, among them: Life: Our creator bade us to "choose life, that you and your descendants may live" (Deuteronomy 30:19). Beyond the obvious "Do not murder," this makes life an intergenerational right. Even indirect limitations on others' lives (e.g., our warming the world for future generations) may violate Jewish human rights. Liberty: Our creator is also our redeemer, the God of liberation; we "must not oppress a stranger, for you know the heart of a stranger, having been strangers yourselves in Egypt" (Exodus 23:9). *Cherut* (freedom) and *charut* (engraved, as in the commandments) are linked. Therefore, with liberty comes responsibility. Pursuit of Happiness: Happiness is not a right (though it's strongly recommended), but pursuing it is. One must never infringe on another's reasonable attempts to be happy. Basics like clean water, food, shelter, health care and education should therefore be universal human rights (as in the U.N. declaration thereof). Jewish ethics support this, as elucidated by a whole galaxy of groups engaged in *tikkun olam* who base their commitment on Jewish texts. Indeed, then, as we said in that other, modem scripture, "With a firm reliance on the protection of Divine Providence, let us mutually pledge to each other our Lives, our Fortunes, and our sacred Honor."

Rabbi Fred Scherlinder Dobb
Adat Shalom Reconstructionist
Congregation
Bethesda, MD

REFORM

As slaves in Egypt, we were denied our fundamental human right to freedom. We lived under the yoke of slavery, unable to lead lives according to ancient Israelite laws and practice. When our redemption came, it was not only a political one, in which we gained back our civil rights, but a theological one, in which we gained back the freedom to worship in our own manner. We gained freedom from tyranny and oppression as well as freedom to serve God and follow God's teachings in the Torah. Torah quite frequently reminds us that we were once slaves in the land of Egypt. The repetition of this phrase is an indication of its significance in our collective understanding of what it means to be a Jew. Our liberation from Egypt comes with an obligation never to forget that experience. We are reminded of it daily in our tefillot (prayers) and at moments in our annual holiday cycle, especially during Passover. Our collective memory of our slavery is the foundation for understanding how we should treat those around us. We were once slaves in the land of Egypt—this is the underlying principle for why we as Jews have an obligation to fight for the freedom of the oppressed and the civil rights of those who are treated inequitably.

Rabbi Laura Novak Winer
Union for Reform Judaism
Fresno, CA

CONSERVATIVE

All obligations toward our fellow human beings are rooted in the biblical teaching that the human being is created in the divine image with the sacred right to life, freedom and dignity. Each person's right to life obliges us to come to his or her aid when threatened. From Talmudic sources it is possible to infer that the individual is entitled not only to life but to health, security from harm and the ability to make a living. Another human right is encapsulated in the principle that in the eyes of the law all people are equal (Leviticus 19:15). Finally, in the Book of Exodus we learn that people are entitled to be free.

As rabbinic law developed, it came to protect fundamental human rights by prohibiting people who have more strength, money and status from oppressing those who have less. Judaism does not limit human rights to the avoidance of exploiting people; it also mandates positive action to take care of people. The laws of supporting the poor are examples of this. What is phrased as an obligation on the giver became a right on the part of the receiver.

Rabbi Amy Wallk Katz
Temple Beth El
Springfield, MA

MODERN ORTHODOX

There is a standard gambit in response to this question: Judaism does not talk about rights (that is, it does not use the language of entitlement); instead, it focuses on duties (what we owe to God and to fellow human beings). I believe that this conventional wisdom is mistaken. Traditional sources do not use the language of rights because such concepts were unknown in ancient times. However, the Torah and Talmud speak of fundamental dignities which confer the equivalent of rights. These biblical and post-biblical sources strongly influenced the early modem thinkers who shaped the emergence of democracy and constitutional rights.

Specifically, the Torah states that every human being, male and female, is "created in the image of God" (Genesis 1:27). The Talmud derives three fundamental dignities of every human being in the divine image: Infinite value ("Saving one life is equivalent to saving a whole world"), equality and uniqueness (Sanhedrin 37a). Honoring these dignities involves granting all the rights and ethical treatment that constitute the sum total of democratic rights. Equality yields equal treatment before the law and prohibition of discrimination, tyranny and slavery. It implies the right to be treated respectfully and to have equal access to education and information. Infinite value brings with it the right to economic justice and economic security, access to adequate medical treatment and the obligation to provide welfare and tzedaka for the poor. Uniqueness implies the right to education and freedom of speech. In the end, the Messianic vision—a world of no poverty, hunger, war or oppression—is the (projected) universal actualization in the real world of the rights conferred by these intrinsic dignities.

Rabbi Yitz Greenberg
New York, NY

ORTHODOX

Judaism believes that every human being is endowed with the right to be and feel of infinite value. No human being is better or less than another, and there is no source for the absolute equality of all human-kind outside of the biblical verse that states, at the very beginning of Genesis, that God Almighty created every human being in His image. Without that verse, what seems evident to us is the blatant inequality of man. Some are taller than others; some are prettier than others; some are brighter than others. Some are rich, some are poor. Yet the Bible says that none of that matters because we are all equal in the eyes of God. Another right involves human uniqueness. There is no one in the world quite like me, and there never will be. This does not make me better than anyone else; it simply asserts that I am essential. My being is not a contingent existence but a necessary one. The same is true of every other person. The core of Judaism is its insistence on freedom of choice. Each and every one of us is born without our lives previously scripted. There is no fate, no astrological chart. What we will become in our life is dependent entirely on what we will do and how we will behave.

Rabbi Shmuley Boteach
Englewood, NJ

SEPHARDIC

Judaism has always placed greater emphasis on the commitment and responsibility requested *from* human beings than on the rights or enti-tlements granted *to* human beings. Even when it comes to protecting the ostensible "rights" of citizens of the world, the Torah speaks the language of obligation and commandment rather than divine "endowment." It seems to me, then, that the notion of "rights" is not especially compatible with Jewish theology. The notion of "rights" elevates the individual's significance and influence to heights of which he or she, as mere creatures of a benevolent creator, may not realistically be worthy. Instead of focusing on the empowerment of persons, our concern should be with the health, success, progress and welfare of creation in general. Of course, crafting a harmonious and peaceful—not to mention enlightened—society entails respecting the just claims to life, liberty and property made by all human beings. But such respect should not be surrendered by society to each person because we feel compelled to submit to any and all demands made in the name of individual "rights"; rather, it should be freely and generously given—out of a sense of moral duty to promote the happiness, growth and spiritual advancement of all of God's creations.

Rabbi Joshua Maroof
Magen David Sephardic Congregation
Rockville, MD

Are there things that can't be forgiven?

T his was a High Holidays question; we asked it in fall *2019, when the tornados of online "cancel culture" were approaching gale force, and numerous people found their job, career or platform terminated over a moment of online stupidity or an offensive or reckless tweet. You won't find much sympathy for the cancel impulse among rabbis, who work with real people, replete with flaws; nor in Judaism generally, with its elaborate rituals for asking and granting forgiveness.*

Still, the impulse toward forgiveness also has its limits, even on the Day of Atonement: Cases that trouble the rabbis include ex-Nazis, abusive parents and those who express no remorse for their deeds. (Published in 2019.)

INDEPENDENT

The most unforgivable king in Jewish history was Menashe, son of Hezekiah, who led his kingdom into idolatry. As they carried him off to Babylon in chains, he desperately turned to God for forgiveness. But the angels blocked the heavens with heavy furniture and nailed in extra boards to prevent that *mamzer*'s plea from being heard. What did God do? While the angels were engaged in choir practice, He bored a tiny hole in the boarded-up heavenly floor so that He could hear Menashe's plea (Midrash Devarim Rabbah 2:20).

But that's God's thing. For us mere mortals, it depends. If someone accidentally bumps a cart into you in the supermarket, you can forgive instantaneously. On the other hand, if someone bumps you with an SUV, you may not be so quick to forgive as they fit your legs, hip and nose with prosthetics—because you're human, and you hope he loses all of his teeth except one, and that one has a toothache! However, if we do transcend our mortality and forgive the sins committed against us by others, "God in turn will dismiss our sins" (*Talmud Bavli*, Rosh Hashanah 17a).

Rabbi Gershon Winkler
Walking Stick Foundation
Fontana, CA

HUMANIST

Few people have never been mistreated or hurt others. Jewish tradition makes demands of both parties. If we've hurt someone, we are required to seek rapprochement, prompted by sincere teshuvah, the recognition of our misdeeds, alongside our resolve not to re-offend. Conversely, when we're hurt by someone who has sought forgiveness following genuine teshuvah, we are asked to forgive. In most human interactions this is the best path to reconciliation. Humanistic Jews recognize the wisdom of this. Whether through love, empathy or the knowledge that forgiveness is necessary for us to move on, we generally endorse efforts to extend it to others. We realize that the way to a better world is solely a human endeavor, one that must certainly include reconciliation.

But what about those who do not offer remorse, or whose misdeeds are simply too monstrous to forgive? Here, there are no clear answers—in Judaism or in Humanistic teachings. Even a belief that the world requires reconciliation cannot impose a duty to forgive. Ultimately, the decision must be left to individuals as we balance costs and benefits to ourselves and others.

Rabbi Jeffrey Falick
Birmingham Temple Congregation
for Humanistic Judaism
Farmington Hills, MI

RENEWAL

It depends on what we mean by "forgive." Jewish law deemed some acts so heinous that only death atoned, and then only with repentance (*Talmud Bavli*, Yoma 86a; Hilchot Teshuvah 1:1). And even then, how can we absolve genocide, murder, sex crimes, child abuse and life-destroying lies?

But "forgiveness" isn't absolution. We can "forgive" even if someone doesn't deserve it—because we ourselves deserve the peace that can come by releasing pain and grudges. That's forgiveness. It doesn't absolve wrongs or withhold justice, but helps us live resiliently amid brokenness. It's among our most powerful spiritual tools—and sometimes difficult to use.

Consider the 2015 Charleston church shooting—domestic terrorism targeting innocents. The triggerman confessed to wanting a race war. How does anyone "forgive" that? But the victims' families found the inner power to forgive—not to inhibit justice, but to seek peace for themselves. Such forgiveness evokes grace—in Hebrew, *chein*, one of the Thirteen Attributes of God's self-revelation to Moses after he shattered the first tablets on seeing the Golden Calf (Exodus 34:6). Grace can't be deserved: It's a spiritual gift we receive because we are. And this same God of *chein* was also a God of justice. We can forgive in that same way—in God's grace, after the shattering, to seek peace.

Rabbi David Evan Markus
Temple Beth El
City Island, NY

RECONSTRUCTIONIST

Most forgiveness is partial. Our lives are lived on slippery slopes, in gray zones. Tradition posits a hypothetical *rasha gamur*, entirely evil person, and *tzadik gamur*, entirely righteous one—with 36 of the latter mythically roaming around. But the rest of us are in between— maybe perched right on the fulcrum, where our next altruistic or selfish act could tip the entire personal and cosmic scale. We've all done "unforgivable" things, and we've all been at least partially forgiven, with further chances to yet make good. Consider climate change: Carbon from the gas I burned driving to visit the sick endures in the atmosphere "even unto the third and fourth generation." Endangered species, coastal dwellers and our own grandchildren can scarcely "forgive" us for our short-sighted emissions and slowness to change—yet every positive change measurably moves the needle, limits further suffering and bends the arc (slightly yet truly) back toward sustainability and justice. In short: Can we be fully forgiven for past sins? No, some damage done is permanent. Should we move forward, measuring our deeds, trying harder, doing better? Heck yes.

Rabbi Fred Scherlinder Dobb
Adat Shalom Reconstructionist
Congregation
Bethesda, MD

REFORM

Only a wronged person can grant forgiveness, so only he or she can answer. One might consider three questions. First: When wounded physically, spiritually, psychologically or materially by another, we must face the basic humanity of that person with all their faults, failings, prejudices and imperfections. Jewish tradition recognizes that we all have flaws and make mistakes. No matter how egregious the wrong, are we ready to see the wrongdoer's humanity?

Second: Has justice been served? According to Jewish law, it is appropriate to ask for recompense from the wrongdoer. This may be as simple as a sincere apology, or it may involve facing legal or material consequences for one's actions. We should not be cruel by withholding forgiveness from those who have made amends.

Third: how might forgiving or withholding forgiveness help me? The Talmud's rabbis noted the social, emotional, spiritual or even health benefits of forgiveness; we should too. If we find ourselves wrapped in clouds of stress, resentment, anger or intolerance, then finding a way to move toward forgiveness would be to our benefit.

Rabbi Dr. Laura Novak Winer
Fresno, CA

CONSERVATIVE

Jewish tradition instructs us to forgive those who have wronged us if they make restitution and apologize. If they don't, each individual has to decide the limits, if any, of forgiveness.

Eva Mozes Kor, who died in July at age 85, challenged me to think about this question. Kor was in Auschwitz and was among the 1,500 sets of twins upon whom the Nazi doctor Josef Mengele conducted horrific experiments. Kor publicly forgave those who had tortured her and all who had participated in the genocide. When I first learned of this, I was shocked that a survivor could forgive any Nazi, ever. I do not think one person could or should absolve all those who participated. And I do not like the public nature of Kor's behavior. But I now recognize a certain wisdom in Kor's action. One forgives not to ease the offender's conscience but to let go of the anger and hurt. Never to forgive is ultimately to allow those who wronged us to continue hurting us. It hurts only the victim.

As for forgetting—we really can't. There's no delete button for the brain. We don't forget the pain, we just learn to live with it.

Rabbi Amy Wallk Katz
Temple Beth El
Springfield, MA

MODERN ORTHODOX

I am very resistant to the idea of any sin being beyond forgiveness. I would like to think that given God's loving nature and "compassion for all of God's creatures" (Psalms 145:9), no bad action is beyond being overcome by God's infinite goodness. However, in sins between one human being and another, the Talmud says that God won't forgive unless/until the sinner regrets and repents, returns what was stolen or damaged and wins forgiveness from the victim. For murder, there can be no forgiveness, because the victim cannot be made whole or asked for forgiveness.

The Holocaust struck me as unforgivable, and for 50-plus years, I would never buy a German product nor set foot in Germany, lest my actions profit one of the perpetrators. In the late 1990s, I told myself that those who had carried out this monstrous crime were mostly gone, and children should not be punished for the (unforgiven) sins of their fathers (Deuteronomy 24:16). I relaxed my boycott and traveled to Germany for a conference on Jewish-Christian relations. It helped that the German government had taken responsibility for the Shoah and paid significant reparations (albeit no amount of money can make whole the losses). Germany had also become the most dependable, supportive ally of Israel in Europe out of a sense of accountability for Nazi crimes. This does not constitute forgiveness. But it paves the way for new generations to work together to prevent recurrences of the unforgivable sin.

Rabbi Yitz Greenberg
Riverdale, NY

ORTHODOX

The Talmud speaks lovingly about the power of forgiveness; it's not mandatory, but almost. When people are asked, they should do the right thing and forgive. But there are two caveats. Forgiveness is not a pro forma declaration of "OK, you're forgiven." It means the person actually forgives—which is not so easy to do. Also, the Talmud says certain things do not demand forgiveness. After physical injury—some commentators extend this to emotional injury—it may still be admirable to forgive if asked, but the expectation is not there.

The Talmud says God Himself cannot forgive transgressions between people. If Reuven harms Shimon, and Reuven repents sincerely but doesn't ask Shimon to forgive him, God cannot grant that forgiveness. In a famous incident recounted by Simon Wiesenthal in *The Sunflower*, Wiesenthal, a prisoner in the camps, was called to an infirmary where an SS officer lay dying. The officer wanted to confess and ask forgiveness for his crimes against Jews. In his last moments, he asked Wiesenthal to forgive him, as a surrogate for the Jewish people. Wiesenthal exited the room. He subsequently wrote that while he felt the urge to forgive, those who were actually in a position to forgive were not there, so he couldn't do it.

Rabbi Yitzchok Adlerstein
Cross-Currents
Los Angeles, CA

SEPHARDIC

There are! But they are not the same for everyone. One person might be unable to forgive parental apathy, but another might empathize with the apathetic parent. That latter person might not forgive a child who escaped from home, while the first one will forgive and embrace even his own child who did so.

If we search for an objective answer, we should first ask if regret was expressed. If not, forgiving is more like letting go of a grudge and forgiving oneself. If regret was expressed, we should ask: 1. Was the apology sincere? 2. Would others of my culture and upbringing consider the act an offense? (If the person committing the offense might see it differently, maybe there's room for forgiveness.) If most people would agree it was an offense, and you feel it is unforgivable, then it should not be forgiven. I think most people would agree that crimes such as murder, rape, sexual assault or criminal negligence that caused irreparable damage to body or soul fall in this category. True, there are programs that bring together victims' relatives and murderers, which reportedly provide some closure for the relatives and generate remorse. But the relatives can forgive only for what they have endured, not for what the victim has suffered. Finally, some crimes should not be forgiven, by individuals or society, to deter potential criminals.

Rabbi Haim Ovadia
Potomac, MD

CHABAD

"What is crooked will not be able to be straightened, and what is missing will not be able to be counted" (Ecclesiastes 1:15). Some misdeeds have severe, irreversible effects and are seemingly beyond forgiveness. At the same time, at the core of Judaism is forgiveness. We are taught to emulate G-d and forgive, just as G-d is all-forgiving.

How do we reconcile these apparently contradictory ideas? We sometimes find ourselves in situations where the betrayal and pain are so great that we are justified in not forgiving. At those times, we need to remember the saying that "Not forgiving someone is like drinking poison and expecting the other person to die."

Forgiveness does more for the provider than the recipient. It does not magically make the pain go away, but it allows one to move past the hurt and begin healing. Not forgiving amplifies the consequences of a misdeed and perpetuates its negative effects. Better to forgive and move on to a brighter future than hold on to an unforgivable offense and be stuck in a dark past.

Rabbi Simcha Backman
Chabad Jewish Center of Glendale
and the Foothill Communities
Glendale, CA

Does Jewish law forbid racism?

*J*udaism's central texts predate by many centuries the codify-
ing of the term "racism" as a concept. But it's part of the job
of rabbis to keep freshening those texts by applying them to
the problems we face. Jewish tradition is hardly immune to
racially tinged and occasionally outright racist thinking, both
about other groups and about our own; that's all the more
reason to sort through and reckon with it.

   We asked this question in the summer 2019 issue amid con-
troversies that, though serious, hardly anticipated the fury
with which public anger at racism, inequality and police bru-
tality is raging today; the answers have only gained urgency
since then. (Published in 2019.)

INDEPENDENT

Neither Jewish law, lore nor history addresses race in any way that can
be construed as problematic. In fact, the ancestor of the Jewish people,
Shem son of Noah, is described by the midrash as having been Black
(*Pirkei D'Rebbe Eliezer*, beginning of Chapter 24). The most fundamental teachings of Judaism clearly dismiss racism altogether, such as "You
shall love the stranger like yourself" (Leviticus 19:34), or the reminder
in Genesis that all of us—regardless of race, color or belief system—
were born of the same mom and dad: Adam and Eve. "Why did God

create swarms of bees, prides of lions, herds of deer, schools of fish, and flocks of birds, and only one human couple? So that no one can say to another 'My ancestry is superior to yours'" (Mishnah, Sanhedrin 4:5).

Rabbi Gershon Winkler
Walking Stick Foundation
Fontana, CA

HUMANIST

The question of Jewish law and racism cannot be separated from that of anti-Semitism. Distrust and hatred of Jews played an important role in the attitudes that Jews formed about others. With our history of suffering, we should not be surprised that our literature (law and lore) records feelings of animosity toward others and even outsized claims of Jewish superiority. Even so, any expressions of hostility sit right alongside higher moral expectations. The Torah repeatedly urges us to engage our empathy, commanding us 36 times to show our concern for strangers among us. Our creation myths and midrash remind us of the common origin of all human beings.

Jewish tradition is old and broad enough to include contradictory teachings; some condone bigotry and racism, others promote solicitude for all people. As Humanistic Jews, we are always delighted to encounter the more enlightened passages and practices. Yet they are not the source of our beliefs. A commitment to furthering human dignity and universal human rights stands at the center of our ethical concerns irrespective of Jewish attitudes from the past.

Rabbi Jeffrey L. Falick
Birmingham Temple Congregation
for Humanistic Judaism
Farmington Hills, MI

RENEWAL

I don't think racism is a term recognized in Jewish law, although a few remarks in Jewish tradition about people of color have been understood in disparaging ways. More essentially, the Torah insists that we treat both neighbors and strangers with *ahavah*, love—a recognition that we are in relationship with one another. Jewish law forbids reminding converts to Judaism of their earlier background; we might extrapolate from that to a prohibition on, for example, asking Jews of color in shul whether they are actually Jewish, which seems to go on all the time. The larger question is how Jewish tradition bids us view the relationship between Jews and non-Jews, which can sometimes take on a "racist" or essentialist disparagement of the other. We have in our background both glorious universalist sentiments and virulent hostility to non-Jews. In that we are no different from other religions or cultures; the urge to define "us vs. them" is, ironically, one of the most universal principles of humankind. The contradiction plays out in two books of the Bible—Ezra, which advances a quasi-racial opposition to the non-Jews living in the land of Israel after the Exile, and Ruth, which makes the case for a much more positive view of non-Jews. Nothing keeps one safe from "othering" except perpetual vigilance and a constant choosing of our *yetzer hatov* or good inclination (unity) over our *yetzer hara* or evil inclination (separation).

> **Rabbi Gilah Langner**
> Congregation Kol Ami
> Arlington, VA

RECONSTRUCTIONIST

In 1963 the Rev. Martin Luther King, Jr. convened a conference on "Religion and Race." The second speaker was Rabbi Abraham Joshua Heschel, who suggested that perhaps the conference should have been called "Religion or Race," for true religion and racism are antithetical. Racism is a "treacherous denial of the existence of God," he said.

Judaism's foundational story is about God's taking the side of the victims of racism and economic oppression. "At the first Conference on Religion and Race," Heschel began his speech, "the main participants were Pharaoh and Moses." Egyptians were racist: Though Joseph was second only to Pharaoh, he ate by himself, "for the Egyptians could not dine with the Hebrews, since that would be abhorrent to the Egyptians" (Genesis 43:32). It was racism that led to such brutal oppression by Pharaoh that God broke through nature and history to hear the Israelites' cries. Judaism teaches that God is on the side of those who struggle for freedom; the Torah's great principle is that every human being is created in the image of God. These are the principles on which all of Judaism rests. Jewish law is and should be an expression of those principles, and therefore I believe that racism is absolutely against Jewish law.

Rabbi Caryn Broitman
Martha's Vineyard Hebrew Center
Vineyard Haven, MA

REFORM

The Talmud teaches that all people are descendants of a single person so that no person can say, "My ancestor is greater than yours." This foundational belief in the equality of all humanity was established in the opening chapters of the Torah. Regardless of whether we believe this creation story, its position as one of the very first lessons of the Torah gives it a place of high priority: All human beings are created equal. This belief in equality compels action in response to discrimination, racism and racial injustice.

In the Reform movement, the work of racial justice reaches back before the civil rights movement. We have an obligation to learn about racial diversity, confront our implicit biases, challenge the deep systemic and cultural sources of those biases and address the racial disparities that plague our society. To create racial justice in America, we must look deeply into and change our own beliefs about our neighbors. And we must change the systems and structures that perpetuate racial injustices. This is not easy work to do. It is our sacred obligation.

Rabbi Dr. Laura Novak Winer
Fresno, CA

CONSERVATIVE

The Torah teaches the equality of all human beings created in the image of God (Genesis 1:27) and is positive toward non-Israelites. Rabbinic literature similarly contains numerous positive statements about gentiles. We can't deny that there are passages in rabbinic literature, Kabbalah and medieval philosophical works that depict gentiles as inferior to Jews and sometimes even as less than human. Some can be explained as normal reactions to the cruel treatment of Jews by non-Jews, be it the Roman Empire, the Church or others. Some, however, go far beyond that, positing an exclusivist theology.

In the 21st century, though, there is only one correct answer to this question: Yes. Leviticus 19 begins, "You shall be holy, for I the Lord your God am holy." The halachic authority Nachmanides (1174-1270) says this means Jews must obey not just the letter but the spirit of the law. The spirit of Torah is clearly conveyed in Genesis 1:27: If all humanity is made in God's image, then clearly any kind of prejudice or racism is forbidden. Nachmanides introduces the phrase *naval b'rshut ha-Torah*—being despicable within the permitted boundaries of Torah. Loosely defined, this means that being holy means not engaging in disgusting behaviors that are not specifically forbidden but are not right either.

Rabbi Amy Wallk Katz
Temple Beth El
Springfield, MA

MODERN ORTHODOX

The Talmud makes clear that every human, as an image of God, is endowed with three intrinsic dignities: infinite value, equality and uniqueness (*Talmud Bavli*, Sanhedrin 37a). This statement completely demolishes racism. However, over millennia of gentile persecution, a lot of antagonism crept into Jewish attitudes. Thus, one rabbi in the Talmud lashes out, "You [Jews] are called Adam [that is, the image of

God] but idolators/gentiles are not." Considering ongoing Christian and Islamic denigration of Jews as less than human, such backlash is understandable. In modern times, though, great rabbis such as Rav Abraham Kook in Israel and Rabbi Joseph B. Soloveitchik in the United States reaffirmed the universal dignity of all people.

Still, narrow-minded, socially isolated fundamentalist Orthodox rabbis often seize upon past texts of anger and rejection and seek to apply them to gentiles today. Recently, Channel 13 in Israel broadcast videotapes revealing that important rabbis at a pre-army Mechina (training program) openly endorsed racism. They claimed that racial theory proved Jewish superiority. They justified permanent annexation of the West Bank on the grounds that the Arabs are an inferior race and would welcome being subservient to Jews. Such comments are especially disgusting coming after the Holocaust and the evidence that racism leads to hatred and genocide. The prophet's cry "We have one father: One God created all of us" (Malachi 2:10) rebukes such vicious attitudes. Sadly, Orthodoxy has a lot of work to do to root out racist and anti-other attitudes in its religious leadership and culture.

Rabbi Yitz Greenberg
Riverdale, NY

ORTHODOX

If I had to make a strong halachic argument for some provision attached to one of the preexisting categories of the Torah forbidding racism, I'd be hard pressed. I don't think I could make the halachic guidelines that plastic. Rabbi Shlomo Luria, nearly 500 years ago, argued that with the exception of great moral deficiencies like murder, stealing and deception, the Torah mostly describes behavior between Jews and relies on secular law for the rest. So it's not so surprising that there's no outright prohibition against being a bigot. Nonetheless, I think racism violates some important meta-principles of the Torah, particularly the thinking of Maimonides, for whom there is a 614th commandment, Thou Shalt Not Be an Idiot. Racism is objectionable for two reasons. One is that it's just stupid. We are taught as Jews to notice differences rather than group things together. Racism is by its nature a failure to take note of the great differences between people within a group, and as such it is intensely anti-Jewish. Second, in practice, it creates a *chillul hashem*, a desecration of God's name, when people who are charged with keeping God's word alive ignore those fundamental distinctions in their dealings with other people.

Rabbi Yitzchok Adlerstein
Cross-Currents
Los Angeles, CA

CHABAD

As per the Torah, I am a creationist, and thus for me the answer is yes. If we agree that G-d is everything, then He is every color. Anything less would be a limitation, and He is unlimited. One is anti-Semitic not when one dislikes someone Jewish, but when one dislikes them merely because they are Jewish. Likewise, disliking someone of another race because of something they did is one thing; judging them or treating them poorly merely because of their race is racism, upon which the Torah frowns. People of any color may convert to Judaism if they choose to accept the Torah and its guidelines for life. If you believe G-d created and sustains the world and everything in it, then there is no place for hate or discrimination merely because of skin color.

Rabbi Levi Shemtov
Executive Vice President, American
Friends of Lubavitch
Washington, DC

SEPHARDIC

To ask if Jewish law forbids racism is to ask if you have ever read the first chapter of Genesis. In it, the Torah presents the most revolutionary idea of ancient times, which, judging by the xenophobia, racism and bigotry that are still prevalent, remains one many cannot easily digest. That idea is contained in two Hebrew words: *b'tzelem Elohim*, the image of God, and it is very carefully inserted into the larger context of the creation story: "Elohim created man in His image, male and female He created them" (1:27). The Torah emphasizes that the image of God is a concept embedded in men and women equally. The idea is reinforced in Genesis 5:2: "Male and female He created them, and He blessed them, and He named them Adam." The woman is Adam—created in the image of God—just as the man is.

The message of these verses is much greater than equality between men and women. It is about the equality of all humankind. The binary difference between men and women is one's first instinctive reaction upon seeing a human being (the inability to clearly define a non-binary person is probably the reason why there is so much bigotry towards them). By equating men and women, the Torah states that the image of God is not expressed physically. Racism is therefore a rejection of the very foundation of the Torah. This is not to say, however, that there are no racist Jews.

Rabbi Haim Ovadia
Potomac, MD

Does Judaism encourage arrogance?

Answering this question demands as much psychology as moral philosophy. As the rabbis point out, arrogance is often the flip side of insecurity. Though understandable in light of centuries of oppression, exile and other experiences that bruise the ego, arrogance and insecurity alike are identified here as malign forces with which the rabbis have little patience. Not surprisingly, the cure they prescribe is study: Jewish text is the antidote to arrogance with its humbling complexity and "the constant Jewish teaching that you are not God." (Published in 2014.)

INDEPENDENT

One of my favorite books is the late Rabbi Abraham Joshua Heschel's essay collection *Moral Grandeur and Spiritual Audacity*. I think the title sums it up. Judaism stands for, is founded upon and thrives from its in-your-face arrogance, which has preserved it since Abraham first took a daring step outside the boundaries laid down for him by voices other than his own. Even the Voice of God responded in kind and—unlike in the prevalent translations—did not tell him to "Get thee forth" but, more literally, to "Go to thyself."

Every culture throughout history that attempted to swallow us failed and ended up behind glass in our local museums. We are like cockroaches. You cannot get rid of us or destroy our ways. It is precisely because of this innate arrogance that God chose the Jews to be the keepers of the Torah. There is no better candidate for the eternal preservation of this embodiment of Divine Revelation than a motley rabble of stubborn, arrogant, obnoxious and argumentative clans who refuse to be like everyone else, choose torture and death over conversion and relentlessly challenge the dictates of authorities, even their own. And no religion has produced so much religious literature in which we admonish ourselves for those very traits, urging us to direct the audacity that characterizes us toward maintaining and fostering the moral grandeur that defines us.

Rabbi Gershon Winkler
Walking Stick Foundation
Thousand Oaks, CA

HUMANIST

The best, though unfortunate, example of Jewish arrogance is our perennial bragging about the disproportionate number of Nobel Prize winners who are Jewish—a practice that encourages an attitude of Jewish intellectual and genetic superiority. The real source of this kind of smug Jewish self-congratulation is God's unabashed favoritism in singling out the Jews as the "chosen people." This appointment to be the "light unto the nations," thankfully rejected by most contemporary Jews, historically gave permission for racial narcissism, Jewish chauvinism and an assertion of aristocracy. Of course, such grandiosity is also undoubtedly a form of psychological compensation for being oppressed and powerless. At least, we could claim, we're smarter than our persecutors, though it's unclear how much balm and comfort that really provides.

The antidote to this smugness is humility, grounded in the biblical notion that all humans share a common origin, the dust of the earth, or, in terms of today's knowledge, the stardust of billions of years ago. And the corollary: We will eventually return to that same dust. Beauty is vain (Proverbs 31:30), the hope of mortals is worms (Avot 4:4), and, said Hillel (Leviticus R 1), "humility is my exaltation."

Rabbi Peter H. Schweitzer
The City Congregation for
Humanistic Judaism
New York, NY

RENEWAL

The Hebrew word for arrogance, *y'hirut*, comes from a root meaning "to exceed limits." To be arrogant is to exceed healthy boundaries in relation to self and other. In Mussar (ethical) literature, arrogance and humility are matters of great spiritual concern. To be humble is not to become a doormat but to know how much room to take up: to know when it is appropriate to be "big," to let your talents shine, and when to make a *tzimtzum*, a contraction, to make room for others to shine. The lack of awareness of *tzimtzum* is the essence of arrogance. Even the Holy One made a *tzimtzum* so all things could come into being! Humility is realizing that every human being is created in the image of the divine. Let everything be your teacher: Nothing we build or attain is done through our virtue alone. At the same time, our historical self-understanding of chosenness, embodied in the Aleinu prayer, can lead to a sense of separation from other peoples, even a kind of tribal arrogance. The literature of Jewish ethics balances this chosenness with the awareness that we, the human family, are intimately interconnected.

Rabbi Chava Bahle
OHALAH: Association of Rabbis
for Jewish Renewal
Suttons Bay, MI

RECONSTRUCTIONIST

Our history, key values and sacred texts all insist on humility, not arrogance. Arrogance brings down the Tower of Babel (Genesis 11), kings and nations, including ours (Deuteronomy 8). In daily liturgy, we confess our sins and name our smallness. Hubris hurt Israel in 1973, and neither Israel nor America is immune today. Abraham's tweetable "I am but dust and ashes" (Genesis 18:27) should be printed on slips of paper, fortune cookie-style, and pulled from our pockets to return us to our place whenever our arrogance arises—or so suggested Reb Simcha Bunim two centuries ago.

But the other pocket, Bunim added, needs the opposite message: "For my sake was the world created." When we're down, we pull out that verse, bringing ourselves up. Calling ourselves to account from the place of our strength is a middah, or value, we must develop. Societies, too, should be strong enough to name their faults and address them. Today the whole world must walk this tightrope: The hubris of our single species now drives countless others to extinction, and our carbon-spewing generation threatens all who follow us. To flourish, let's be strong enough to practice humility.

Rabbi Fred Scherlinder Dobb
Adat Shalom Reconstructionist
Congregation
Bethesda, MD

REFORM

Pride and arrogance are opposite sides of the same coin. As Jews, we should be proud of and uphold our heritage, traditions and values. Yet under what conditions does that pride transform itself into arrogance? Consider the story of Abraham arguing with God (Genesis 18). God had declared the destruction of Sodom because of the Sodomites' pervasive wicked behavior. Abraham humbly challenged God to save the town should he find even only 10 righteous men there. One might say that this is the quintessential example of arrogance, yet tradition upholds Abraham's behavior as that of a righteous and holy man who proudly stood by his belief in the value of human life. Or consider the incident of the Golden Calf (Exodus 32). Aaron, in the absence of Moses, in response to the people's doubts and, some might

say, in hope of becoming the leader of the Israelites, arrogantly mis-
leads the community by permitting and orchestrating the creation of
the Golden Calf. Aaron's arrogance leads both God and Moses to punish the Israelites.

Judaism upholds humility and righteousness and scorns arrogance.
Our challenging task is to know when doing right and feeling pride
become overshadowed by the egocentrism and desire for self-promo-
tion that are the symptoms of arrogance.

Rabbi Laura Novak Winer
Fresno, CA

CONSERVATIVE

The concept of a Chosen People can be misunderstood and encourage
arrogance. Without an understanding that we are a covenanted people
expected to embrace the Torah and its teachings, it is easy to assume
we are chosen because we are better. Isaiah says: "I the Lord in My
grace have summoned you, and I have grasped you by the hand. I created you and appointed you." (42:6) The prophet Amos, on the other
hand, anticipated the possibility that this idea could be seen as promot-
ing arrogance and chauvinism. He reminds the Israelites that, by being
chosen, they will be held to a higher standard: "You alone have I singled
out, of all the families of the earth; that is why I will call you to account
for all your iniquities."(3:2)

Amos teaches that we are not chosen because we are better. Rather,
because we are chosen, God will demand we take responsibility for our
sins. Later in Amos, God tells the Israelites, "To Me, O Israelites, you
are just like the Ethiopians…True, I brought Israel up from the land of
Egypt, but also Philistines from Caphtor and the Arameans from Kir."
(9:7) When we understand that chosenness means we are held account-
able to a Torah-mandated standard of behavior, we guard against
assuming an attitude of arrogance.

Rabbi Amy Wallk Katz
Temple Beth El
Springfield, MA

MODERN ORTHODOX

Judaism teaches monotheism. There is one universal God/Creator who cares deeply for humans and communicates revelation and instruction. The emphasis on the Universal One lends itself to a potential abuse: Spokesmen and teachers may present their message not as interpretive guidance but as definitive, literal divine instruction. That can imply the right to delegitimize other views—or even coerce other people to do it exactly their way.

This unconscious arrogance is sometimes encouraged by the classic teaching that a human being is an image of God. The human mind is godlike, and people are encouraged to develop their mind and other capacities to become even more godlike. It is not a big jump from that to think of themselves as all-knowing and unimpeachable. Terrible injustices have been inflicted—sometimes even killing of others has been justified—because of this wrong extension of the idea of God's centrality.

The corrective for this tendency is the constant Jewish teaching that you are not God; you are a finite, flawed image of God. The rabbis in the Talmud developed the method of *machloket*—debate, argumentation and multiple approaches to the text and the law to establish the best interpretation. But each side acknowledges the legitimacy of disagreement and multiple analyses. "Both these and those [School of Hillel and School of Shammai] are the words of the living God." Though not foolproof, this method keeps people aware of their own limitations and checks, even contradicts, the tendency to arrogance.

Rabbi Yitz Greenberg
Riverdale, NY

ORTHODOX

If we believed half of the things our admirers and critics say about us—that we control world markets, that we have all the Nobel laureates, that we clannishly stick together to protect our interests—it would certainly create room for arrogance. Hannah Arendt wrote in *The*

Origins of Totalitarianism (1951) that the idea of chosenness never really got Jews in trouble during hundreds of years of persecution. People didn't mind the claim to specialness when it just meant God had picked us to have brit milah, to not eat things, to get up early and put funny straps on our arms. Rav Abraham Isaac Kook (1865-1935) said something similar. In Jewish tradition, no personality trait is all good or all bad—for instance, anger has a place—but the one exception is *ga'ava*, pride. Rav Kook disputed that and said there can be "*ga'ava d'kedusha*"—holy pride. *Ga'ava* usually tells a person he or she is different and better; it's pride in what one has that others haven't. But when the *ga'ava* comes from something given to you by God, it doesn't lead to arrogance, because you share that with everyone else.

And that's what so much of Jewish tradition keeps telling us. So, you have 20 IQ points more than your neighbor? Don't be arrogant; that's just a genetic inheritance, a gift. Your hedge fund is doing well? Another gift. I'm probably not as humble as I should be, but I find that daily involvement with Jewish texts, particularly Gemara, on a deep level, keeps you humble. The text is so complex that every time you look at it for more than five minutes, it cuts you down.

Rabbi Yitzchok Adlerstein
Cross-Currents
Los Angeles, CA

CHABAD

All the letters of the Hebrew alphabet, says the Rabbi of Kotzk, can be made larger but still retain their identity—except the small letter called "Yud," a word that in Yiddish also means "Jew." If it is made larger, Yud becomes another letter, "Vav." So it is with the Jew when he becomes bigheaded: His identity, his Jewishness, vanishes. To me, that aphorism perfectly describes Judaism's conception of arrogance. Pride is a spiritual cannibal, devouring empathy, gratitude and love and pitting person against person and G-d.

How do we combat this danger? Judaism brought to the world the idea of one all-powerful Creator. And that concept is the antidote against arrogance. In G-d, you come up against a being who is, in every respect, infinitely superior to yourself. Therefore, you are humbled in comparison. As long as you remain egotistical, you have not encountered G-d.

The humility that an awareness of G-d brings us is not incompatible with greatness. The greater the person, the more humble he is likely to be. Moses, the greatest hero of Jewish tradition, is described as "a very humble man, more so than any other man on earth" (Numbers 12:3). Humility does not mean undervaluing oneself. It means valuing others. It means the "I" is quiet so that I can hear the "you," the voice of another that calls me to relieve its loneliness with love.

Rabbi Dov Greenberg
Rohr Chabad House, Stanford University
Palo Alto, CA.

What does Judaism say about love?

I s romantic love just another Western value, antithetical to Jewish tradition? Is it illusory or shallow? As it turns out, Judaism has a lot to say in support of romantic and sexual love, though the rabbis also draw attention to the solid framework of other loves undergirding human happiness—love of family, attachment to community, or that Jewish favorite, love expressed through action. Many wrestle with the inherent implausibility of the commandment to love God—can you be mandated to feel an emotion?—while also suggesting that it's the foundation stone that holds the whole thing up. (Published in 2011.)

INDEPENDENT

Love is defined in Hebrew as *ahavah*, which is rooted in the Aramaic word *hav* and literally translates as "give." Rather than translate *Bereishit*, the first word of the Torah, as "In the beginning," one can say "In the first gift." Creation originated in the Creator's will to give. We refer to the nature of this gifting as love because it involves not only giving of oneself, but also stepping back to enable the existence and flourishing of the other. God thus models what love entails: selfless gifting accompanied by withdrawal to enable the other to emerge. Therefore, the ancient rabbis defined authentic love as not contingent on any factor because if it is, and then that factor is gone, so is love.

But romantic love does have contingencies. It requires compatibility and trust because it involves intimacy. The Talmud admonishes, "A man should never marry off his daughter but to the one whom she finds favorable." Is romantic love then a step down from altruistic love? Not at all. It is rather a step into the inner sanctum of love, a sampling of the World to Come, where love is not merely a state of grace but a state of bliss.

Rabbi Gershon Winkler
Walking Stick Foundation
Thousand Oaks, CA

HUMANIST

What is love? An emotion? Is it defined by what it is not? The opposite of hate? Like the theological challenge of defining God, does love defy being pinned down? Perhaps the most familiar references to love in our tradition come from two verses: "Love your neighbor as yourself" (Leviticus 19:18) and "You shall love your God with all your heart, with all your soul, and with all your might," (Deuteronomy 6:5).

I have always been intrigued by the idea that love could be mandated. I thought true love was voluntary, from the heart. Rashi, the 12th-century commentator, seems to have understood my problem. He distinguished between acting out of fear and acting out of love. Fear may induce basic obedience, but it won't build loyalty. Love, on the other hand, will be met with love and a readiness to give back even more in return.

For Rashi, "love your God" meant "performing commandments out of love." What matters is how we carry ourselves, how we treat others, how we act with loving intentions. The mandate isn't necessarily a mandate to love God. In fact, God doesn't even need to be part of the equation and is conspicuously absent in the instruction to love our neighbor as ourself.

Rabbi Peter H. Schweitzer
The City Congregation for
Humanistic Judaism
New York, NY

RENEWAL

The Torah commands: Love God "with all your heart, with all your soul and with all your might," "Love the stranger" and "Love your neighbor as yourself." You are asked to receive God's love in the form of Torah, community, history and the wonders of nature. These commandments constitute the most simple and the most complicated challenge of living a holy life. Love is the "measure" for my Jewish practice. Every mitzvah I keep, every prayer I say, is done and said with the intention of adding more love to this world, opening my heart, connecting myself to the divine essence that is hidden in all things. Psalm 34 asks, "Who is the one with a passion for life, loving every day and seeing the good?" Jewish wisdom ignites my passion for life, reminds me to pay attention to the quality of my loving every day and points me toward the essential goodness of being. Learning to love and be loved is the most rigorous spiritual path there is. Every day, we must ask, "How do we love God and receive God's love through this world?

Rabbi Shefa Gold
Center for Devotional, Energy
and Ecstatic Practice
Jemez Springs, NM

RECONSTRUCTIONIST

For romantic love, see the Song of Songs. But the word love in Torah is primarily an activist commandment: Love your neighbor and the stranger; love God. Even to love God (says Talmud Yoma 26a) means we should behave divinely toward others, "making God beloved, through us." And Maimonides brought an almost ecological consciousness to loving the One in the *Mishneh Torah*: "When we study God's many wondrous works and creations, and thus comprehend God's infinite wisdom, immediately we love, and praise."

The prophets warn us to pair every prayer with acts of love. As 20th-century Jewish philosopher Martin Buber taught: "Love of the Creator and love of that which God has created, are finally one and the same."

Still, can feelings of love really be commanded? In the rabbinic mind, these mitzvot demand actions. Here we should emulate our Unitarian-Universalist cousins, whose "Stand on the Side of Love" campaign takes the logic of love to its fullest by organizing for universal health coverage, same-sex marriage equality, caring for creation and more. In short: Love the stranger, whether documented or undocumented. Love your neighbor, regardless of whom they love in turn. And through these loving actions, you love God.

Rabbi Fred Scherlinder Dobb
Adat Shalom Reconstructionist
Congregation
Bethesda, MD

REFORM

The Jewish expression of love is a triangle: love of self, love of another and love of God. Leviticus 19:18 teaches us, "Love your neighbor as yourself." To love another, one has to first feel and express love for oneself. We all know that this is not always easy to achieve, but it is vital. Finally, a loving relationship is seen as Jewish when the partners acknowledge, value and name that relationship as holy. Two people in love see the divine. Think of Jean Valjean in *Les Miserables* singing, "To love another person is to see the face of God."

Ultimately, our understanding of God informs how we love ourselves and another. We must uphold the Jewish value of *b'tzelem elohim*, that we are created in the image of God. In so doing, we continuously strive to see that holy essence in ourselves and in others. With holiness as that measure for how we treat, care for and love each other, we can build truly loving relationships.

Rabbi Laura Novak Winer
Union for Reform Judaism
Livermore, CA

CONSERVATIVE

The Bible suggests that loving relationships can be either sexual or platonic. The Song of Songs vividly describes sexual love. It is unique in the Bible because its purpose is to describe the power of love between men and women. Talmudic rabbis understood the Song of Songs to be an allegory: It used a man and a woman to explain the love between God and the Jewish people and suggests the high regard Judaism has for male-female love and sexuality. The Bible also offers two images of platonic love: one between Ruth and Naomi and one between Jonathan and David. The circumstances around both are complicated, but nevertheless demonstrate a strong, sincere bond. Naomi was Ruth's mother-in-law, a relationship that is not always associated with love. To make matters worse, Ruth was from Moab, an enemy of ancient Israel. Still, the women's relationship flourished after Ruth's husband died. David and Jonathan's friendship survived even greater tension: Jonathan, King Saul's son, was assumed to be the heir to the throne, while David, the leading soldier in Saul's army, was the popular choice to become king. Our texts teach us that love has multiple meanings and comes in multiple forms.

Rabbi Amy Wallk Katz
Temple Beth El
Springfield, MA

MODERN ORTHODOX

"Love makes the world go round"—that is Jewish wisdom. According to Kabbalah, God created the world because love needs another to love. Three times a day, traditional Jews say in the Ashrei prayer: "God is good to all [in the world because] God's mother love extends to all God's creatures" (Psalms 145:9). So consuming is God's love that Hashem brings a flood to wash out evil and start again. But Hashem also promises never to do that again and instead enters into a covenant to accept humans as they are. With all of their flaws, God partners with humans to build a perfect world (*tikkun olam*). We are called to return

God's love. Says the Torah: "You shall love the Lord your God with all your heart, with all your soul and with all your might." All commandments and rituals are meant to express our love for Hashem. In the Jewish ideal, every person finds the unique one destined for him/her to love totally (body, emotion, mind) to become fully human and together create and nurture more life. Such a love can mature through life—and beyond. "Love is stronger than death" (Song of Songs 8:6).

Rabbi Yitz Greenberg
New York, NY

SEPHARDIC

Judaism acknowledges that love —both of God and our fellow human beings—is a beautiful part of life that plays an important role in our emotional, spiritual and intellectual development. The Bible famously describes love as an extraordinarily powerful force that is "stronger than death." That being said, love, especially of the romantic variety, is not without its limitations and pitfalls. Western culture, in particular, has a tendency to exaggerate the significance of romantic love, portraying it as the be all and end all of happiness. I believe that the skyrocketing divorce rates are a sign not of more failing marriages but of the prevalence of unrealistic expectations about love that can only lead to disillusionment and frustration. This is why my favorite biblical verse about marriage is in Ecclesiastes: "Enjoy life with the woman whom you love all the days of your futile life…." In other words, enjoy love for what it is worth, but do not expect it to provide you with more satisfaction or fulfillment than it can. Otherwise, you will inevitably find yourself disappointed.

Rabbi Joshua Maroof
Magen David Sephardic Congregation
Rockville, MD

ORTHODOX

Love is the gravity that pulls the universe together. Hatred is the anti-matter that rips it apart. Love between a man and woman is life's loftiest goal. But it must be accompanied by lust. The tenth commandment orders a man not to covet his neighbor's wife, which, by clear implication, means he should be coveting his own. Erotic love is most fully expressed in the Song of Songs. Interestingly, the man and woman are never named. We do not know if they are even married. This teaches us that love best flourishes when it is both mysterious and sinful.

How can marriage, a legal institution based on familiarity, attain these twin attributes? Having a monthly period of sexual separation in which husband and wife are forbidden to each other heightens, in the illicit physical period, the role of conversation in which the inner and ever-deeper layers of human personality are slowly manifest. Love between a man and woman is even more exalted than the unbreakable bond between parent and child, which is why G-d's relationship with the Jewish people, which encompasses both aspects, is ultimately described as a marriage. Romantic love embodies choice, whereas genetic love, however strong, is compelled by a blood relationship. The Jewish people are, therefore, G-d's chosen.

Rabbi Shmuley Boteach
Englewood, NJ

Should Jews strive
to be happy?

Perhaps this is the ultimate way of asking whether, or how well, Jewish values map onto the ones that drive our society. The rabbis refine the question and break it down into parts—what makes us happy in the first place? Should we strive for wealth, popularity, stability, length of days? Should we seek happiness only in doing good deeds? Still, they take care to acknowledge that the drive for happiness is part of what makes us human. "What kind of a question is this?" one rabbi asks. "Should Jews strive to eat?" (Published in 2014.)

INDEPENDENT

No. Jews should never strive to be happy.

Happiness should not be something to strive for. It should be solidly entrenched deeply within us, born of a sense of mystery, a sense that defies reason and definition. We are here for the very purpose of not knowing why. And in the not knowing, we rejoice and laugh in the face of every imaginable fate. This is the audacity of Torah, which challenges us to dance on Simchat Torah with numbers etched into our arms, to dream tenaciously about Jerusalem in spite of 2,000 years of exile, to sing joyful melodies on Saturday even if we know a pogrom is pending on Sunday. We are a people that has been subjected to unimaginable tragedy, genocide, expulsion and conquest for longer periods and with far more frequency than any other group in human history. Yet at the same time, we are a people known for our humor, our laughter, our joy. Happiness for us is much more than an emotion. It is a theology, an essential and enormous divine imperative (*Likutei Moharan*, Tanina, Ch. 4). Without it, we risk slip-sliding into subjection to a finite, mortally fashioned reality along with all of its empty promises, painful disappointments, disempowering illusions and short-lived exaltations. Happiness, Judaism teaches, is knowing that you don't know.

Rabbi Gershon Winkler
Walking Stick Foundation
Thousand Oaks, CA

HUMANIST

The first really big thoughts I ever had were as a young child pondering the possibility of life both before me and after me. How, I wondered, could there be a world without my existence? Who hasn't had similar questions?

The corollary to the "before" and "after" query is what to make of the "during"—the in-between. What, we ask, is the goal, aim or purpose of life? Some people aren't bothered by these questions—or don't have the luxury to sit and reflect on them. Others lose sleep over them. Life, they say, must be more than just survival or making a living. Happiness and self-worth must mean more than the material possessions and wealth we acquire.

I believe that for Jews and Judaism, happiness is not a goal in and of itself. Rather, it is the reward for doing deeds of loving-kindness (loving our neighbor as ourself); performing acts of justice ("Justice, justice you shall pursue"); learning for learning's sake; thinking critically, staying true to our values and celebrating our heritage. Follow this path and happiness will come as a matter of course, along with dignity and a worthwhile sense of purpose.

Rabbi Peter H. Schweitzer
The City Congregation for
Humanistic Judaism
New York, NY

RENEWAL

Rabbi Nachman of Breslov teaches, "If you don't feel happy, pretend to be. Even if you are downright depressed, put on a smile. Act happy. Genuine joy will follow." While at first glance this might appear to be disingenuous, the Rebbe is inviting us to be fully human. Joy, once activated, opens us to our aliveness, our *chiyyut*. It draws us to the state of *mochin d'gadlut*—spacious mind—from which we can see things from a G!d's-eye view.

Putting on a smile is not intended to cover over anything but rather to make room for what is here—the presence of Yah—in each breathing, sacred moment. The smile which leads us to joy, which leads us to wonder, calls upon the child within to live with curiosity and creativity.

To "strive to be happy" is the response to G!d's call, *U'vacharta b'chayim, l'ma'an tichyeh*, "Choose life so you may live" (Deuteronomy 30:19) so that we may, with G!d's help, be fully alive.

Rabbi Mark Novak
Minyan Oneg Shabbat
Washington, DC

RECONSTRUCTIONIST

Real happiness is profound. Beyond smiles and good feelings, it denotes meaning and purpose, as in the opening of the familiar prayer "Happy [Ashrei] are those who dwell in Your house" [Psalm 84]. So Rabbi Nachman of Breslov was right: "*Mitzvah gedolah lihyot b'simcha tamid*, the overarching Jewish imperative is to strive always to be happy." Likewise, for Mordecai Kaplan, being happy is truly divine: God is "the Power that makes for Salvation [i.e. deep happiness, fulfillment of potential]." Pursuit of happiness, an inalienable right, is ingrained in human nature; simply, we'll do what it takes. That self-centered impulse, our *yetzer hara,* is actually deemed "very good" in our tradition. But it must be constantly balanced with helping others be happy, too. That ethical impulse is our *yetzer hatov* (Bereshit Rabbah 9:7, as taught by Ira Stone).

When it's grounded and meaningful, indeed, as Pharrell Williams' hit song has it, "Happiness is the truth." Yet its evil twin, immediate gratification, gives happiness a bad name. Seeking happiness exclusively for oneself, or too impulsively, is destructive. Defined broadly, however, pursuing everyone's happiness for the long haul is our *mitzvah gedolah*, our purpose. Everything we hold dear—family, Torah, self-actualization, tikkun olam, art, education, truth, peace, you name it—it's all about striving toward our own happiness, and that of others, simultaneously.

Rabbi Fred Scherlinder Dobb
Adat Shalom Reconstructionist
Congregation
Bethesda, MD

REFORM

I am reminded of a recent conversation I had with a group of high school students who were debating the question, "Do we have control over our own happiness, or is that something for which we must rely on others?" Maimonides teaches, "It is natural for man's character to be drawn after the thoughts and actions of his friends and associates, and for him to follow the norms of the people of his country. Therefore, one must associate with the righteous and be constantly in the company of the wise, so as to learn from their deeds" (*Mishneh Torah*, Hilchot Deot, ch. 6:1). Maimonides proves this point with a text: "Happy is the man who has not followed the counsel of the wicked... rather, the teaching of Adonai is his delight" (Psalms 1:1).

In other words, achieving happiness requires action, doing righteous work for the benefit of oneself and others and surrounding oneself with a community of shared values. If those around you are happy, you will be too.

Of course we should strive to be happy. Is happiness in our control? Our tradition affirms that happiness comes from the choices we make each day, how we live and with whom we are in relationship. Those choices are surely in our control. I encouraged those students to adopt

such a mindset and to strive for happiness in that way each day.
Rabbi Laura Novak Winer
Fresno, CA

CONSERVATIVE

Happiness can have many meanings: serving God with joy, rejoicing on special occasions, appreciating small pleasures, feeling happy or contented. Let's focus for now on practicing Judaism with joy.

Our Sages declared that we should strive to bring simcha (happiness) to all Jewish living—worship, observance of mitzvot and study—and serve God with joy. The Sages argued that commandments should be performed with joy (*simcha she' mitzvah*). Indeed, the Sages argued that one can develop a close relationship with God only by bringing joy and happiness to the performance of the commandments. Similarly, it was considered important to study Torah with a positive attitude and a sense of joy.

The great medieval commentator Rashi suggested that God does not reside with a person unless that person is joyous in fulfilling God's will. When the Hasidic movement was founded in the late 1700s, its premise was that Jewish life was parched. Jewish observance had become tedious; there was no joy in serving God. The early Hasidic rabbis strove to infuse joy and spirit into all expressions of Judaism.

The first chief rabbi of Palestine, Rabbi Abraham Isaac Kook (1865-1935), is quoted as saying, "Delight and joy must accompany your every spiritual endeavor." If we strive to make this so, Kook argued, we will strive to live a better life.

Rabbi Amy Wallk Katz
Temple Beth El
Springfield, MA

MODERN ORTHODOX

What kind of question is this? Striving to be happy is a universal human phenomenon. Why should Jews not do the same? Would you ask: Should Jews strive to breathe? Should Jews strive to eat?

Maybe you meant: Is there a distinctive Jewish way to be happy? I doubt it. Jews, like most people, are happy when they are given the right to "life, liberty and the pursuit of happiness." This last phrase means that most people are happy not so much when they are in an actual state of fixed or permanent happiness, but when they are striving for happiness. Most people tend to be happy when they experience love or are treated with dignity, when they are physically healthy and well fed, clothed, sheltered and have constructive work to do. There is nothing particularly Jewish about these conditions.

The question does draw attention to the fact that happiness is highly rated in Jewish tradition. Yes, Virginia, joy and not guilt is the top Jewish message. However, usually the reference is to the joy of fulfilling a mitzvah or doing a good deed. The Psalmist says, "Serve God with joy; come before God with shouts of gladness" (Psalms 100:2). Maybe Rabbi Nachman of Breslov put it best: "It is a great mitzvah to be in a state of happiness, always."

Rabbi Yitz Greenberg
Riverdale, NY

ORTHODOX

How could we not try to be happy? Of course, being happy is not the only value—there are lots of things we should be doing—but happiness is certainly a value to pursue. I'm very fond of the beginning of *Mesillat Yesharim* (*The Path of the Just*), a great Hebrew literary classic written in 1740, in which Moses Chaim Luzzatto, the Ramchal, begins the first chapter, "Man is created to take pleasure." He then, cleverly, once he has your attention, says that the real pleasure in life is closeness to Hashem and that nothing can compete with the pleasure of being near G-d, who is the source of all pleasure. But he does take it for granted that the idea of pursuing pleasure is going to resonate with traditional Jews who are turning to his book to learn how to pursue the ethical high road.

An important distinction can be made between pleasure and happiness. At least the way we use the word in English, pleasure can be transitory and ephemeral, something that is stimulating or even titillating in the moment but quickly vanishes. Happiness is usually something you have to invest in, that grows slowly and takes a good deal of work and sometimes sacrifice and even pain to achieve. But the pursuit of happiness is something so natural that we have no recourse but to presume that G-d engineered us in order to pursue it and then gave us the guidance to pursue it ethically.

Rabbi Yitzchok Adlerstein
Loyola Law School
Los Angeles, CA

CHABAD

Happiness is usually understood in the context of pleasure derived from a goal achieved. As Jews we are an *or l'Goyim*—a light to the nations—striving to bring about a perfected world. Not all that much to be happy about. Yet the Torah complains that "you did not serve the Lord, your G-d, with happiness and with gladness of heart, when [you had an] abundance of everything" (Deuteronomy 28:47).

When we are conscious that we are working as part of G-d's plan, trying to bring the world into alignment as well, then we have personally achieved the goal of oneness with the divine. So, as Jews, we should be happy to strive.

Rabbi Yossi Serebryanski
Chabad of South Denver
Denver, CO

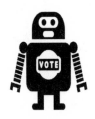

PART FIVE

POLITICS

T hough relatively few in number, American Jews have been consistently active in politics. They also mostly vote for Democrats, for reasons that the community loves to debate (that taste for argument coming out again) but that is often attributed to do with the experience of being "the stranger"—immigrants, sweatshop workers, religious minorities. That could change, of course—or not. The increase in political polarization gripping the United States is certainly reflected in the Jewish community, making political subjects more fraught than ever to discuss.

While support for Israel drives a good deal of American Jewish political involvement, and also a good deal of our political argument, these questions mostly focus on Jewish political behavior here at home. It's no coincidence that we've asked them all in presidential election years.

Are we commanded to vote?

T his question is more complicated than it may appear at first glance. One might view voting as a paramount ethical obligation, yet separate this from the question of whether it is a commandment. The distinction can be traced in the contrasting answers from Reform, which explicitly takes ethics as Judaism's core, and Orthodoxy, which explicitly states that it relies on halacha, Jewish law, rather than general ideas of what is a good thing.

In practice, though, these paths frequently converge: "There are a lot of warm, fuzzy reasons to vote," Orthodox Rabbi Yitzchok Adlerstein observes, "but as a halachist, I am limited to citing two compelling reasons why one is actually obligated to do so." (Published in 2016.)

INDEPENDENT

Not necessarily commanded, but it was long ago suggested that we do what we can to contribute to the general welfare of the lands in which we sojourn. One could argue that voting may be a part of this contribution. The suggestion came to the prophet Jeremiah in a message from God, which he forwarded to our exiled ancestors following the destruction by the Babylonians of the First Jewish Commonwealth more than 2,400 years ago:

To all [those] I have exiled from Jerusalem to Babylon: "Build houses and settle down; plant gardens and eat of their yield. Start families, have children, and help your children start families, so that they too may have sons and daughters. Increase in number there; do not decrease. Also, seek the peace of the village to which I have exiled you, and pray to God on her behalf, for in her state of peace shall you too find peace" (Jeremiah 29:4-7).

Rabbi Gershon Winkler
Walking Stick Foundation
Thousand Oaks, CA

HUMANIST

Let's start by pointing out how remarkable this question is, because it presumes that Jews are enfranchised to vote in the first place. We take this for granted now, but it wasn't always the case. In the original American colonies under British rule, the right to vote and the right to hold office were restricted to white, Protestant, land-owning men. Over time, these restrictions were overturned—for Jews as well as for women and African Americans. Even now, a number of states, including Maryland and Mississippi, still prohibit any person who "denies the existence of a Supreme Being" from holding state office. This carve-out, if it could be enforced—and it probably can't—would effectively eliminate secular, non-believing Jews from running for election, perhaps even Bernie Sanders, who has said he believes in God, but not in a traditional manner: "I am what I am, and what I believe in, and what my spirituality is about, is that we're all in this together."

In a normal election year, a secularly inclined candidate like Sanders might pay at the polls for not being an ardent synagogue-goer. Since this is hardly a normal election year, another challenge arises: Many Republican voters, and presumably some Jews among them, are considering not voting at all. Are they, or we, commanded to vote? No. Should we take for granted the right to vote? No. Should we work to protect those voting rights and expand them for everyone? Absolutely!

Rabbi Peter H. Schweitzer
The City Congregation for
Humanistic Judaism
New York, NY

RENEWAL

Every Jew has a duty to vote in the democratic elections in one's nation of citizenship. Jewish law mandates the creation of civil government (*Talmud Bavli*, Avot 3:2, Avodah Zara 4a) and obliges all who benefit from public services to help provide them (Bava Batra 7b, Bava Metzia 108a). Voting follows from this Jewish communitarian value against free-riding and from a "social compact"—recognized by Jews 700 years before Enlightenment democratic thought arose in Europe—by which Jews opting to live in a society thereby agree to support its government and laws (Rashbam, Bava Batra 54b). Most of all, Judaism views voting to be a holy act of divine partnership. Before selecting Bezalel as master builder, God told Moses to consult the people (Berakhot 55a); the modern elective franchise continues this legacy "for the sake of heaven" (*Shulchan Aruch*, C.M. 163:1). It follows that all government policies—from public order and foreign policy to education and the environment—are issues on which Jews are called to help renew and repair the world in holy partnership at the ballot box.

Rabbi David Evan Markus
Temple Beth-El
City Island, NY

RECONSTRUCTIONIST

We may not be commanded, exactly, but we're fools, hypocrites and worse if we fail to vote. Judaism puts values front and center, and in a democracy, voting is the core expression of values. Think we should "pursue justice" (Deuteronomy 16)? Vote. "Love the stranger/immigrant" (Deuteronomy 10)? Vote. Keep humans and Earth, *adam* and *adamah*, connected (Genesis 2)? Vote. Love our own, protect others (Leviticus 19) and honor all who are created in the Divine image (Genesis 1)? Vote.

Jewish history is instructive, too, for we've always fared best in open societies. True democracies with robust electorates rarely fight one another, are more stable and generally enfranchise not only the majority but, crucially, the minority as well. Here, our two great centers, Israel (with a Jewish majority) and America (just 2 percent Jewish), inform each other. How exactly should voters treat minorities? What to do when demagogic voices, in either land, seek to exclude and divide?

Exodus 23:2 says, in a hard-to-translate passage, that there is an obligation of *aharei rabim l'hatot*, which may mean to "incline after the majority"—a principle that has grounded Jewish democracy for more than 2,000 years and allows legal matters to be settled by a majority of judges. Ironically, the passage is also sometimes read as meaning the opposite—that one should not side with the mighty but bolster the minority. Either way, we must honor everyone (Avot 4:1), without fail. Where to start? Vote.

Fred Scherlinder Dobb
Adat Shalom Reconstructionist
Congregation
Bethesda, MD

REFORM

A man once came before the Chazon Ish (a Russian-born Orthodox rabbi, 1878-1953) and explained that he didn't have enough money to pay his taxes and, therefore, would not be allowed to vote in an upcoming election. The Chazon Ish responded: "You should sell your tefillin and pay the taxes... tefillin, you can borrow from another, but the right to vote you cannot get from someone else."

As this story illustrates, there have been times when Jews faced barriers to voting, or, though allowed to vote in theory, were unable to do so. (Of course, there were far worse times when legislation affirmatively stripped Jews of their rights, such as the Nuremberg Laws in 1930s Germany.) Thankfully, in the United States, the 24th Amendment protects one's right to vote regardless of taxpayer status.

The Chazon Ish story tells us that voting is so important that one should sell one's tefillin—a symbol of one's commitment to observing the mitzvot, or commandments—in order to do so. I would suggest that for us, today, voting is more than a right or a privilege. It is an obligation incumbent upon us as equal citizens in a democratic society.

Rabbi Laura Novak Winer
Fresno, CA

CONSERVATIVE

The Bible comes up short in conceptualizing the "democratic ideal" as we know it today. In the Torah, there is a clearly defined hierarchy of leadership. The Kohanim and Levi'im are granted religious privileges not open to everyone else. The Prophets describe, and usually castigate, the kings of Israel and Judah. Although there were kings whom the Prophets applauded, the bulk of their writings describe monarchy as an immensely flawed form of government.

It is in rabbinic literature that the value of democracy is put forth (*Babylonian Talmud*, Berakhot 55a). Rabbi Isaac said: "One does not appoint a leader for a community without consulting the community. How do we know this? It says in the Torah: 'See, the Eternal One has singled out by name Bezalel' (Exodus 35:30). God said to Moses, 'Moses, is Bezalel worthy in your opinion?' Moses answered God, 'Ruler of the Universe, if he is worthy before You, how could he possibly not be worthy before me?' God said to him, 'Even so, go and ask them [the people] . . .'"

It is abundantly clear from this text that God demands our participation when appointing a leader for our community. In other words, yes, it is a mitzvah to vote!

Rabbi Amy Wallk Katz
Temple Beth El
Springfield, MA

MODERN ORTHODOX

It does not say in the Torah, "Thou shalt vote; I am the Lord." The Torah's laws generally take off from where the society is; they try to move the standard situation closer to the ideal. The Torah does not advocate voting for political leadership because it was given in a culture that was neither egalitarian nor democratic. The Torah does instruct that the king and the leaders be and act under the rule of law—but it does not deal with the population at large or with the selection process.

The prophet Jeremiah does say that the Israelites should join in the country where they live, should build it, seek its welfare and pray for it. Voting is a key way to assure the well-being of the country. I believe that democracy is the political system most likely to advance the Torah's goal of tikkun olam—to repair the world—so that every human being is treated as an equal, valuable and unique image of God. But the mitzvah to vote will have to be written in by the Oral Law—the unfolding tradition.

Rabbi Yitz Greenberg
Riverdale, NY

ORTHODOX

The use of the word "commanded" makes this question easier. There are a lot of warm, fuzzy reasons to vote, but as a halachist, I am limited to citing two compelling reasons why one is actually obligated to do so. The first is an overarching principle of Jewish life that translates again and again into normative behavior: *Hakarat ha-tov*, recognizing the good that someone or something has provided you. This is a great country for Jews. It is a minimal expectation of citizenship that we participate in the electoral process, and I see it as nothing less than obligatory to show our appreciation of this great country by acting on that expectation.

The second reason may be more controversial. In 1984, Rabbi Moshe Feinstein, the preeminent halachist of the late 20th century, wrote in a letter that all observant Jewish citizens of this country are obligated to vote. He wrote this during an election season in which many people felt the outcome was a foregone conclusion and any individual vote would have no value. Nonetheless, Rabbi Feinstein wrote—at the urging of some people in the know—that there are always people scrutinizing the voting habits of different communities, and that Jews have an obligation to vote in such a way that they will do the most good for their community. And he called it an exercise in *"nosei b'ol ha-tzibbur"*—the rabbis command one not only not to shirk community responsibility, but to seek out ways in which one may help ease the community's burdens. So, he argued, where there are consequences for the community—consequences that he did not spell out—all Jews should vote.

Of course, one could theoretically imagine an election where all the choices were so terrible that it would be better not to vote. But that's just a hypothetical.

Rabbi Yitzchok Adlerstein
Loyola Law School
Los Angeles, CA

CHABAD

There are many sources in Torah that talk about the imperative for civic engagement: the obligation for a system of justice in the Noahide Code, the very Noahide Code itself, the imperative to "pray for the welfare of the government" and many more. But saying that we are commanded to vote would be focusing on the symptom rather than the cause.

We are commanded to do what we can to "correct the world under the sovereignty of G-d"—to make our world better and more in tune with its innate goodness and sanctity. To the extent that this can be achieved at the ballot box, voting can be seen as an expression of our core Jewish values. But remembering to focus on the underlying imperative and aim can help to ensure that we maintain the right attitude toward it—an attitude within which political engagement is all about upholding our highest aspirations of ethics and love of a fellow, even those with whom we might happen to disagree.

Another reminder provided by voting: We each count. Every one. And each person counts for no more—and no less—than one. Although that may be arguable at times in the vagaries of our politi-

cal structures, it never varies where it truly matters—in our absolute
and essential value in the eyes of G-d.

Rabbi Dov Wagner
Rohr Chabad Jewish Student Center,
University of Southern California
Los Angeles, CA

Does politics belong on the bima?

This is a perennial question; indeed, we've asked it several times from slightly different angles, and two of those variations—from 2008 and 2012—are included below, overlaps and all. On one level, this first question is legal: What kinds of things said from the bima (podium) would cost a synagogue or religious institution its tax exemption? Equally pragmatic, though harder to predict: What kinds of things said from the bima will get a rabbi fired? Beyond that, it's a matter of personal preference and knowing your audience, and every rabbi has a story to tell, though not necessarily from the bima. (Published in 2008.)

INDEPENDENT

The nexus between religion and political life invites us to revisit the roles of priest and prophet in biblical society and discuss their relevance today. Historically, the Tanach separated civil and religious authorities. In "Priest and Prophet," Ahad Ha'am describes the prophet as an uncompromising zealot who seldom engages in diplomacy. Moses is not a people pleaser; if Moses had led our ancestors into the Promised Land, he might well have engaged in holy war against the Canaanite nations to fulfill the divine command. Moses' successor, Joshua, shows a priestly personality when he makes covenants with the surrounding Canaanite nations.

The Hebrew word for prophet, *Navi*, means "speaker." Neither seers nor clairvoyants, the prophets spoke out against society's evils. Not afraid of condemnation or incarceration, they were among the first to stage demonstrations against governmental oppression. Jeremiah wore an ox's yoke over his shoulders to demonstrate the heavy burden of King Jehoachim's rule. Prophets also challenged the priesthood when it engaged in practices that negated fundamental principles of religious belief and doctrine.

The roles of priest and prophet should not exclude one another, particularly in this election year. *Kadosh* translates as both "holy" and "other," and Martin Buber says, "Holiness is otherness." Therefore, the synagogue would be amiss if it were not involved in presenting dissident political views. The synagogue should maintain its three-fold function as the house of prayer, study and gathering.

> **Rabbi Harold S. White**
> *Senior Jewish Chaplain,*
> *Georgetown University*
> *Washington, DC*

HUMANIST

Rabbis have long championed the idea of "freedom of the pulpit" that entitles them to speak out on issues and to voice opinions that may not necessarily be popular among their members. However, while some communities welcome these pronouncements, others discourage them.

As an old joke goes, a rabbi was once hired for a new position and advised that he could talk about any subject he wanted as long as it wasn't about politics or religion.

To be a good rabbi one needs imagination. That is, one needs to imagine that somebody is paying attention to what you have to say. Naturally, I'm glad when members listen to my ideas. I am equally gratified when I can learn from them and be guided by them. These days, in fact, we all have access to the same news and op-ed writers. Rabbis cannot claim some special insight into the affairs of the world. If anything, our specialty is less about understanding the working of society than it is about understanding the working of individuals. Of course, we may make pronouncements on politics if we care to, and our synagogues can host public discussions on the issues, but we serve our members best when we address their concerns—their hopes and fears—as well as our visions and ideals.

Rabbi Peter H. Schweitzer
The City Congregation for
Humanist Judaism
New York, NY

RENEWAL

An evangelical Christian pastor said that Bible-loving Christians come to different conclusions about the issues of our day, including abortion. He concluded that it was not his work to tell them for whom to vote, but to remind them of their loyalty to the Kingdom of God.

I resonate with him. If politics in the synagogue means endorsing one candidate or party over another, then I don't want politics in my shul. (Besides, it's not legal, at least in the U.S.!) However, it is appropriate to focus on the criteria we use to choose our governments.

A congregant asked me whether I would rather live in a town with no limits on wealth where some would always be poor, or where there would be no poor because there were limits placed on wealth. He was surprised when I said the latter. I explained to him that the Torah mandated sabbatical and jubilee years designed to accomplish this purpose and that the higher ethical principle was to minimize poverty.

Expressing a commitment to bringing these ideals into practice is a way to evaluate the merits of governments. Without it, Judaism is a hollow shell. With it, it is vibrant, alive with the reality of God and committed to a higher purpose.

Rabbi Daniel Siegel
Alliance for Jewish Renewal
Philadelphia, PA

RECONSTRUCTIONIST

Judaism, as a tradition of values, demands our involvement in public affairs. From Isaiah to Maimonides to Judith Plaskow, thoughtful Jews concur with Elie Wiesel: "Indifference is not an option."

Where we gather in real time (*bet knesset*), we address issues of the day. Where we study (*bet sefer*), the learning must lead to action. Even public prayer (*bet tefilah*) requires nine others. Every function of a synagogue demands our engagement with current societal needs.

Congregations discuss values, and with them, political issues. But promote political parties? Prohibited. Candidates? We can't.

Internal Revenue Service regulations rightly steer synagogues clear of endorsing parties or candidates. We should be humble about our own positions, while honoring shuls as "big tents." Rabbis' leanings may appear in the paper, but not the pulpit. Resources from groups like the Interfaith Alliance help us walk that ethical and legal line.

Yet we must not bifurcate between "spiritual" and "political." The *yotzer* nature blessing should motivate us to stem global warming; our "Redemption Song," Mi Chamocha, should recall those too impoverished or oppressed to be free. These are political and spiritual concerns in which upcoming elections loom large. Avoiding them, we risk irrelevance.

Bless the tradition that encourages us to grapple, to take respectful action, and to vote for whomever we deem likeliest to heal our country and our world.

Rabbi Fred Scherlinder Dobb
Adat Shalom Reconstructionist
Congregation
Bethesda, MD

REFORM

Issues, not individuals. Policies, not partisanship. Concerns, not candidates. These guidelines should direct synagogues as they chart their critical role. Global warming, Middle East peace, health care reform, the role of government in securing a safety net for Americans in need, immigration policy, confronting terrorism effectively, economic hardship—these are just some of the great moral issues and political challenges confronting America. Synagogues have long been powerful prophetic voices in American public life and must continue to be so. Educational debates and presentations are candidates for rabbinic sermons; adult education classes, social action, social service and advocacy programs constitute appropriate ways of raising awareness of such issues.

Traditionally, Jews vote at much higher rates than other Americans, yet some studies indicate a fall-off among those under 40. Therefore, every synagogue in the nation should engage in voter registration campaigns, ensure that every member is registered when they turn 18 and undertake "Get Out the Vote" efforts, using phone banks, email and listservs. This is particularly important with our young, because habits forged in first elections will last a lifetime.

The key legal limitation on synagogues is that they cannot spend one penny, or one second of staff time, supporting or opposing a candidate or party. It is also good policy: The last thing we need is to tear our synagogues apart over which candidates they should oppose or support. By sticking to issues and not candidates, synagogues can fulfill our obligation of prophetic witness without violating the law.

Rabbi David Saperstein
Religious Action Center
of Reform Judaism
Washington, DC

CONSERVATIVE

Recently, I was urged to teach my congregation about the developing situation between Israel and Iran because it might be a mortal threat to Israel. Since I have no greater expertise than many members of my community, I responded, in part, by speaking of "the belief that I share with all my rabbinic predecessors that knowledge of Torah and Jewish spirituality are the bedrock of strength and tenacity in any Jewish community. That's my post, and I shall not abandon it to take on someone else's assignment. God forbid that we should ever turn all of our rabbis into political analysts and military advisers. Judaism, and thus Israel itself, would be dangerously, if not disastrously, impoverished."

On the other hand, when it is argued—to take one example—that torture can be tolerated in extraordinary times because mortal threats to the nation override normal legal and ethical constraints, I am duty bound to teach that (a) Judaism has never believed that all steps are legitimate when attempting to save a life; (b) one may not simply assume without argument that threats to a nation are different from threats to individuals in this respect; and (c) torture in interrogation desecrates the divine image in every human being to which an abundance of classical texts testify.

On such issues, I do preach and teach. When one does so, however, one should never lose the ability to say to oneself those four very civilizing words: "I might be wrong."

Rabbi Gordon Tucker
Temple Israel Center
White Plains, NY

MODERN ORTHODOX

This question offers a classic case of "on the one hand . . . on the other hand." On the one hand: Judaism asks us to live religiously in every aspect of life. The prophets challenged kings' moral failure, royal exploitation of the people and favoritism to the powerful and wealthy. Therefore, rabbis should discuss burning political issues, apply Torah principles to them and maybe even endorse (or reject) candidates.

On the other hand: Most rabbis know less about politics than well-informed analysts—who may be their congregants. So rabbis are likely to dissipate their credibility by indulging in political analysis.

Furthermore, religious interventions frequently harm the political process. Democracy depends on negotiations and compromises amid constantly changing conditions. Religious approaches tend to wrap issues in the mantle of absolute values and eternal, unchanging divine commandments, which block compromise. Religious interventions have led to extremist, sometimes violent politics. Who can forget how right-wing, religious rabbis denounced Israel's offer of territorial compromises and two important Orthodox rabbis spoke menacingly about the right to kill Israel's prime minister?

In the U.S., polarization, government gridlock and the culture wars of the past two decades reflect, in part, the evangelical intervention in American politics. Jews also worry that "Christianization" of American politics may roll back Jewish gains in becoming fully equal in American public life.

So on which hand should we act? Since it is illegal under American law for non-profit, tax-exempt organizations to take part in politics, rabbis in synagogues should not be in politics.

Rabbi Yitz Greenberg
New York, NY

SEPHARDIC

Politics is inappropriate for discussion in mixed company. Political opinions are considered highly personal and extremely sensitive in our culture. The advocacy of any particular viewpoint in a place of worship is almost certain to cause offense and is likely to alienate congregants who disagree. To ensure that our synagogues are warm and comfortable "homes away from home," it is imperative that the pulpit not be used as a political soapbox.

On the other hand, a rabbi's primary role is to serve as a teacher and spiritual guide, and any light that the Torah's wisdom may shed on political matters is certainly worthy of being shared with one's congregation. Thus, the approach I adopt is twofold. I attempt to model the application of traditional Jewish methods of critical thought and moral analysis to matters of public policy by demonstrating how one must try to penetrate beneath the surface of political debate, cast aside the rhetoric and then clearly identify and precisely define the issues.

Furthermore, I like to encourage my congregants to assume full responsibility for their "take" on a given political point, diligently studying it from all sides, contemplating its nuances rigorously and not allowing the media or "spin doctors" to do their thinking for them. All the while I strive to keep my personal views out of the picture and hope that the tools with which I equip my congregants help them in their quests to develop well-informed and reasonable ideas.

Rabbi Joshua Maroof
Magen David Sephardic Congregation
Rockville, MD

A re there times when a rabbi must express his or her political opinion from the pulpit, even if it is likely to spark controversy? (2012)
Though it covers some of the same ground, this second version of the question applies even to rabbis who answered "No" to the first one. Rabbis who are reticent about sharing their political views may experience a "Thus far and no farther" moment and speak out. Others, citing the prophetic tradition, draw a distinction between a declaration of partisan politics and one of moral principle.

INDEPENDENT

When someone once asked me where I stood on Israel, I responded: "Mostly in Safed, and then a week in Jerusalem, and, where possible, on the sidewalk." And when recently I was asked if I believed in same-sex marriage, my response was: "I believe married couples should try to be more creative and not have sex the same way all the time."

During all the years that I served as a pulpit rabbi, I never once introduced my personal political opinions. It is my deep, deep belief that rabbis should use the pulpit as a rare and precious opportunity to share the richness of our ancient tradition. The pulpit is the only venue through which most Jews these days are likely to get a smidgen of a semblance of Jewish knowledge. Political opinions they can get from the opinion-saturated media, Jewish and otherwise. When national or world politics affects us as Jews, the rabbi's role is not to pontificate personal political opinions but to help the congregation explore what is so unique about being Jewish that it should matter to us at all. It is not our place to sway but to inspire. And that is my personal political opinion.

Rabbi Gershon Winkler
Walking Stick Foundation
Thousand Oaks, CA

HUMANIST

I have always thought congregations ought to be open communities where a range of views can be tolerated side by side. We don't all hold the same theological beliefs, and we don't all subscribe to the same political opinions. In my community, while there may be a preponderance of atheists and agnostics, there are also those with abstract god-beliefs, albeit not ones that include personal prayer. Likewise, we may be mostly center-to-left in our politics, but we have members who sit on both sides of the aisle—even within the same family.

Rabbis have a special opportunity, by virtue of their unique bully pulpit, to speak out on an array of topics from the mundane to the controversial. While I believe in the idea of a "free pulpit," I don't think a rabbi's voice has much weight or credibility unless it is already bolstered by the overwhelming support of the community that has engaged his or her services. In this sense, rabbis really are hired to preach to the choir. A congregation doesn't generally hire a leader for the purpose of sparking controversy. Excitement, maybe, but turmoil, no. More active participation, certainly. Deeper and more honest self-accounting, sure. But castigation and condemnation and taking highly unpopular positions, not at all.

I know that some rabbis seek out opportunities to be provocative. This is not my style. I prefer to examine issues on a meta-level. Why, for example, is such an issue so controversial? What is at stake? What makes it so difficult for opposing sides to hear each other? How do we resolve our differences if there is such a divide? Can we find common ground? And if not, how do we manage to coexist? These, in my mind, are the real provocative questions.

Rabbi Peter H. Schweitzer
The City Congregation for
Humanistic Judaism
New York, NY

RENEWAL

"Rabbis and politics." To get an animated discussion going in a group of rabbis, just say those three words. The same thing would happen if I were to say these words to members of my congregation. My president would start to wonder what I was planning and whether I might endanger our precious 501(c)3 status.

Despite all of that, I believe there are indeed times when a rabbi can, should and even must discuss a political opinion. If there is an issue (not a candidate) about which a rabbi is passionate, and if there is a solid tie-in to Jewish ethics or tradition, then I believe the rabbi owes it to the congregation to be open and candid. A topic for me that strikes this chord is LGBTQ rights, and I have talked about this issue at different times, especially in connection with marriage legislation. It was my topic for Yom Kippur afternoon this year. I made clear what I felt and why I felt that way, and I invited others to consider my opinions. However, I never suggested how someone should vote—just that they need to do so every election they can, whether they vote for or against any issue or person.

Rabbi Shafir Lobb
Temple Beth El Israel
Port Saint Lucie, FL

REFORM

Reform Judaism attempts to follow in the footsteps of the prophets, and one of its hallmarks is the emphasis on leading an ethical life, incorporating ethical mitzvot into our daily deeds and activities and striving always to create a world of peace, justice and freedom. Reform Judaism calls upon each of us to find within Judaism the moral and ethical lessons that can guide our behavior and our decisions. It is with these moral teachings in mind that a rabbi can—and sometimes should—address political issues from the pulpit. Without expressing her own personal opinion, a rabbi has the responsibility to teach her congregation about Jewish values and the Jewish obligation to act justly. A rabbi need not tell others what to believe. A rabbi should not abuse the pulpit to benefit one political position over another, which, by the way, could jeopardize a congregation's tax-exempt status.

Like the prophets, a rabbi should lead his congregation in wrestling with the issues and in speaking up and speaking out when peace, justice and freedom are at stake. Those moments are not always so clearcut, though. What appears unjust for one might seem just to another. So, as Reform rabbis, we should bring our congregants to Torah so they can make meaning of it for themselves.

Rabbi Laura Novak Winer
Fresno, CA

CONSERVATIVE

I do not shy away from controversy. Sometimes my role as rabbi demands that I say things my community does not want to hear. I understand that I am a leader in the community and that this means sometimes taking an unpopular stance.

Rarely, if ever, do I express my political views publicly. I think it presumptuous to suggest that I know the right course of action when considering issues as complicated as national security and economic competitiveness. I am proud that my congregants do not know how I vote.

Several years ago, as our country debated health care reform, I noticed that many of my colleagues were endorsing President Obama's proposed legislation and encouraging their congregations to do the same. I was uncomfortable taking such a stance. I believed that my role as rabbi was to show that Judaism has wisdom to consider when debating health care. I wrote an article that outlined how Jewish values might inform a conversation about health care, and I gave a sermon in which we studied some relevant texts. I suggested that both access and affordability are Jewish values, and I encouraged my congregation to apply these values to the public debate and decide which proposal would cause a reality most in line with the Jewish values we had discussed.

My practice is to teach Jewish texts and encourage my congregants to draw their own conclusions about the political issues of our times.

Rabbi Amy Wallk Katz
Temple Beth El
Springfield, MA

MODERN ORTHODOX

Yes, there are moments when a rabbi must speak out from the pulpit—whether on a political question or on a spiritual/moral/religious one—even though this will spark controversy or even strong backlash. Rabbis are meant to be spiritual, moral and communal leaders. If they never challenge their congregants, they are not leaders. They are schleppers—or panderers. On the other hand, if they are clueless or overdo this confrontation—if they cannot judge the limits of their people—they may lose their congregation, or even their job. The classic statement on this issue is Rabbi Israel Salanter's: "Any rabbi whose congregation never considered firing him [her] is no rabbi. Any rabbi whose congregation does fire him [her] is no mensch."

I can't write a general description in advance that will identify the moment when it is mandatory to speak out no matter what the cost. But, as with pornography, I will recognize it when I see it. I believe that rabbis with genuine stature have an inner compass that tells them: Now.

Rabbi Yitz Greenberg
Riverdale, NY

ORTHODOX

The answer is, of course, when those political opinions directly affect values issues. Support for Israel is an obvious example. If President Obama demands a halt to building in Jerusalem, Israel's eternal and undivided capital, rabbis must speak out. Conversely, if George H. W. Bush wanted to tie Israel's hands with regard to Soviet Jewish immigration, the same would have been true.

And consider the recent gas attack in Syria. The Jews are entrusted by God in the Torah with the commandment, "Thou shalt not stand idly by the blood of your neighbor." How can we allow innocent Arab children to be gassed to death and do nothing? Rabbis have an absolute responsibility to speak out against genocide and mass murder.

The same applies to many other issues. Take, say, the persecution of gays in Arab countries, where they are murdered as alleged collaborators with Israel. Or the debate over whether Egypt should receive military aid, or whether the United States has a responsibility to object to Vladimir Putin's continued encroachment on human rights in Russia. Rabbis must be values exponents.

Rabbi Shmuley Boteach
Englewood, NJ

CHABAD

Judaism never saw itself as a religion with a specialized interest in just spiritual matters. It is a tool for living that informs and enriches all areas of life, private as well as public, personal as well as civic.

So should a rabbi address issues that are being debated in the public arena and present the perspective that Torah and Judaism bring to these issues? The answer is: Of course! What should he talk about—things that have no bearing upon people's lives? Things that are of no practical consequence to us as a society?

That an issue "is likely to spark controversy" might at times be all the more reason to speak out and make a difference for a person whose job description is to teach the Torah's approach to life.

As for speaking out in support or denunciation of a specific person or party, I aspire to follow the principled example set by the Lubavitcher Rebbe, who had the ability to articulate a Torah-based perspective on so many issues, including contentious ones, without mentioning names or political parties. I find it more effective to speak about the issues themselves, without the divisiveness and one-upmanship that has unfortunately come to dominate our political discourse.

Rabbi Eliezer Zalmanov
Chabad of Northwest Indiana
Munster, IN

Is democracy a Jewish idea?

O ne of the endless left-right disputes in politics is whether American constitutional democracy is fundamentally religious in inspiration or a secular product of the Enlightenment. The two sides mostly talk past each other: Church-state separation! In God We Trust! Beyond the polarization, though, there is some common ground. Here, it's the two Orthodox rabbis who are most specific and emphatic in crediting one foundational Jewish concept as the root and basis of democratic self-governance: b'tzelem Elohim, the idea that every human being is created in the image of God.

In other contexts, such as human rights, b'tzelem Elohim is often invoked in support of liberal or even leftist views; in this case, though the liberal rabbis appreciate democracy and lay claim to various aspects of it, their claims are more varied and pragmatic. But many still find a way to say yes. This isn't surprising either. When an idea is as central and as widely revered as democracy, it's hard to resist taking at least some credit for it. (Published in 2012.)

INDEPENDENT

Democracy is not a Jewish idea. In fact, it falls short of the Jewish idea.

We unanimously accepted the guidance of Torah at Sinai (Exodus 24:3 and 7) and committed ourselves to its system of social, economic and national law—thus, democracy. But this system included accepting our tribal elders and judges as the sole authorities who could interpret those laws (Deuteronomy 17:11)—elders appointed by other elders or divine ordination, not popular vote. The sages did rule that such authorities could not enact decrees, divinely ordained or not, which the majority of the community would find difficult to implement (*Talmud Bavli*, Baba Batra 60b). And the rules were often suspended or outright abrogated in response to the special needs of the times or of individual circumstances (Berachot 54a). So while Jewish law and practice are not decided by majority vote of the nation, as in a democracy, Judaism traditionally looked askance at blanket codification and considered it akin to "burning a Torah scroll" (Terumah 14b). The application of Torah must remain fluid, addressing not only the ideals of the nation but the needs and concerns of the individual.

> *Rabbi Gershon Winkler*
> *Walking Stick Foundation*
> *Thousand Oaks, CA*

HUMANIST

Jews have a long history of overcompensating for our equally long history of victimization, belittlement and exclusion by extolling our great contributions to Western civilization. So we have laid claim to inventing human dignity, freedom and equality; equitable laws; a day off each week; an elaborate system of care for the indigent and impoverished, and so on.

But can we say we invented democracy? Or, if we give this one to the Greeks, can we assert that we embrace its ideals? It depends what time period we're talking about. Historically, we were the people of theocracy. Theocracies are based on divine revelation, not deliberative debate. Leaders were divinely appointed. Priests, and later rabbis, ruled autocratically. Theocracies stifle discussion and personal freedom, while democracies tend to nourish freedom of expression and human rights. Since the Enlightenment, democracy has been the best safeguard for Jews. That is why we laid claim as soon as we could to our rights—and should work just as hard to protect these rights for all peoples, whose democratically guaranteed equality and freedom will secure our own.

Rabbi Peter H. Schweitzer
The City Congregation for
Humanistic Judaism
New York, NY

RENEWAL

In Deuteronomy 17:14-20, the Torah sets limits to the powers of a king. He must not pile up wives or wealth for himself or horses for his army. He is forbidden to "send the people back to Mitzrayim" [Egypt] to buy horses. This probably meant that the king must not impose harsh taxes or forced labor to pay for an army; cavalry were so expensive that only an aggressive empire such as Egypt could afford them. The king was also required to write—and then to read every day—a copy of the Deuteronomic protections for the poor and the limits on his own power. Levites were to be present to oversee his reading.

Most modern scholars think the book of Deuteronomy emerged from a time of social upheaval when there were actual Israelite kings. The prohibitions on what a king may do fit well with what Solomon and his tyrannical son Rehoboam did. So the passage may be analogous to the rebukes of King George in the U.S. Declaration of Independence. Are these rules, then, the roots of democracy? Some Jewish communities have adopted the practice of reading this Torah passage each July 4 and then reading the Declaration as the prophetic Haftarah—blessings, trope and all.

Ancient Israel was not a democracy, but neither was the United States in 1776. Perhaps we can see this Torah passage as the roots of constitutional monarchy—a challenge to tyranny that could slowly ripen toward the democracy that we have even now not quite achieved.

Rabbi Arthur Waskow
The Shalom Center
Philadelphia, PA

RECONSTRUCTIONIST

Of course, classical Judaism didn't foresee every facet of modern democracy, and yes, non-democratic tendencies also abound. But democracy is Jewish just like Shabbat (ancient Babylon's calendar had a special seventh day), the Afikomen (a Greek import), or Maimonides' *Guide for the Perplexed* (influenced by Greek and Islamic philosophy).

Certain ideas, latent in early Judaism, become central through encounter with the larger world. Though Torah emerged in a pre-democratic era, it still has hints: "Would that all God's people were prophets" (Numbers 11:29); "You all stand here today" (Deuteronomy 29:9). The Talmud always records minority opinions in debates and legal proceedings. Its rabbis upend Torah in order to establish majority rule (Baba Metzia 59b misreads Exodus 23:2 to say "Incline after the majority"). And they admit a communal role in judicial matters ("Torah is only received via havurah [community/fellowship]", Berachot 63b).

Eighteenth-century democracy's spirit of expanding enfranchisement bore Jewish fruit in early Reform efforts. And in the last century, Reconstructionist founder Mordecai Kaplan offered a thorough synthesis of democratic and Jewish ideals. Judaism always has evolved, Kaplan reminds us, and always will. Thank God, Jewish evolution has taken us permanently toward democracy.

Rabbi Fred Scherlinder Dobb
Adat Shalom Reconstructionist
Congregation
Bethesda, MD

REFORM

In the book of Samuel, the prophet, priest and judge, we witness one of the biblical conversations about governance and its underlying values. The Israelites, frustrated with their governance system, ask Samuel to anoint a king. Neither God nor Samuel thinks this is a good idea; they fear that a king would take advantage of the people and usurp God's place as sovereign of the universe. But they listen to the Israelites and anoint Saul, a secular leader. Samuel remains nearby as an adviser to Saul, a religious leader and a prophet—God's voice to the people.

While staying within a religious framework, this narrative demonstrates the roots of democratic values in this ancient Jewish community. A dialogue takes place between the people and God, through Samuel. The Israelites have a voice in establishing their system. Without destroying their covenant or denying God's sovereignty, they are able to create a system in which day-to-day governance is overseen and shared by the people—in which there are checks and balances, self-government and pluralism and the secular leader is answerable to the people he serves and ultimately to God.

Rabbi Laura Novak Winer
Fresno, CA

CONSERVATIVE

Democracy has four key elements. It chooses and replaces the government through free and fair elections. It provides for the active participation of citizens in politics and civic life. It protects the human rights of all citizens. And its laws apply equally to all. Democracy in its entirety is not a traditional Jewish idea, since, according to the Bible, the ideal form of government is a theocracy that rules according to God's law. In practice, this doesn't work, because God's law is interpreted and enforced by human beings, who are always fallible and sometimes corrupt. Modern Western thinking, informed by the abuses of theocratic forms of government, holds that democracy is the best form of government for delivering the four elements listed above.

Although the Torah emphasizes a polity that looks to God, other biblical values promote the rule of law, including equality of all before the law, rejection of absolute rule by autocrats who put themselves above the law, and separation of powers among kings, priests and prophets. These Jewish ideas and practices, radical in their time, are echoed in the values of contemporary democracy.

Rabbi Amy Wallk Katz
Temple Beth El
Springfield, MA

MODERN ORTHODOX

Democracy is not a Jewish idea—if you mean that Judaism taught the world the idea or that Jews practiced it first, as they did with monotheism. Democracy was not practiced in biblical times or in the diaspora, although, in the Middle Ages, lay people in the Jewish community had more input in their government than their Christian neighbors had in theirs.

However, some fundamental building blocks of democracy are derived from Judaism. The tradition's core concept is that every person is created in the image of God. According to the Talmud, this means that every person has the intrinsic dignity of infinite value, equality and uniqueness. Those dignities are honored best in a democracy. The Torah taught that there should be equality before the law and that the king (or any ruler) is not above the law. Add to that the central Jewish messages of liberation for the slaves, the right to rest on Shabbat for all persons of whatever rank and station, laws that frame and guide the society (as with our Constitution) and the obligation for society to assure the basic needs of the poor through tzedakah, and you have the basis not only of democracy but of a welfare state.

Rabbi Yitz Greenberg
Riverdale, NY

ORTHODOX

I have long lamented that so many Jewish values have been appropriated by other nations without attribution. The Jews gave the world God, but his name today is Jesus and Allah. We gave the world the Sabbath, but today it's called Sunday. And we gave the world the Ten Commandments, but today the concept is called ethics or morality.

Nowhere is this more dramatic than in the Bible's pronouncement that every human being is created equally in the image of God, a concept today called democracy.

Democracy is absolutely counterintuitive. The blatant inequality of man seems evident. Why should someone with little knowledge of economics have the same vote as, say, Milton Friedman on fixing the economy? Why should someone utterly unversed in foreign affairs have equal political voice with Henry Kissinger? Because the Bible says all people are equal, not by virtue of knowledge, resources, intelligence or area of expertise but because each is a child of God, stamped with the divine image. And there is no source for the equality of man—the very foundation of democratic ideals—other than the Bible.

Rabbi Shmuley Boteach
Englewood, NJ

CHABAD

Democracy is most certainly a Jewish idea. So are monarchy, theocracy and even a little bit of anarchy. Let me explain with a story. The sixth rebbe of Chabad, Rabbi Yosef Yitzchak Schneersohn (1880-1950), was once approached by two men who wanted him to settle an intellectual argument: Whether communism or capitalism was closer to the economic system espoused by the Torah. Rabbi Yosef Yitzchak answered, "Capitalism and communism are both imperfect systems, and yet each contains some aspect of truth as well. The Torah, in contrast, which is the essence of good and truth, transcends and combines the positive elements of both." In other words, no one economic system, or philosophy, or sports team, or flavor of ice cream is the "official Torah-endorsed" variety. The same is true of government. There are certainly elements of democracy represented in Torah's values, but Torah cannot be limited to just one approach. That is the difference between the finite and the infinite.

Rabbi Shais Taub
Chabad.org
Pittsburgh, PA

SEPHARDIC

Many of the ideals of democracy are indeed deeply rooted in Jewish tradition and teachings. The attitude of the Torah to democratic government is far less clear. On the surface, the Bible appears to endorse (somewhat hesitantly) the institution of monarchy, and it presents the philosopher or theologian king, best represented by King David, as its prime example of political leadership. On the other hand, a minority of our sages, most notably Rabbi Avraham Ibn Ezra and Don Isaac Abarbanel, understood the Torah's acceptance of monarchy as a compromise reluctantly introduced to meet the needs of a nation that knew no other way.

Democracy serves to prevent tyranny by placing power in the hands of the people. However, this very distribution of power is also a weakness, since it assigns equal weight to the opinion of the wise and the foolish, the experienced and the sheltered, and the educated and the ignorant. The result is a culture in which, rather than guide the populace to think critically and discourse intelligently about policy and values, politicians manipulate the masses with commercials, sound bites and photo ops in order to win their votes for all the wrong reasons. Ultimately, as the Bible states, a society in which the wisest thinkers and finest leaders determined policy without having to bow to public opinion would undoubtedly be ideal. Realistically, though, such a society might be vulnerable to a takeover by violent extremists, corrupt demagogues or elitist tyrants. So in the absence of divine guidance in our choice of a king, the survival of civilization as we know it depends upon democracy.

Rabbi Joshua Maroof
Magen David Sephardic Congregation
Rockville, MD

PART SIX

THE NATURE OF THE UNIVERSE

Even for the most disputatious of peoples, there's a point when argument breaks down. The truly universal questions—life, death, consciousness, redemption—are an invitation to indulge in unquestioning belief, or galloping imagination, or maybe some combination of the two. Is the universe best understood rationally or mystically? Can time be described prosaically or only in poetry? In this era of string theory and post-Einsteinian quantum physics, it's hard to broach ultimate topics without mingling all these vocabularies.

Just a little tweak, and some of these questions could have been asked in the chapter on science: What's really out there? How can we know for sure? In spite of the lack of evidence, though—or, more likely, because of it—the rabbis and their predecessors here outdo themselves, taking us on a journey over vast stretches of time and space.

What is the Jewish relationship to time?

C oncepts of time are threaded through Jewish tradition. Some are foundational to Western civilization, while others are metaphorical or even whimsical. Asked to muse, the rabbis rise to the occasion, ranging through geology and physics, eternity and memory. Though expressed in different terms, all reflect a central sensibility of a religion with a deep appreciation of the here and now. (Published in 2017.)

INDEPENDENT

Time is an invitation. Both words share the same root: *z'mahn*. It is written: "The life of man is like a breath exhaling; his days are like a passing shadow" (Psalms 144:4). The midrash adds, "Not like the shadow of a tree, but like the shadow of a bird while she is flying": The shadow of a tree vanishes when the sun shifts, but the shadow of a bird moves with the bird in flight.

"We journey with and within time," my teacher, the late Rav Efraim Zeitchik, taught. "We ride the waves of time, whether the tides are high or low. We eat time, we drink time, are shadowed by time. How can we truly know life when whatever happened is already past, and what is going to happen is yet unknown, and we are oblivious to what is happening?" The missing link is the "invitation," the knowledge of time in the present, the shadow of our wings while we are in flight. Otherwise, "We can live even a thousand years and still feel like it's been only a single day" (*Zohar,* Vol. 1, folio 223b). Time is the thread, and we are the weavers. And our lives are the fabric waiting to be woven.

Rabbi Gershon Winkler
Walking Stick Foundation
Cedar Glen, CA

HUMANIST

From creation until the end of days, Jews have been and will forever be fixated on time. Historically and traditionally, we locate ourselves on a continuum from the six days of creation until the messianic or apocalyptic end of days. In principle, and often in practice, we parcel out time into smaller pieces: a continuum of weeks with their Sabbaths, months with their new moons and years with their new beginnings.

Once we marked time by the stars and the moon and became expert observers of the skies. But we had a problem when the lunar year lagged behind the solar year and the holidays threatened to rotate untethered away from their seasons. So we developed a sophisticated calendar that periodically adjusts lunar and solar timetables with our own Jewish version of a leap year. This system gave rise to another quality of our relationship with time: flexibility. Some years, we say, the Jewish holidays are early; some years they are late. But one thing they are not is on time. And so we have to adjust ourselves constantly to this slippery timetable. Whether time rushes on or stands still, we have a choice: to live in the past, in the future, in the moment, or maybe even in all three phases simultaneously!

Rabbi Peter H. Schweitzer
The City Congregation for
Humanistic Judaism
New York, NY

RENEWAL

Jewish practice gives me the opportunity to start over each day, each month, each year. What a gift! I get to wipe the slate clean and begin again. And while the whole world is complaining about not having enough time, I have Shabbat, the experience of timelessness. On Shabbat I shrug my shoulders and say, "Oh, well! Can't get anything done." I turn off my computer, put my to-do list aside and wait for the kiss of the Infinite.

I get some respite from the seemingly relentless engine of my ambition. And I do return—renewed, refreshed and sometimes even laughing, with a wider perspective, a deeper breath. Shabbat is my teacher, showing me how to relax and giving me a larger context for my life. It teaches me to engage with my time-bound work differently. The experience of timelessness gives me access to a different source of creative energy.

Each Shabbat, we are invited into that place beyond the confines of time, as we commemorate the Exodus from Mitzrayim (narrow places). Shabbat sets us free from the narrow places—in this case, our addiction to the time-bound world of achievement, consumption, buying and selling, quantifying and comparing.

Rabbi Shefa Gold
Center for Devotional Energy and
Ecstatic Practice
Jemez Springs, NM

RECONSTRUCTIONIST

One of the great insights of Einsteinian physics is that time is the fourth dimension. One of the ancient insights of Jewish and other religious traditions is that time has a sacred dimension as well. In ordinary or secular time, one moment is just like the next. In Judaism, there are times that stand out, times when the past, present and future meet. These are holy times or, as Marilynne Robinson wrote in *Gilead*, the time of "the eternal breaking in on the temporal."

The first mitzvah in the Torah commanded to the Israelites as a people is about making time holy. "This month shall mark for you the beginning of the months; it shall be the first of the months of the year for you" (Exodus 12:2). "For you," the sages teach, meaning it is you, human beings, who have the power to make time holy. You set the calendar. You can live according to the dings and dongs of your phone or according to the flow of sacred and ordinary time. Traditionally, Rosh Hodesh (the beginning of the Jewish month) has to be declared by witnesses who see the new moon. It doesn't just happen. We have to commit. Those moments, whether they mark passages in our lives, mark the week with Shabbat or mark the year with holidays, are made by our attention to them.

They are also made in community. The word in the Torah for sacred time, *moed*, is also the word for gathering place, *moad*. When we gather together at our appointed times with a full heart and full awareness, we can experience "the eternal breaking in on the temporal."

Rabbi Caryn Broitman
Martha's Vineyard Hebrew Center
Vineyard Haven, MA

REFORM

The Talmud states that each Jew is obligated to say 100 blessings a day. This compels a person to mark discernible sacred moments—giving thanks before and after eating, or taking notice of beautiful sights such as a rainbow or a majestic tree—as well as those we might not normally consider sacred, such as using the bathroom or hearing distressing news. Each hour of our day, each day of our week and each week of our year presents us with occasions to find the holy in the quotidian.

Rabbi Abraham Joshua Heschel taught that when Jews lost our collective connection to sacred space, the Temple in Jerusalem, we had to shift our collective focus to sacred time. Our holidays align with the seasons of the year; our prayer life aligns with the rising and setting of the sun as well as with the generations of those who lived before us and will live after us. Many Jews joke about living on "Jewish standard time," which is to say that we always run ten minutes late. But in fact, to live on Jewish time is to see each day as sacred and worthy of blessing.

Rabbi Laura Novak Winer
Fresno, CA

CONSERVATIVE

Sadly, I sat down to answer this question just after sitting shiva for my oldest brother, David Ira Wallk. It made me remember how Judaism uses time as a tool. In Judaism, time brings focus, structure and meaning to our weeks (Shabbat), our years (Passover, Shavuot, Sukkot) and our lives (Rosh Hashanah and Yom Kippur). Besides these communal experiences, Judaism also uses time to guide the individual. Long before modern psychology discovered "grief work," the rabbis established a staged series of steps to manage mourning. There are six basic phases of the bereavement cycle. Each has a specific time period and rituals that assist the mourner through the grieving process. The nature of our relationship to the deceased varies, but Judaism assumes that there is something universal about grief.

I have been a mourner three times: My father died 25 years ago, my mother two and a half years ago and my brother last month. In all three instances, I have greatly appreciated how my experience was grounded by Judaism's use of time to mourn.

Rabbi Amy Wallk Katz
Temple Beth El
Springfield, MA

MODERN ORTHODOX

Jews practically invented time, or at least its significance and meaning. Jewish religion broke from the pagan and Stoic-Hellenist understanding that time loops in endless circularity, going nowhere, in an eternal recurrence. Judaism taught that time has a positive direction. The world is moving from its present state of conflict, suffering and war toward an ultimate redemption—a messianic state where war, conflict, oppression and poverty will be overcome. (The Bible teaches that humans, in partnership with God, must do their share to make this happen. The purpose of human life is to build a just society and repair the world.)

Other cultures taught that the sequence of history was decline— from an original golden age to a silver to a bronze/copper era, to the present time which is the lowest ever. Judaism, as it were, invented progress. (Thomas Cahill pointed out that Jews gave the gift of "new and improved" to the world.) The end of days would outstrip the present. The world would become a Garden of Eden.

For 2,000 years of exile, Jews lived in time—in history and in their sacred calendar—without the rootedness in space that normal nations require. In our time, wholeness was restored as Jews became grounded again in space and homeland, alongside our roots in time and eternity.

Rabbi Yitz Greenberg
Riverdale, NY

ORTHODOX

The first time God spoke to the Jewish people as a community, he gave them a mitzvah that had to do with time, *hachodesh hazeh lachem rosh chadashim*, the commandment to identify the time of the new moon. This meant that human beings were going to call the shots. If they needed to delay a month, or add a new month to the year, they had that ability. God seems to be telling them, "Not only am I going to redeem you from the mindset of slavery, I'm also going to help you transcend what seems impossible to transcend, the last frontier, time." The fact that time only works in one direction is a bit of a mystery to us. We're used to every other physical movement or reaction going in two directions; time doesn't. It's a dimension of life we can't get a handle on at all. But Jews assert that it's not natural, that it was created and that the God who created it can transcend it. Stick with me, God says, and you can transcend time.

Rabbi Yitzchok Adlerstein
Loyola Law School
Los Angeles, CA

CHABAD

Time has always been essential to Jewish practice. There are specific times to pray, to welcome Shabbat, to rejoice and to reflect. But there is also a deeper relationship between time and Jewish practice. In explaining why a missed opportunity to fulfill a mitzvah can never be made right, Rabbi Schneur Zalman of Liadi, the founder of Chabad Hasidism and author of the *Tanya*, explains that each positive mitzvah at each particular time draws a unique energy into the world. So an opportunity to sanctify any given moment which is missed is an opportunity forever lost. The world will permanently be lacking that unique gift of divine light.

It was 50 years ago that his successor, the Rebbe—Rabbi Menachem M. Schneerson, of righteous memory—launched the mitzvah campaigns encouraging his Hasidim to reach out to Jews, including individuals they would likely never meet again and who might never engage Jewishly again, and offer them the opportunity to perform a mitzvah. These campaigns are credited with bringing Jewish pride and important Jewish precepts into the public consciousness. But equally important, the Rebbe taught us in a very tangible way about the intrinsic value of each and every moment. Each point in time has infinite potential, no matter what may have occurred before or what is to come after.

Rabbi Chaim A. Landa
Brooklyn, NY

Do Jews believe in an afterlife?

T he dramatic variety of answers to this question is fitting for a subject about which, as one rabbi notes, "By the time we know for sure, it'll be too late to tell." The rabbis don't just disagree about what will happen after we die; they disagree, some quite categorically, about what Jews think *will* happen.

Any religious or philosophical tradition can be expected to spend some thought on the unknowable matter of what happens after death. Judaism, in the popular view, is less focused on this than most; its bias toward this world and its struggles is pronounced. Still, 4,000 years of reflection have created an underappreciated wealth of philosophical, moral and metaphysical speculation. (Published in 2011.)

INDEPENDENT

Some Jews do; some Jews don't. The Torah makes no mention of what happens after death, only that we join our ancestors. Its emphasis is on life and living. While our ancient teachers taught about the world to come and how the soul lives on after death, they nonetheless encouraged humans to "walk before the Lord in the land of the living" (Psalms 116:9). I find it harder to believe that this life is all there is than to believe in an afterlife. Reward? Punishment? Seems to me we get plenty of both right here and now. When Rabbi Chanina tried to console his very sick colleague Rabbi Abba, he assured him that his suffering here and now would earn him a greater reward in the afterlife—to which Rabbi Abba responded, "I can do without this suffering or its reward, thank you very much."

Rabbi Gershon Winkler
Walking Stick Foundation
Thousand Oaks, CA

HUMANIST

Most people I know believe that this is the only life we'll ever know. They think that death means the demise of our physical being, and they don't put any stock in some kind of everlasting spiritual survival in a world to come. Nor do they place any bets on some kind of delayed system of reward and punishment to make up for the injustices of this world. Life is to be lived and appreciated in the here and now. Yet this down-to-earth orientation doesn't negate the possibility of an afterlife. Only it is an afterlife that continues where we have spent our lives. We all know the idea that we live on in our deeds and the ripple effect they spread out into the world. Likewise, we live on in the memories that people hold dear and cherish. And of course, we live on in our descendants who bear our names. More subtly, we also live on in the quirky mannerisms that we bequeath to the next generation. We laugh or tilt our head in a certain way that is likely to get replicated and be recognized in our offspring. How often also do we catch ourselves saying not only "just what my mother would have said" but with the same tone? Despite our determination to be our "own person" we inevitably internalize messages that have been passed down to us and now live on through us.

Rabbi Peter H. Schweitzer
The City Congregation for
Humanistic Judaism
New York, NY

RENEWAL

Two famous explanations of why we say Kaddish are: (1) the daily discipline supports the living through the grieving process; (2) the Kaddish's description of a realm of perfection beyond words helps the soul of the deceased travel to the next world. We have no way of telling the difference between these two views. Our experience of a relationship with the deceased is our main source of information about the soul's journey after death. Jewish tradition affirms a variety of beliefs about the afterlife. All are grounded in our sense of connection with important people in our lives who have died. For example, we may meet someone we feel we have more to say to in our dreams. Such meetings support the view of Moses Maimonides that people live on in spiritual form, available to reunite with us in a universal spiritual resurrection.

If we have had a difficult relationship with someone, we may go through a process of coming to terms with their misdeeds and their effect on us. This process supports the Talmudic view that some souls travel through purgatory. We do not know which view is empirically true, only which is consistent with our experience. In either case, Jewish tradition provides a year of community support during these powerful transitions.

Rabbi Laura Duhan Kaplan
Or Shalom
Vancouver, Canada

RECONSTRUCTIONIST

Congregants asking about an afterlife are usually seeking reassurance that a loved one is not entirely gone. In my pastoral role, I respond, "Yes, she lives on, through her influence on you and others, and through the difference she made on earth, which spreads like ripples on still water, starting clearly then slowly diminishing, but never disappearing entirely. And beyond that, who knows? Perhaps her soul is indeed still out there: hovering, loving, whole and happy at last."

For further exploration, I always suggest *Jewish Views of the Afterlife*, by Simcha Paull Raphael. The author outlines just how radically these views vary across centuries and continents. In short, Jewish views are resources, not dogma. The 13th-century scholar and poet Immanuel of Rome's Dante-esque yet deeply Jewish "Hell and Paradise" is great as myth, while rationally I'm with the neo-Kantian Hermann Cohen's notion of "social immortality," where legacy alone defines one's afterlife. Once we know for sure, it'll be too late to tell. But in memory and deed, and perhaps in spirit, as Raphael suggests, "Between the world of the living and the world of the dead there is a window, not a wall."

> *Rabbi Fred Scherlinder Dobb*
> *Adat Shalom Reconstructionist*
> *Congregation*
> *Bethesda, MD*

REFORM

I sometimes dream about my grandmother Rose Finkelstein, *z"l*. I awake in the morning contemplating what Nanny Rose came to tell me. I want to believe that she lives on in a different space but knows when I need her guidance. I want to believe that her nighttime visits guide me as she did when she was alive.

It isn't unheard of in Jewish tradition to speak about an afterlife. Our liturgy and texts often make mention of a "world to come." In *Pirkei Avot*, Rabbi Jacob said, "This world is like a foyer to the world to come. Prepare yourself in the foyer so that you may enter into the banquet hall" (4:21). Despite these allusions, we are urged to keep our focus and energies on this life we are living now. We are God's partners in striving for the perfection of this world. Abraham Joshua Heschel writes in *God in Search of Man*, "True, this world is only a 'vestibule to the world to come,' where we must prepare ourselves before we enter the 'banquet hall.' Yet, in the eyes of God, the endeavor and the participation are greater than the achievement and perfection." What awaits us after we die is immaterial. As Jews, as God's partners in creation, we have an obligation to do our part in living meaningful, ethical, productive lives here and now.

Rabbi Laura Novak Winer
Union for Reform Judaism
Fresno, CA

CONSERVATIVE

Simply put, yes—Judaism does assume that there is a world beyond this world. For example, the second blessing of the traditional Amidah prayer describes God as *michaye hamateem*—God who resurrects the dead. Maimonides made belief in the afterlife one of the Thirteen Principles of Faith. When I speak with students or congregants, I like to explain that there is life after life, but we cannot know exactly what it consists of because our human understanding is limited. Two excellent books written by Conservative rabbis can help the interested reader understand Jewish views of the afterlife. *The Death of Death*, by Rabbi Neil Gillman, explores the argument that while early books of the Hebrew Bible include little evidence of firm views on any kind of afterlife, later sources definitely discuss both eternity of the soul and bodily resurrection. *Does the Soul Survive?* by Rabbi Elie Spitz explores both his own experiences and classical Jewish texts. Spitz is certain that the soul survives long after the body dies.

Rabbi Amy Wallk Katz
Temple Beth El
Springfield, MA

ORTHODOX

Belief in the afterlife—a world to come in which the righteous get their true reward and the wicked get their deserved comeuppance—is a central teaching of traditional Judaism. This belief stems from the conviction that a loving God would not allow injustice to win. When the facts of life did not fit the Bible's emphasis on reward and punishment in the here and now, this faith in the afterlife was emphasized. In the

Middle Ages, when Jews suffered so much while enemies ruled the world, the stress on the world to come grew stronger. Some religious teachers taught that this life is "unimportant," and that one should live only to be worthy of eternal bliss. This view spilled over into asceticism and less respect for the body and material activity.

Early modernizers reversed direction. They validated Judaism and dismissed Christianity by insisting that Judaism is interested only in doing good in earthly life. Christianity was criticized as otherworldly, repressive and dreaming only of getting to heaven. It was described as cruel for condemning people to eternal damnation. This modern one-sided emphasis on mortal life robbed Jews of the profound consolation of eternal life and justice for all who suffered unjustly and innocently.

What is needed is the classical Jewish ability to hold both sides of a tension. Such a Judaism would inspire people to find God in the secular, to unite body and soul, to work for tikkun olam (repairing the world) in the here and now. At the same time, it would uphold the reality of the spirit and the immortality of the soul. This faith offers the consolation of a final reunion—with those we have loved and lost and with the *El Maleh Rachamim*, the Infinite God of Compassion.

Rabbi Yitz Greenberg
Riverdale, NY

SEPHARDIC

The Hebrew Bible alludes to the existence of an afterlife in several places. There is little doubt that Jews in biblical times subscribed to a belief in some kind of life after death. After all, there was no nation on earth without such a conviction, and there is no indication that the Jews differed from their gentile neighbors in this regard. The nature of the afterlife as understood in Judaism, however—as with the nature of God and the nature of the human soul—is purely metaphysical, shrouded in mystery and thus deemed inaccessible to our limited intellects. When dealing with such esoteric subject matter, the Bible's approach is to keep its verbiage to a bare minimum rather than offer grossly inaccurate anthropomorphic descriptions. Whereas the Talmud and Midrash tend to offer more colorful depictions of the world to come, these are understood by our tradition to be elaborate metaphors rather than representations of literal truth. The essence of our belief is that the purely spiritual component of a human being does not perish with the death of the body; instead, it continues to perceive and enjoy the infinite wisdom of the Creator for all eternity.

Rabbi Joshua Maroof
Magen David Sephardic Congregation
Rockville, MD

CHABAD

Consistent with its "this world" orientation, Judaism believes in an afterlife, but remarkably, it is here on this earth. While Judaism embraces a belief in Eden, heaven and paradise, these are all transitory places where the soul goes after death until it is ultimately reinvested in a body when the world achieves a perfect state in the messianic era. This topic, which constitutes a monumental and fascinating disputation between Maimonides and Nachmanides, is a subject to which I devoted an entire book, entitled *The Wolf Shall Lie with the Lamb*.

But in a wider sense, everyone—atheists and agnostics included—believes in an afterlife. One year on the eve of Yom Kippur, I debated atheist Christopher Hitchens and made the point that none would dispute that a man's good acts live on as an eternal legacy after him, which is why Judaism has always emphasized the importance of positive action. But just as the Talmud says that the patriarch Jacob never died because his children continue the tradition he taught them, the same can be said of Martin Luther King Jr., whose commitment to racial harmony we continue to embrace, or of the Lubavitcher Rebbe, whose pioneering work in returning Jews to their heritage continues to influence every strand of world Jewry.

Rabbi Shmuley Boteach
Englewood, NJ

Are we hard-wired to believe in God?

N euroscience and evolutionary biology offer powerful explanations of a wide swath of human behavior. By 2012, when we asked this question, neurologically inflected insights into everything from infant bonding to adolescent lawbreaking were common and increasingly influential in public policy. It's only a small jump to the idea that this wiring extends to such fundamental human qualities as the capacity for worship and wonder.

You might expect rabbis to balk at reducing the religious sense to "wiring," and some do, but others are willing to run with the metaphor, extending it to "wireless" versions of contact with God (in Rabbi Yitz Greenberg's vision, "The human soul is constantly sending out homing signals" until it "connects" on the Divine wavelength) or suggesting that in fact, what's hard-wired isn't belief in God but the unstoppable drive to challenge and question it. (Published in 2012.)

INDEPENDENT

If we were hard-wired to believe in God, there wouldn't be any atheists. Nowhere in the entire Torah are we commanded to believe in God. We are asked to love God, serve God, be in awe of God, but nowhere to believe in God. You cannot mandate belief. Instead, we are encouraged to arrive at our own conclusions, not through blind faith but through experience and reason. "You shall know" is the wording throughout the Bible (Deuteronomy 4:35 and 39, First Kings 20:13, Psalms 100:3, Isaiah 49:23, Ezekiel 17:21, etc.). Knowing is more powerful than believing. The 11th-century Rabbi Bachya ben Joseph ibn Paquda taught that we should periodically wrestle with our belief, not merely presume it (*Chovot Halevavot, Sha'ar Hayichud*, Chapter 3). That we should believe in God is the last thing on God's wish list. On top of that list is that you believe in yourself. As the 19th-century sage Rabbi Tzadok HaKohen put it: "Just as it is important to believe in God, it is just as important to believe in yourself" (*Tzidkat Hatzadik*, No. 154). And to the atheist in us, God whispers: "Whether you believe in me or not, know that I believe in you."

Rabbi Gershon Winkler
Walking Stick Foundation
Thousand Oaks, CA

HUMANIST

Why not flip this conundrum on its head and ask instead, "Are we hard-wired to question belief in God?" In fact, for hundreds of millions of people, secularity, and with it skepticism and critical thinking, are at the core of their basic existence. For us, faith and belief in a deity are not innate but are actually baffling concepts. A 2005 Eurobarometer study found that one-third of the French and around a quarter of Dutch, Belgians, Germans and British do not believe in God or any sort of spirit or life force. Those figures go up dramatically in Korea, Japan and China.

Among Americans overall, depending on the survey, anywhere from 12 to 20 percent are atheists or agnostics. When you narrow it to Jews, that figure soars to around 50 percent. Many of us may have been raised with traditional teachings, but they were not instinctual. As soon as we could grapple critically with these concepts, we raised questions and challenges that eventually led to discarding these beliefs. We didn't choose to be secularists any more than someone chooses to be lesbian or gay. We're just hard-wired that way. And that's fine with us.

Rabbi Peter H. Schweitzer
The City Congregation for
Humanistic Judaism
New York, NY

RENEWAL

A 2009 article in the British newspaper *The Daily Mail* quotes Yale University psychologist Paul Bloom as saying, "There's now a lot of evidence that some of the foundations for our religious beliefs are hard-wired. All humans possess the brain circuitry, and it never goes away." Whether or not we accept that science has proved this, there certainly seems to be a great deal of anecdotal evidence that it is the case. The visceral elation we feel at the sight of a glorious sunset, an inspiring sunrise or the birth of our offspring indicates a spiritual connection to something greater than ourselves. Our sense of awe is also a shared human emotion that points to belief in an entity or an energy beyond ourselves.

We acknowledge that we are emotionally moved by music and are often deeply inspired by words. Ecstatic dance and jubilant chant can be universally elevating. These are also shared human experiences, and whether we categorize them as spirituality or religion, they are undeniably hard-wired in our psyches. Finally, the truism "There are no atheists in a foxhole" suggests that we may indeed be hard-wired for belief in G-d.

Rabbi Yocheved Mirrtz
Congregation Pnai Tikvah
Las Vegas, NV

RECONSTRUCTIONIST

To varying degrees, and taking into account varying views of God, the answer is yes. Most people are primed to perceive the godliness around us. We're hard-wired (despite some occasionally loose circuits) to appreciate and celebrate the very fact of our existence and to respond to the universe and to each other with wonder, *yirah*, or, in the words of Abraham Joshua Heschel, "radical amazement." Perhaps we are indeed hard-wired for Godbelief, though maybe it's simply for goodness or for reflection.

As we encounter the world and one another, the "better angels of our nature" (per Abraham Lincoln) do point us toward gratitude and interdependence. Our wiring was not laid down at once by God-as-hardware-developer; it's actually the product of billions of years of evolution. And that itself is the real miracle: not some freak suspension of the natural order, but rather the very fact of nature, where atoms slowly become molecules, cells, organisms, communities.

"We are grateful to You... for Your wondrousnesses and goodnesses which are with us always, evening and morning and afternoon" (Modim prayer). God didn't write our internal code, but She/He/It is behind the whole schmear. God is "the Life, Love, and Intelligence of the Universe," according to Mordecai Kaplan; God is the Process, the Power, behind these holy miracles of our ever-evolving existence. To love God is never to take these miracles for granted.

Rabbi Fred Scherlinder Dobb
Adat Shalom Reconstructionist
Congregation
Bethesda, MD

REFORM

Tradition teaches that at Mount Sinai, when Moses is given the Torah, we are taught the first of all commandments: "I, the Lord, am your God who brought you out of the land of Egypt, the house of bondage: You shall have no other gods besides Me." This first commandment, as a statement of God's existence and connection to our people, may lead us to presume that we are hard-wired for belief in God. Throughout the Torah, we read stories of conversations and debates with and pleas to God. Our ancestors turned to God in times of joy and sorrow, for guidance and thanksgiving. Yet in our real-life living rooms and coffee-house conversations, we know that not all people believe in God. We struggle, we question, we doubt. No, we are not hard-wired for belief in God. Rather, we are hard-wired to ask questions about God. As self-reflective, conscious, conscientious human beings, we have it in our make-up to ask those existential questions: Who am I? Where did I come from? Why am I here? What happens to me after I die? Our answers are dependent upon our own understanding of the existence and role of God in the universe. Torah illustrates how our ancestors answered these questions. With the Torah's lessons, the traditions of Judaism and the support of the Jewish community, we each have the opportunity to find our own answers. It is our prerogative, even obligation, as Jews to seek out our answers to these questions.

Rabbi Laura Novak Winer
Union for Reform Judaism
Fresno, CA

CONSERVATIVE

"We were born believing," wrote Ralph Waldo Emerson. "A man bears beliefs as a tree bears apples." Does this mean we are hard-wired to believe in God? Or is belief in God a result of humanity's experiences in this world? I don't have answers, but I do believe Emerson understood a universal truth: Faith seems to be innate. In a recent Gallup Poll, nine out of ten Americans said they believe in God. They are in good company. Throughout history, regardless of nationality or culture, people have expressed faith in some kind of deity or greater power in a variety of ways. Why do people believe in God? What motivates people today to embrace a religious tradition? I suggest several answers; there are, of course, many more. First, the world we live in is awesome in many ways. Religious tradition gives us language for expressing gratitude and appreciation. Second, faith in God can give comfort, meaning, stability and purpose to our lives as we confront the bewildering circumstances we will all encounter. Finally, throughout history, groups of people have sought to create a community with a shared purpose and vision. Faith in God can lead to religious observance, which in turn provides a path for connecting with that larger community.

Rabbi Amy Wallk Katz
Temple Beth El
Springfield, MA

MODERN ORTHODOX

Some evolutionary biologists argue that humans are hard-wired for belief in God. Jewish religious language offers three other explanatory metaphors: 1) Human beings have a mission. The search for purpose has been planted in them by an infinite God/Creator who has a plan to perfect the world (tikkun olam). The instinct for purpose motivates humans to seek out the divine plan and participate in it. 2) As life in human form becomes more Godlike in its understanding, it seeks meaning. As civilized humans move beyond the elementary struggle for existence, they strive to find their place in nature and their calling in this life. This leads to God. 3) God has planted in humans a capacity and drive to pursue a higher purpose. This leads humans to seek out a relationship to the hidden but ever-present Creator in whose infinity all life is grounded.

There is also a Jewish "wireless" version. The Lord created the human being—man and woman—"in the image of God" (Genesis 1:26). The image of God is in harmony, in rhythm and resonance, with the God whose image it is. The human soul is constantly sending out homing signals—until it homes in on the same wavelength as the Divine and connects to God.

Rabbi Yitz Greenberg
Riverdale, NY

CHABAD

There's something strange about the human being. He sends a space-ship to the moon and proclaims, "I have conquered the universe!" He prescribes a drug that makes him feel better and declares, "I have decoded the human soul!" He wires together a little box that addicts him to incessant chat with his friends and determines, "Reality is a wired box! We are all wired boxes! G-d is in the wiring!"

If humans were benign fuzzy critters, this would be fine. Given our history of fascism and genocide, however, the belief that everything, including our deepest beliefs, is a product of our "wiring" is downright nefarious. If you add that we are poised to unleash genomic technology into a world that has yet to shed its brutal dictators and greed-driven corporations, things get downright scary. I'll quote the chilling words of neurologist/psychiatrist Viktor Frankl, who was "absolutely convinced that the gas chambers . . . were ultimately prepared not in some ministry or other in Berlin, but rather at the desks and in the lecture halls of nihilistic scientists and philosophers," who had reduced the human being to "an automaton of reflexes...a mind machine." As we reduce the human being to a string of genotypes, nothing is more crucial than to recognize that a divine image lies there as well; that human life cannot be price-tagged in a laboratory because within each one of us breathes the image of G-d. It's with that precious knowledge that we can channel our technology toward tremendous good rather than the unspeakable opposite. Last I checked, the divine image was wireless.

Rabbi Tzvi Freeman
Editor, chabad.org
Thornhill, Ontario

SEPHARDIC

In order to answer this question, we must first distinguish between two forms of religious belief. Insofar as belief in God satisfies certain primal emotional urges and makes a person feel good, it is quite possible that it is genetically determined or hard-wired. In this respect, belief should not be different from any other psychological phenomenon that is ultimately reducible to the combination of biological and environmental factors that generated it.

However, there is another kind of religious belief—belief based on abstract thought, reasoning from evidence and rational conviction. Such belief takes shape in the soul or intellect of a person, not in his heart or psyche. Whereas the former, more immature or simplistic sort of faith may indeed be traced to the same biological causes that are responsible for other emotions, the more sophisticated form of belief is the product of conscious, deliberate and painstaking thought, which is far from a natural or evolutionarily directed process. And it is the latter type of belief in God that the Torah commands us to develop, as it is written, "And you shall know today, and continually impress this upon your heart—that the Lord is God in the Heavens above and in the Earth below; there is no other."

Rabbi Joshua Maroof
Magen David Sephardic Congregation
Rockville, MD

Are Jews still expecting a messiah?

nswering this question is all about defining your terms. Who or what is a messiah? This question may have drawn the widest range of answers of anything we've ever asked. (It's also one of the few with an entry labeled "ultra-Orthodox"—a term we probably wouldn't use today.) Like all these questions, and particularly those involving any tinge of the apocalyptic, a great part of the answer lies in the mirror, or, as in the title of a book recommended by one rabbi, There Is No Messiah and You Are It. (Published in 2012.)

INDEPENDENT

Very few of us ever expected the Messiah. We spent most of our history hoping for one. And one day, indeed, the dove will return with those hopes grasped firmly in its beak. But it is up to us to do what Noah did—open the window of the Ark.

Truth be told, the Messiah has probably been here a few hundred times but got spat at on the way to school, or told he wasn't Jewish enough and had to re-convert, or gotten ousted from a temple board meeting because he couldn't pay dues. Who knows? The second-century Rabbi Bibi bar Abaye taught that "If ever a *Ro'chom* (desert buzzard) would chance to sit on the earth and sing 'Rak rak,' it is a sign that the Messiah has come" (*Talmud Bavli*, Chulin 63a). I believe that one day the Ro'chom will alight upon the earth and go "Rak rak," restoring within us what has become fragmented. Since buzzards carry the lifebreath of struggle, she will sing her messianic song with the same breath we sighed at moments of challenge in our lives. Then all our grief will be transformed into dance (Psalms 30:12), our weeping into song (Psalms 126:5), and every sigh you ever breathed will be breathed back into you as renewed life and joy. "Rak rak!"

Rabbi Gershon Winkler
Walking Stick Foundation
Thousand Oaks, CA

HUMANIST

Years ago, a popular evangelical bumper sticker read, "I found it." The Jewish version would read, "I'm still looking for it." In contrast to Christians who assert that the Messiah has come, Jews would never be satisfied with any applicant for the job. Messianic claimants have all fallen short in the past and will in the future. Waiting around for messianic redemption is therefore a distraction from life's immediate challenges. Our focus should be on bringing redemption in our own lifetime and with our own two hands.

The idea of a messiah supports a top-down model of power that invests far too much influence and responsibility in one solitary supermensch who will single-handedly save the day. I prefer a different mythic construct that promotes the worth of every person: the legend of the 36 righteous people on whom the world is sustained on account of their goodness and unpretentious deeds. Because the 36 are concealed even from themselves, it is incumbent on us to treat everyone—family, neighbors, co-workers and ourselves—as one of them. Just think of the ripple effect that would bring to the world. It could even bring peace.

Rabbi Peter H. Schweitzer
The City Congregation for
Humanistic Judaism
New York, NY

RENEWAL

The messianic belief—whether in Judaism, Christianity, Islam or even secular capitalist and communist worldviews—can lead to complacency if it means a belief that human history is inevitably progressing toward complete harmony. If God or history dictates the necessary linear progression to *olam ha-ba* (the world to come), or the final conflict, then we need only wait patiently for its arrival, though it may tarry.

But we do need to worry, and we cannot afford to wait patiently while the ice caps melt and economic disparity grows worse each year. So what do we do with this age-old vision of harmony and resolution for which we pray in Oseh Shalom?

Isaac Luria's vision of tikkun olam—repairing a broken world—has been reinterpreted in our time to acknowledge that there is nothing inevitable about its realization. It depends upon us. We must also acknowledge that there will always be something that needs fixing—even after we restore ecological balance and have eliminated all chauvinisms and corruption. Perhaps the goal will always lie ahead of us. So *mashiach* might not be a moment in time, but rather a moment in eternity. It may be the eternal vector by which we direct our efforts to perfect the world toward a *malkhut Shaddai*—a kingdom of G-d.

Rabbi David J. Cooper
Kehilla Community Synagogue
Piedmont, CA

RECONSTRUCTIONIST

Only in Israel could a smash 1985 pop song about a recession be titled "Waiting for the Messiah." For fans of Israeli culture, Shalom Chanoch's text is now a touchstone: "'The stock exchange collapsed, people chose to leap off the roof; Messiah jumped too, and they reported he died'... *mashiach lo ba* [he's not coming], *mashiach gam lo m'talpen* [he won't even call]."

Chanoch's sarcastic refrain warns of misplaced faith, whether in free markets or in messiahs. Yes, the best Jewish teachings discourage searching for wonder-workers. But to deny all messianic possibility is defeatist. Moderate messianism leads us to enlightened activism.

Like many progressive Jews, I hold out for a messianic era, a distant vision that inspires and sustains today's necessary work. For our descendants to realize someday that they brought *mashiach*, we must begin now by enfranchising everyone, saving the ecosystem, eradicating poverty and broadening what we mean by salvation. As Rabbi Leila Berner added to our Havdalah ceremony, "Miriam the prophetess, strength and song in her hand: Miriam, come dance with us, to enlarge the eternal song, to repair the world."

Rabbi Fred Scherlinder Dobb
Adat Shalom Reconstructionist
Congregation
Bethesda, MD

REFORM

Every year at Passover, we set an extra cup of wine at our Seder tables for the prophet Elijah. At baby naming and bris ceremonies, we set a seat of honor for Elijah. Each Saturday night, as Shabbat comes to a close with Havdalah, we sing about Elijah.

Who is Elijah? We meet him in the Hebrew Bible, in Kings I and II. He is a prophet like many others who speaks to the people of Israel, imploring them to cleave to their Israelite ways. Later, in the Book of Malachi, Elijah is understood to be the harbinger of the Messiah. As we sing during Havdalah, Elijah is the one we hope will come soon, in our time, and bring with him the Messiah, son of David.

Who is Elijah? We all are Elijah. As Jews, we are each God's partner in the creation and the ongoing perfection of the world. God calls upon each of us to heed the prophets' call to heal the sick, feed the hungry, fight injustice and bring about a time of peace, prosperity and wholeness. This work gives us hope and looks ahead to the messianic time.

An individual messiah cannot and will not do that for us. We are all part of the messianic process.

Rabbi Laura Novak Winer
Union for Reform Judaism
Fresno, CA

CONSERVATIVE

Traditional Judaism teaches that there will be a leader, an individual who will bring about redemption. In some ways I like to imagine that this is true. At a bris or baby naming, I imagine the many ways this bundle of love will influence and change the world. It seems easy to sit back and hope that a messiah will come. Although I have no idea whether or not most Jews are expecting the Messiah, I am certain that most Jews recognize there is much suffering and great sadness in our world. Speaking for myself only, I am not waiting for a personal messiah who will bring a kingdom of God on earth. I prefer a more active approach. I believe that each of us is created in the divine image. We increase holiness when we accept personal responsibility for bringing about a "messianic age." Our tradition teaches that human beings have the power to help God save the world, by effecting justice, finding cures for diseases and fighting poverty. For more on this worldview, I recommend Robert N. Levine's book, *There Is No Messiah and You Are It.*

Rabbi Amy Wallk Katz
Temple Beth El
Springfield, MA

MODERN ORTHODOX

By continuing to live as Jews, all Jews are stating that the Messiah has not yet arrived. Jewry pledged at Mount Sinai and elsewhere that as long as the world is not totally redeemed, we will go on with our testimony as Jews. As long as there is poverty, hunger, oppression and war, the world is still not perfected. We maintain this against the Christian claim that the Messiah has arrived and against secular messianic redemptive movements (Nazism, communism, socialism) that claim they have brought the true, final perfection. This continuing testimony of "not yet" is why would-be world redeemers have hated and persecuted Jews.

After great catastrophes, many Jews lifted their level of expectation because of the need to rebalance the world toward the victory of the good. In this post-Shoah generation, some Lubavitchers and followers of Rav Abraham Kook were convinced that the Messiah had arrived or was almost here. Unfortunately, all celebrations have been premature.

It would appear that secular Jews have renounced belief in the Messiah. But I believe that the choice to continue living as a Jew is the statement "I still believe the world will be perfected" and, by implication, "I will work to bring the Messiah."

Rabbi Yitz Greenberg
Riverdale, NY

SEPHARDIC

It is impossible to accept the notion that God would create a deeply flawed world, filled to the brim with injustice, corruption and immorality, for all eternity. We must therefore proceed with the conviction that one day, humankind will achieve true enlightenment and will abandon the endless pursuits of power, wealth and selfish pleasure that have dominated its consciousness since the dawn of time and are responsible for the disharmony and conflict that prevail on earth. Like all social and political movements, this transformation will take place under the guidance of a wise teacher, a brave pioneer with the courage to stand up and to fight for principles of eternal value and enduring truth. Like all revolutionaries, this leader will initially be ignored, later reviled and finally resisted until the sheer power of his message can no longer be denied. At that moment, our civilization will attain its greatest spiritual breakthrough; the search for wisdom and justice will supplant hankerings after material wealth and instantaneous gratification; and human beings will live in peace and harmony, united in the service of the Almighty. The architect of this cultural upheaval is the person we call the Messiah. And our faith in his arrival is a necessary corollary of our belief in God: that a perfect and omnipotent Creator would not allow His handiwork to wallow in imperfection forever.

Rabbi Joshua Maroof
Magen David Sephardic Congregation
Rockville, MD

CHABAD

As much as a Jew may wrestle to rip away from his G-d and his people, the undercurrent of indignation remains endemic to his Jewish psyche, a gnawing conviction that the world is not the way it should be. The Jew aches with expectation and blatantly demands that the world act according to the beauty it inherently contains.

Do we await a human messiah? The last century left us deeply scarred with a wariness of demagogues, of glorifying any individual beyond the humanness of all others. So we yearn yet more for a truly Jewish messiah—less about power and more about empathy, education and insight into life. A leader like an orchestral conductor, directing musicians from their fragmented discordance into a magnificent symphony. After all, by now all the instruments are in place—instruments to plunge the fathomless depths of our universe, to know its oneness and the oneness of its Creator, to make hunger both for food and for knowledge obsolete. What's missing is a singular voice of wisdom, universally respected, a voice for the human soul. A very human, modern-day Moses.

No, we don't expect a messiah. We want, need, pray in every prayer: *Mashiach* now!

Rabbi Tzvi Freeman
Editor, chabad.org
Thornhill, Ontario

ULTRA-ORTHODOX

Maimonides, codifier of Torah law, lists 13 principles of faith that are incumbent on a Jew. The 12th of these is "I believe with complete faith in the coming of the Messiah, and even though he may delay, nevertheless I anticipate every day that he will come."

Torah literature contains many references to the Messiah. We are told that the Messiah may come at any time, if Jews deserve it by following the teachings of the Torah. However, there is a fixed point in time at which the Messiah will come even if Jews are not meritorious.

It was predicted that prior to the coming of the Messiah, Jews will experience great anguish and suffering. Prayers are rendered that we be spared this agony, but many see the Holocaust as this pre-Messiah ordeal. At the end of the Talmudic volume of Sotah, there is a frightening description of the degeneration of morals and ethics in the world prior to the coming of the Messiah, with flagrant rejection of all authority, parental or otherwise. Some of the esoteric writings predict that prior to the coming of the Messiah, the people of Ishmael (Muslims) will dominate the earth.

These harbingers have unfortunately occurred, and we anticipate the imminent coming of the Messiah.

Rabbi Abraham J. Twerski
Founder, Gateway Rehabilitation Center
Teaneck, NJ

AFTERWORD

A refreshing rejoinder in divided times

Rabbi Shira Stutman

T he wall of my first office at the Sixth & I Historic Synagogue in Washington, DC was filled with about a dozen framed pages from *Moment Magazine*. *Moment* was an important part of my childhood and adolescence, and not just because my father for many years edited its humorous "Spice Box" feature. *Moment* was required Shabbat reading for me as an aspiring Jewish communal nerd. Now that I'm a rabbi myself, it continues to be an ongoing help in my duties. Countless times I've searched for an answer to a question (in the field we call this "asking a *shayla*—a question—of Rabbi Google") only to come upon *Moment*'s "Ask the Rabbis" section. I read it thoroughly and always come away learning something new.

As Amy Schwartz points out in her introduction to this book, the most striking part of "Ask the Rabbis" is that the lines of demarcation between the rabbis are somewhat surprising. One never knows when or how the rabbis' opinions are going to line up, the Humanist rabbi with the Chabad one, the Reconstructionist with the Sephardic Orthodox one. One also never knows which rabbi is going to give one firm answer and which one is going to say, in pure rabbinic fashion, "On the one hand," and, one line later, "On the other hand," implying that for them as well there are multiple answers. What a refreshing rejoinder to this moment we are in, in which one's opinion on everything from science to love depends on the denomination or political party with

251

which one aligns, and in which too many are convinced that they hold the one and only Truth.

I write this at a time when we are divided: by class, race, political party, geographic location. Even within our own religion, we are gutted by ways that our co-religionists feel radically differently from us about issues that we hold close to our hearts and minds, including fighting anti-Black racism, how best to support the State of Israel, and other issues. And yes, there are rabbis that I think are wrong and even offensive in the ways that they use our tradition to score one political point or another. I know there are rabbis who feel the same about me; I have the emails to prove it! On the other hand (there's that phrase again), this is what Jews have done for millennia—disagree, sometimes radically, sometimes unkindly. We put those disagreements down on paper, and we let the test of time determine, in true Hillel/Shammai fashion, who is right, and who is wrong, and—one can only hope—how we can dredge even the tiniest bit of Torah from everyone.

In those moments when we can't get a rabbi on the phone—or even better, in those moments in which 10 rabbis' opinions are better than one—we can turn to books like this one, to be reminded that Judaism, like any life well-lived, is multifaceted, vibrant, meaningful, able to evolve, grounded in its history, provider of guidance in difficult and uncertain moments—and sometimes quite funny as well.

A QUICK GUIDE TO DENOMINATIONS

HUMANIST

An American stream of Judaism, founded in 1963, that disavows belief in God but instead celebrates human beings' role in creating religion and the pleasure and benefit that Jewish practice can bring its adherents. Holidays and life cycle events are celebrated, often with prayers and blessings rewritten to avoid reference to a deity.

RENEWAL

A network of congregations under the umbrella organization ALEPH: Alliance for Jewish Renewal in Philadelphia, Jewish Renewal was founded in the 1960s by Rabbi Zalman Schachter-Shalomi (1924-2014) with the aim of infusing Judaism with new spirituality and passion. On its website, the Renewal movement calls itself "a trans-denominational approach to revitalizing Judaism" that combines "the socially progressive values of egalitarianism, the joy of Hasidism, the informed do-it-yourself spirit of the havurah movement, and the accumulated wisdom of centuries of tradition."

RECONSTRUCTIONISM

Originally part of the Conservative movement, Reconstructionism broke off from it in 1955 under the leadership of Conservative rabbi Mordecai Kaplan (1881-1983). The movement deemphasized literal belief in God or revelation and declined to be bound by halacha, traditional Jewish law, instead defining Judaism as "the evolving religious civilization of the Jews" and giving the past "a vote, not a veto." While valuing traditional practices, it gives a great deal of deference to individuals and congregations. The movement began ordaining female rabbis in 1974, accepted gay rabbinic students in 1984 and has been welcoming to interfaith couples. Kaplan is credited with holding the first bat mitzvah, of his daughter Judith in 1922.

REFORM

The largest American denomination, Reform started as a radical modernizing movement in Germany in the early 19th century, as Jews gained new rights and access to mainstream society and sought a Judaism compatible with this new milieu. Reform's founders rejected most traditional forms of observance—from Shabbat prohibitions and kosher laws to Hebrew prayers—and instead located the core of Jewish identity and practice in universal moral values, ethical monotheism and the prophetic vision of a just society. Reform came to America with German Jewish immigrants and flourished, later softening its opposition to traditional ritual practices and emphasizing progressive political activism, egalitarianism and openness to interfaith families and same-sex marriage. It ordained women in 1972 and gay and lesbian rabbis in the late 1980s. Reform recognizes patrilinear descent, meaning that one can be Jewish with only a Jewish father—a departure from the traditional view that Judaism is passed only through the mother.

CONSERVATIVE

Once the largest movement in American Judaism, now about 18 percent of the community, Conservative Judaism is often seen as a middle ground between Reform and Orthodoxy. It was formed in the 1880s to "conserve" more of traditional Jewish practice in reaction to Reform Judaism's rejection of it. Unlike Reform, Conservative thought holds that Jewish practice is bound by halacha but also that the law changes over time through a process of study and rabbinic deliberation. (The approach was exemplified by a mid-20th-century ruling that Jews, traditionally forbidden to "ride" on the Sabbath, could drive to synagogue—but only to synagogue—rather than not go at all.) Through this process, the movement eventually permitted the ordination of female rabbis in 1985 and largely relaxed restrictions on gay marriage and ordination in 2006, though alternative rulings exist that allow individual congregations to take other positions.

ORTHODOX

An umbrella term covering many different types of congregations—from Modern Orthodox to haredi, or ultra-traditional—that view themselves as bound by halacha. This means keeping kosher, refraining from many activities on Shabbat and holidays, praying three times a day and generally observing all 613 of the positive and negative commandments found in the Torah, along with many rules drawn from them. Orthodoxy mandates distinct religious roles for men and women, so women are seated separately from men in synagogue, cannot count in the ten-person minimum required for a prayer service, and cannot be rabbis or serve as witnesses in a religious court. Feminism and gay rights are sometimes described as alien values in opposition to Torah. Though often seen as the "real," authentic traditional Judaism, Orthodoxy has also codified and tightened some practices in reaction to the liberal movements.

MODERN ORTHODOX

A wing of Orthodoxy that strives for commitment to halacha in tandem with engagement with the modern world, favoring a synthesis of *Torah u'madda*, religious and scientific knowledge. Within Modern Orthodoxy there are some tensions, particularly surrounding the role of women. Some parts of the community have become more traditional and stricter in their approach to observance, while in the other direction, a subgroup calling itself Open Orthodoxy has moved toward more flexibility. An Open Orthodox yeshiva in New York now ordains women as clergy using the term "Maharat," an acronym for a Hebrew phrase meaning "leader of Jewish law, spirituality and Torah."

ULTRA-ORTHODOX

A general term denoting the more traditionalist Orthodox communities and those most opposed to interaction with the secular world. This term has recently been criticized as pejorative and imprecise, with the word haredi (literally, those who tremble before God) preferred by many.

SEPHARDIC

Sephardic Judaism is part of Orthodoxy and follows the same authorities in determining overall halachic direction, but it arises from a different tradition—the part of the community that came from Sefarad, meaning Muslim Spain, Portugal and the Middle East, rather than from Eastern Europe. Because of this, rulings are sometimes more flexible and the role of the individual rabbi more capacious.

CHABAD (LUBAVITCHER HASIDIC)

Hasidism arose in the 18th century in Eastern Europe during a period of intense persecution. Under its founder, Rabbi Israel ben Eliezer, known as the Baal Shem Tov, it emphasized religious joy and passion over law and study, ultimately developing into a series of smaller groups, each with a charismatic leader. Under modern Hasidism, gender roles remain traditional and separate, and communities adhere to religious law. Chabad is the umbrella organization for the Lubavitcher Hasidim, who migrated from Lubavitch, Russia. Shaped by the highly influential Lubavitcher Rebbe Menachem Schneerson (1902-1994), Chabad developed a distinctive mission of outreach to less observant Jews, a program it pursues worldwide.

A GLOSSARY
OF TERMS

TORAH—Can refer to just the first five books of the Bible (in English, named Genesis, Exodus, Leviticus, Numbers and Deuteronomy); or to the Hebrew Bible; or more generally to the entire corpus of Jewish text and commentary.

TANAKH—the Hebrew Bible, an acronym for Torah, Nevi'im and Ketubim, or Torah, Prophets (which includes Judges, Kings and other historical material about ancient Israel) and Writings (additional books such as Psalms, Proverbs, Ecclesiastes and more).

TALMUD—An umbrella term for a large body of civil and religious law and commentary, composed of the Mishnah, or Oral Law, and the Gemara, or commentaries on it—compiled between the 2nd and the 5th centuries CE. There are two versions, the Babylonian Talmud (*Talmud Bavli*) and the earlier Palestinian or Jerusalem Talmud (*Talmud Yerushalmi*). Both versions are divided into tractates (such as Yoma, Baba Batra, Baba Metzia, etc.).

MIDRASH—Stories, tales and imaginative literature told by early rabbis to fill in and interpret the Torah.

HALACHA—The system of Jewish law, literally "the way" or "the road."

OUR RABBIS
(ALPHABETICAL)

Where more than one affiliation or location is listed, the rabbi may have changed jobs while continuing to answer questions for us. Where a date is listed, it refers to the year the question was asked; the affiliation was current at that time, but may have since changed. Where no date is listed, the affiliation is current or lasted for a long period.

Rabbi Yitzchok Adlerstein
(Orthodox)
Adjunct Chair of Jewish Law and Ethics, Loyola Law School
Cross-Currents
Los Angeles, CA

Rabbi Simcha Backman
(Chabad)
Chabad Jewish Center of Glendale and the Foothill Communities
Glendale, CA (2014)

Rabbi Chava Bahle (Renewal)
OHALAH: Association of Rabbis for Jewish Renewal
Suttons Bay, MI (2014)

Rabbi Rachel Barenblat
(Renewal)
Congregation Beth Israel
North Adams, MA

Rabbi Shmuley Boteach
(Chabad, Orthodox)
Englewood, NJ

Rabbi Caryn Broitman
(Reconstructionist)
Martha's Vineyard Hebrew Center
Vineyard Haven, MA

Rabbi Michael J. Broyde
(Orthodox)
Emory University School of Law
Atlanta, GA (2016)

Rabbi David J. Cooper
(Renewal)
Kehilla Community Synagogue
Piedmont, CA (2012)

Rabbi Fred Scherlinder Dobb
(Reconstructionist)
Adat Shalom Reconstructionist Congregation
Bethesda, MD

Rabbi Jeffrey L. Falick
(Humanist)
Birmingham Temple Congregation for Humanistic Judaism
Farmington Hills, MI

Rabbi Tzvi Freeman
(Chabad)
Editor, chabad.org
Thornhill, Ontario (2011)

Rabbi Manis Friedman
(Chabad)
Bais Chana Institute of Jewish Studies
St. Paul, MN (2009)

Rabbi Shefa Gold
(Renewal)
*Center for Devotional, Energy
and Ecstatic Practice*
Jemez Springs, NM (2011)

Rabbi Irving (Yitz) Greenberg
(Modern Orthodox)
*President, Jewish Life Network
Steinhardt Foundation*
New York, NY (2006-7)
*J. J. Greenberg Institute for the
Advancement of Jewish Life/Hadar*
Riverdale, NY

Rabbi Dov Greenberg
(Chabad)
*Rohr Chabad House,
Stanford University*
Palo Alto, CA (2014)

Rabbi Judith Hauptman
(Conservative)
*E. Billi Ivry Professor of Talmud
and Rabbinic Culture, Jewish
Theological Seminary*
New York, NY (2006)

Rabbi Sherre Hirsch
(Conservative)
Sinai Temple
Los Angeles, CA (2005)

Rabbi Yosef Y. Jacobson
(Chabad)
Yeshiva Chovevei Torah
Brooklyn, NY

Rabbi Miriam Jerris
(Humanist)
Society for Humanistic Judaism
Farmington Hills, MI

Rabbi Laura Duhan Kaplan
(Renewal)
Or Shalom Synagogue
Vancouver, Canada

Rabbi Amy Wallk Katz
(Conservative)
Temple Beth El
Springfield, MA

Rabbi Debra Kolodny
(Renewal)
ALEPH: Alliance for Jewish Renewal
Silver Spring, MD (2011)

Rabbi Chaim A. Landa
(Chabad)
Brooklyn, New York (2017)

Rabbi Yosef Landa
(Chabad)
*Regional Director
Chabad of Greater St. Louis*
St. Louis, MO (2013)

Rabbi Gilah Langner
(Renewal)
Congregation Kol Ami
Arlington, VA

Rabbi Sari Laufer
(Reform)
Congregation Rodeph Sholom
New York, NY (2014)

Rabbi Shafir Lobb
(Renewal)
Temple Beth El Israel
Port Saint Lucie, FL (2012)

Rabbi David Evan Markus
(Renewal)
Temple Beth El
City Island, NY

Rabbi Joshua Maroof
(Sephardic)
*Magen David Sephardic
Congregation*
Rockville, MD (2005-2014)

Rabbi Goldie Milgram
(Renewal)
ReclaimingJudaism.org
Sarasota, FL

Rabbi Avis D. Miller
(Conservative)
Adas Israel Congregation
Washington, DC (2006)

Rabbi Yocheved Mirrtz
(Renewal)
Congregation Pnai Tikvah
Las Vegas, NV (2011)

Rabbi Geoff Mitelman
(Reform)
Sinai and Synapses
*CLAL-The National Jewish Center
for Learning and Leadership*
New York, NY (2019)

Rabbi Mark Novak
(Renewal)
Minyan Oneg Shabbat
Washington, DC

Rabbi Haim Ovadia
(Sephardic)
*Magen David Sephardic
Congregation*
Rockville, MD (2015–2018)
Potomac, MD (current)

Rabbi Julie Schonfeld
(Conservative)
Rabbinical Assembly
New York, NY (2009)

Rabbi Daniel Siegel
(Renewal)
Director of Spiritual Resources,
ALEPH: Alliance for Jewish Renewal
West Roxbury, MA (2005)

Rabbi Fred Reiner
(Reform)
Temple Sinai
Washington, DC (2005)

Rabbi David Saperstein
(Reform)
Director, Religious Action Center
of Reform Judaism
Washington, DC (2008)

Rabbi Peter H. Schweitzer
(Humanist)
Association of Humanistic Rabbis
City Congregation for
Humanistic Judaism
New York, NY (2005-2018)

Rabbi Yossi Serebryanski
(Chabad)
Chabad of South Denver
Denver, CO (2011)

Rabbi David Shabtai, MD
(Orthodox)
Boca Raton Synagogue
Boca Raton, FL (2019)

Rabbi Levi Shemtov
(Chabad)
Executive Vice President, American
Friends of Lubavitch
Washington, DC

Rabbi Daniel Siegel
(Renewal)
ALEPH: Alliance for Jewish Renewal
Philadelphia, PA (2008)

Rabbi Steve Silvern
(Renewal)
ALEPH: Alliance for Jewish Renewal
Auburn University
Auburn, AL (2008)

Rabbi Gil Steinlauf
(Conservative)
Adas Israel Congregation
Washington, DC (2009)

Rabbi Shais Taub
(Chabad)
Chabad.org
Pittsburgh, PA (2014)

Rabbi David Teutsch
(Reconstructionist)
Center for Jewish Ethics
Reconstructionist Rabbinical College
Philadelphia, PA (2019)

Rabbi Simcha Tolwin
(Ultra-Orthodox)
Executive Director,
Aish Huntington Woods
Southfield, MI (2009)

Rabbi Gordon Tucker
(Conservative)
Temple Israel Center
White Plains, NY (2008)

Rabbi Abraham J. Twerski
(Ultra-Orthodox)
Founder, Gateway
Rehabilitation Center
Teaneck, NJ (2012)

Rabbi Dov Wagner
(Chabad)
Rohr Chabad Jewish Student Center
University of Southern California

Rabbi Mark Washofsky
(Reform)
Professor of Jewish Law and Practice
Hebrew Union College/Jewish
Institute of Religion
Cincinnati, OH (2009)

Rabbi Arthur Waskow
(Renewal)
The Shalom Center
Philadelphia, PA

Rabbi Harold S. White (z"l)
(Independent)
Senior Jewish Chaplain,
Georgetown University
 Washington, DC (2008)

Rabbi David Wilfond
(Reform)
Hebrew Union College
Jerusalem (2009)

Rabbi Laura Novak Winer
(Reform)
Union for Reform Judaism (2011)
Hebrew Union College
Fresno, CA (current)

Rabbi Gershon Winkler
(Independent)
Walking Stick Foundation
(Various locations)
Jewish Chaplain,
Patton State Hospital
Patton, CA

Rabbi Eliezer Zalmanov
(Chabad)
Chabad of Northwest Indiana
Munster, IN (2019)

Rabbi David Zaslow
(Renewal)
Havurah Shir Hadash
Ashland, Oregon (2006)

Rabbi Reuben Zellman
(Reform)
Congregation Beth El
Berkeley, CA (2016)

ACKNOWLEDGMENTS

This book owes its existence to Nadine Epstein, *Moment*'s brilliant editor-in-chief, who dreamed up "Ask the Rabbis" and who has situated it within an exciting and creative magazine. I'm grateful for her encouragement and her generous sharing of opportunities such as this project.

To state the obvious, the book also would not exist without the many rabbis who have answered our questions over the years, gamely taking on whatever knotty moral conundrum or oddly framed inquiry we've thrown their way. Their generosity and willingness to teach, and also to have their insights squeezed into 200 words, deserves a gratitude I may not always manage to express fully to them when we are close to deadline. (That also goes for the many rabbis who help me find other rabbis, notably Chabad's ever-patient Motti Seligson.) I also owe a debt of gratitude to the many rabbis and teachers in my own life; to the colleagues I've learned from at the Jewish Study Center; to Marissa Vonesh and Barbara Werden, who designed the book and its cover; to my daughter, Mimi Koenig, who proofread the entire manuscipt; to *Moment*'s many wonderful editors, staff, proofreaders and fact-checkers, including Ross Bishton, Diane Bolz, Suzanne Borden, Sarah Breger, Sue Driesen, Lilly Gelman, Dina Gold, Terry Grant, Tanya George, Diane Heiman, George Johnson, Eileen Lavine, Pat Lewis, Ellen Meltzer, Wesley Pippert, Johnna Miller Raskin, Debbie Sann, Francie Weinman Schwartz, Ellen Wexler and Larry Wolff. And I'm grateful to my wonderful husband, Eric Koenig, and my long-suffering kids Sandy, Danny and Mimi, who have long since learned to take it in stride when I wave them off, hissing, "Shhh, I'm on the phone with a rabbi!"

ABOUT THE CONTRIBUTORS

Amy E. Schwartz was born in New York City and educated at Harvard College. She worked at *Harper's Magazine* and *The New Republic* before joining *The Washington Post* in 1985. From 1985 to 2002 she worked as an editorial writer and op-ed columnist for the *Post*, specializing in education and covering the culture wars of the 1990s. She was nominated for a Pulitzer Prize in commentary in 1988 and was a three-time winner of the Newspaper Guild's Bernie Harrison Memorial Award for commentary and criticism. After leaving the *Post*, she was guest literary editor and contributing editor of the *Wilson Quarterly*. In 2011 she joined *Moment Magazine* and is currently opinion and book editor, as well as editing *Moment's* popular "Ask the Rabbis" section.

Rabbi Irving (Yitz) Greenberg is president of the J.J. Greenberg Institute for the Advancement of Jewish Life, a division of the Hadar Institute. He is the author of *The Jewish Way, For the Sake of Heaven and Earth, Sage Advice: Pirkei Avot* and the forthcoming *The Triumph of Life*. During his career, he has served as the Chairman of the United States Holocaust Memorial Council; Founding President of the Jewish Life Network/Steinhardt Foundation; and Founding President of the National Jewish Center for Learning and Leadership.

Rabbi Shira Stutman is the senior rabbi at Sixth & I Synagogue in Washington, DC, rabbi-in-residence for the Jewish Federations of North America, and teaches on the faculty of the Wexner Heritage Program of the Wexner Foundation. She was named one of America's Most Inspiring Rabbis by *The Forward*, spotlighted as a Woman to Watch by Jewish Women International, and featured as a notable rabbi by *Tablet Magazine*.

**To read more
of "Ask the Rabbis" visit
momentmag.com/ask-the-rabbis**